D0874016

Physical Order and Moral Liberty

Consciousness and Time

Attention can obviously be sustained. The sense of duration is elementary: in pain for instance the most vivid part of the sensation is often that of dragging through a still persisting past into a future constantly arriving. This is the deliverance of consciousness at such times: it might conceivably be an illusion and we might have before us nothing but the static essence of duration, the changeless idea of change. In fact, however, we can hardly be wrong in predicating ~~that~~ duration and continuity (though not ~~the~~ the scale nor ~~the~~ the limit ~~of our ideas~~ ~~sense of them~~) of the outer world, ~~which is~~ the world in process, and in much more rapid and complex process, than the ~~arithing~~ ~~steadying~~ and ~~cognitive~~ ~~blobed~~ ~~summary~~ data of our senses. Yet the sense of change and continuity is true; there is real change and real continuity in the world and in the psyche which it signifies to us. It is indeed the persistently varying assaults of matter that calls away our attention from whatever we might be inclined to fix and to contemplate: and as this change of objects is not complete, but the two overlap, one waning and the other waxing, we not only change but feel that we change, and that

Previously
Unpublished
Essays
of
George
Santayana

Physical
Order
and
Moral
Liberty

Edited by

John and Shirley Lachs

Vanderbilt University Press *1969*

Standard Book Number 8265–1131–7
Library of Congress Catalogue card number 70–87255

Printed in the United States of America
by Heritage Printers, Inc.
Charlotte, North Carolina
Bound by Nicholstone Book Bindery
Nashville, Tennessee

PREFACE

All but the first of the essays and fragments in this book are published here for the first time. They constitute the bulk of the philosophically interesting manuscripts in the Santayana collections of the Humanities Research Center at the University of Texas and the Columbia University Library. The book itself should be looked upon as another link in the continuing process of bringing to light all of the publishable literary and philosophical product of George Santayana.

In preparing the manuscripts for press, we called upon and received the generous assistance of numerous individuals and organizations. We wish to express our grateful acknowledgment to Daniel Cory for having authorized the publication of these manuscripts. The Research Council of Vanderbilt University provided a grant to visit libraries for an initial examination of the manuscripts and another to enable us to devote free time to their selection, transcription, and arrangement. Dean Robert T. Lagemann of the Vanderbilt Graduate School has earned our gratitude for making funds available to prepare the index, and Herman J. Saatkamp Jr. for completing it rapidly and well.

The kindness and co-operation of officials of the University of Texas and Columbia University Libraries have greatly facilitated our work. Our thanks go particularly to Mary M. Hirth, Librarian at the Academic Center Library of the University of Texas, and Kenneth A. Lohf, Librarian for Rare Books and Manuscripts at the Columbia University Libraries.

We owe a debt of gratitude to Robert P. Emmitt of Vanderbilt University Press for his enthusiasm and patience in helping this project become a reality, and to Professors Donald W. Sherburne and Irwin C. Lieb for effective help in a variety of ways.

J. L.
S. L.

Contents

INTRODUCTION

The reader who goes to the text before he consults the Introduction is not likely to ask for the justification of publishing these essays and fragments. Although they are not, perhaps, on a par with Santayana's polished masterpieces, they are clearly good enough to stand on their own. None need give an embarrassed defense of their literary quality or philosophical contribution: they would, as a whole, be worth having in print even if their author had been a less distinguished man. The fact that they were written by Santayana, of course, places them in a context of significance and endows them with relations that enhance their interest to the philosopher and the scholar. But such value is adventitious: it would be of little comfort to know that these pieces are important to the scholar if reading them gave no wisdom or delight.

For this reason, we invite the reader to weigh the merits of this book by its intrinsic features. He may in the end agree that much of it is thoughtful, creative, and instructive; it is the struggle of a learned and urbane mind to come to terms with some of the most puzzling and most fundamental problems of philosophy and life. The cautious silence you may have felt in your heart upon seeing another volume of posthumous essays by Santayana may quickly turn into the birdsong of joy, if only you allow eloquent reason to address your soul. Admittedly, there is nothing here to match the sustained beauty of *Dialogues in Limbo* or the scope of philosophical argument one finds in *Scepticism and Animal Faith*. Yet even the most cursory reading should be enough to convince us that obscure subsistence in manuscript collections would have been a sadly inappropriate fate for these essays.

Some maintain that once one has gained even a rudimentary grasp of Santayana's philosophical system, reading him further will provide no added enlightenment: although most of his writing is fresh, little of it is new. We may accordingly ask whether there is anything here that has not been thoroughly explored in previously published works.

The answer is a resounding yes. No hitherto published book by Santayana contains a serious and sustained philosophical study of causation; we have the good fortune of printing here no less than two major attempts to deal with the subject, a third shorter essay, along with a related piece entitled "Genesis." Although there is nothing novel in these essays in the sense of views that contradict or are incompatible with Santayana's published system or philosophical perspective, we would look in vain throughout his works for discussions that are as clear and explicit on the relation of sensation to thought as are included in "What Are Data?" "Essences Not Abstractions," and "Pictorial Space and Sentimental Time."

This last essay also contains an entirely novel theory of "critical instants," which is an interesting contribution to Santayana's philosophy of nature. Other pieces go a long way toward clarifying the difficult concept of the spiritual life: in them Santayana comes closer than perhaps anywhere else to admitting that a life devoted to the disinterested contemplation of essences is ultimately unlivable. To these and other important discussions should be added the sensitive observations he makes on pain, his particularly insightful treatment of expectation, superstition, and law, and the forthright and important affirmation of the simultaneity of intuitions with their psychic counterparts. In the end, the reader may well come away with the conviction that the portion of Santayana's work that did not go through his final revision provides a less highly qualified and correspondingly more enlightening picture of some of the most difficult junctures of his philosophical thought more than anything he had published while alive.

This immediately raises the question of the relation of such essays and fragments as these, unrevised and unpublished by Santayana, to the work that bears his final seal of approval. Can the scholar take these drafts as authoritative expressions of Santayana's thought? We do not think that there is a general answer to this question. It is obvious that if the views expressed in these essays were to contradict the philosophical theories defended in Santayana's mature work, we should have to defer to the authority of the "official" doctrine published during the author's life. But this occurs rarely, if at all, or only in a trivially verbal fashion.

We are convinced that it would be a mistake to look upon these pieces as merely inadequate, rejected versions of chapters and essays.

If there were any doubt about the accuracy of Santayana's account in "The Idler and His Works" of his method of composition, a careful study of the three drafts on causation would surely bear him out. Although the central ideas appear in each of the drafts, they are expressed and developed in a different fashion in each. No part of any appears to have been incorporated in any of the others. We are dealing with drafts of a chapter that are successive only in a temporal sense; they are not in any ordinary or simple manner cumulative. Santayana's "dreamful way of composing" is the obvious source of such independent attempts to express the same ideas. By his own account, in writing he would allow his "industrious, playful, automatic self" to spin a spontaneous web of dialectic. He would occasionally salvage portions of these drafts by copying a happy phrase or soaring argument for inclusion in the final version. For the rest (especially in the case of the manuscripts meant for *The Realm of Matter*), he gave them to Cory for comments and eventually set them aside for future reference. Some writers may be ready to do any amount of work to save a hapless draft. Santayana's technique, by contrast, was to achieve perfection by maturing the organ, instead of by the ceaseless revision of its dead product. It was by repeatedly confronting his psyche with the same problem that he honed its response, until it could produce an adequate and spontaneous account of some difficult philosophical subject.

We may conclude, therefore, that there is nothing to the view of those who, in love with the startling and recondite, might wish to urge that these manuscripts reveal our author's *real* doctrine. It would be absurd to suppose that Santayana had the bad judgment or perverse will to withhold from publication the very essays that are the best expressions of his real views. On the other hand, it is worth remarking that the essays in this book, though largely rejected drafts, were probably not left unpublished because they contained opinions that Santayana thought indefensible or false. Given his mode of composition, the fact that he set aside the draft in which a given view occurs is no reason to suppose that he thought it was a bad view or a bad draft. Such varied versions are the inevitable by-products of an active psyche in the process of sharpening its responses. They must be read in the light of Santayana's mature system and are best used in completing the thoughts half-uttered in the published corpus. His ideas on causation, for example, clearly stated here and nowhere else, hover

in the background of much of his philosophy of nature: it is important and interesting to see him develop theories that we could only
uncertainly infer without these manuscripts. Where we deal with a
new view (as in the case of the theory of critical instants) or an apparent conflict between manuscript and previously published treatment, it is best to have no general theory about the authoritativeness
of these essays. The issue should be decided after careful examination
and on its own merits in every case. And if the reader thinks this an
unglamorous and cumbersome procedure, we may well agree, but we
would quietly remind him that it is one that good judgment demands.

Santayana's remarkably steady philosophical convictions combined
with his habit of returning to the same topics again and again make it
virtually impossible to date with any degree of precision most of the
works printed here. Fortunately, the same steadfast vision makes the
issue of the precise date of each manuscript less important and less interesting in the case of Santayana than with philosophers whose views
changed markedly or underwent substantial evolution. However that
may be, some things can be said with confidence. Of the two early
works one is dated by its publication in *The Daily Crimson*, the other
carries its year of composition on the first page in Santayana's hand.
It is highly probable that all the other essays were composed after
Santayana had left Harvard and America in 1912. Some of the pieces
carry internal evidence that they were written before a given date;
the manuscripts of others show physical evidence (uneven lines in a
shaky hand) that they are the work of a very old person. We have
collected all such evidence in notes at the beginning of each fragment.

For the rest we must proceed by intelligent guesswork. We know,
for example, that *The Realm of Matter* occupied Santayana's attention for several years during the 1920s: it is reasonable to assume that
the drafts for it printed here were written during that period. We see
no way of dating them more closely and no reason for it, and we
hasten to warn that even the fact that most of them carry marginal
notes by Cory should not be taken as an indication that they were
written after the time (1927) that Cory first met Santayana in Rome.
Suffice it to say that all the manuscripts here either foreshadow or
develop Santayana's mature philosophical system.

The little dating we can do is enough to show that the categories of
his ontology first occupied Santayana's attention well before 1920.
The changes in his view from that time were mainly verbal—such as

the substitution of the word "spirit" for the earlier word "conscious-ness"—and ones that derive from gaining a clearer and more focused perspective on his commitments. Interestingly enough, the treatment of a number of topics in *The Realms of Being* cannot be looked upon as elaborations or developments of earlier, more general ideas. If we take these manuscripts seriously, the opposite view appears to be more nearly true: Santayana had early developed treatments of a variety of topics, such as that of the complex relations of the mind to time, in far greater detail than the passages published on them in his major works would lead us to suspect.

In preparing these manuscripts for press, we proceeded on the reader's unspoken wish to confront Santayana and not the editors' paraphrase of him, as well as the author's desire, enshrined no doubt eternally in the realm of truth, that his living words not be defaced by the pedant's notes. For this reason, we did the minimum of editing com-patible with pleasant and unhindered reading. We have performed no plastic surgery and applied no heavy makeup to make these maidens more presentable. We changed them only when their author, pre-occupied with tracing the curve of argument, made a minor literary slip. We rewrote nothing: whenever a slip seemed major enough to require work, we simply marked it with the sign "[*sic*]."

The title of each piece, unless otherwise noted, is the one Santayana wrote on the first page of the corresponding manuscript. The note of credits at the beginning of each essay is, of course, by the editors. All other footnotes by the editors are clearly marked as such; notes not so marked are Santayana's own. In the text itself, we are as confident of the accuracy of our readings and transcriptions of the manuscripts as loving care and a substantial investment of time might warrant. The usual clarity of Santayana's calligraphy enabled us to make out most of his words without trouble, and the sense of his sentences along with the context of the relevant discussions helped us in the task of decipher-ing dubious words. As a result, there is only one word, in the essay entitled "Imagination," of which we cannot offer a reasonable reading and, luckily, this word makes little philosophical difference.

Since our aim was to interfere with the manuscripts as little as was consistent with good sense in the text and with minimal standards of literary consistency, we have simply allowed some awkward gram-matical constructions to stand. We have generally refrained from com-ment or correction where Santayana's choice of words or word order was odd and, with the exception of a few places where it interfered with the sense, we have retained his idiosyncratic punctuation.

It was only on the level of spelling that we allowed ourselves the liberty of making some systematic changes in the interest of consistency. In all the essays except the two early pieces, written while he was still in this country, Santayana shows a marked preference for the British spelling of words. Taking this as our clue, we have eliminated the few cases where he reverted back to the American spelling. And since Santayana's "s" is sometimes difficult to distinguish from his "z," we have simply decided to read a "s" consistently in all such words as "realise" and "materialisation." Where Santayana's spelling was idiosyncratic but threatened no harm to sense or sensibility, we have allowed it to stand. We have been careful to set off the few other changes we made, such as the provision of words or parts of words clearly implied by the context, by the use of square brackets for easy identification.

The essays and fragments printed in this book are a part—we think an important part—of Santayana's philosophical output. The serious scholar of his work will discover much that is of interest and value here. Philosophers who chance upon these essays may draw courage from their speculative scope and learn to love the mind that gave them birth. And the general reader may agree with us that in a world in which too little thought is judicious and too little writing good, it would have been a grave loss to have surrendered these works to the dark.

I

Two Early Works

THE PROBLEM OF THE FREEDOM OF THE WILL IN ITS RELATION TO ETHICS

The word freedom has many meanings. When we say that a stream is not free to flow because it is frozen, we do not speak of the same freedom as when we say that a Negro is not free to vote because he is intimidated. For the Negro may still vote if he has courage enough to run the risk; but the frozen stream cannot possibly flow. Besides, a stream is not free to flow except when it is actually flowing, but a man may be free to vote and yet never cast his ballot. Thus by liberty we mean sometimes action and sometimes only permission; in the first case, action becoming possible becomes at the same time necessary, so that freedom means that a given force works unimpeded; in the second case, action remains merely possible, and freedom means that a given obstacle does not exist.

We talk of freedom in still another sense when we say that we do something freely, gladly, or willingly. Here it is not a question of obstacles at all; our attention is not directed to the facility or possibility of the action, but to the pleasure we take in doing it. Not unlike this use is that by which we call what is voluntary or intentional free. Thus if a man has done something unawares, or under the influence of another, we say his action was not free; yet we do not necessarily imply that he was reluctant to do it, but only that he was not conscious of what he did. Suppose, for example, that when the collection-box is passed around, I have only a ten-dollar bill, which I put in sorrowfully rather than appear to give nothing. The gift is not free. But if by some mistake, I think that what I am giving is only one dollar, the gift of the ten is still not free, even if I do not grudge it on discovering my error.

George Santayana, "The Problem of the Freedom of the Will in Its Relation to Ethics," "A junior forensic" published in the *Daily Crimson Supplement*, February 25, 1885.

When we speak of freedom of the will, we usually understand a kind of freedom different from all these. We mean by freedom, that a man, solicited by given motives in a given emergency, may act in various ways. For instance: the fact that I am enjoying a walk does not prove that I went out, or am walking now, of my own freewill; on the contrary, my enjoyment, in so far as it has any bearing at all on my freedom, tends to discredit it; since it would be harder to assign a reason for my action, if I had gone out when to do so caused me trouble and annoyance. We might, in this case, look for such opposed motives as could have influenced me; but we should then be merely evading and postponing the real question. We may assume that men are swayed by motives, and that they are apt to go where the strongest one drives them. What we want to know is this: could I with these same fixed motives have acted differently? Is my choice essentially independent not only of present circumstances, but also of my past circumstances and settled character; so that each act of my will is not a result from their union, but a new force, springing uncaused into existence,—an agent or factor in their union?

It is hard to understand the nature of such a force; and perhaps on this account people are apt, in discussing the freedom of the will, to confuse this special kind of freedom with those others which I have tried to explain. Another source of confusion is the prevailing feeling that the very existence of right and wrong is involved in this question; and therefore men approach the subject with their minds already made up, and do not take the trouble to analyze the problem and see in what sense right and wrong really depend on the answer we give to it.

Let us first consider what are the implications of the determinist view. If our acts depend entirely on our present circumstances and character, and our characters on past circumstances and the circumstances of our parents, it is evident that all things are perfectly determined. For the past cannot be changed, and as the future flows out of the past by a necessary law, the future is itself equally fixed and immutable. Why then, it may be said, should we waste effort in trying to accomplish that which, if not settled already, can never come about? If all things spring necessarily from the seeds sown in the beginning, what need is there that we should till the field of life with our labor or water it with our tears? Let us watch and be patient! we shall reap as much as if we worked. But this is not an inevitable conclusion; on the contrary, that very law which decrees that all things shall follow necessarily from their causes, decrees that our least effort, our most trifling act, shall not lack its proportionate effect. True, all future events are determined, but only because their antecedents were determined first: and so far from the truth is it that we cannot change our destiny, that in fact we cannot but change it. If we work, we turn the current of our lives in one direction; if we do not work, we turn it in the other.

And let it not be said that the zest of life is gone when we know that all is fixed. Do we read a story with less interest because the last page was written long ago? Indeed, the man of clear vision, who can estimate the forces at work in him and around him, is encouraged and emboldened when he feels that he knows what he is to accomplish. To him an opportunity is more than an exhortation, it is a prophecy. Yes, it may be said, very good, so long as the future he can foresee is pleasant, and the action he can forecast is noble; but if he thinks he is fated to be miserable, will that not extinguish his hopes, will that not break his spirit? Certainly, I might answer, and he must have a spirit broken already, who would not rather be sobered by truth than tickled by self-deception. Living is like going to the theatre: if the play is good, it is enjoyed all the more for having been previously read; while if it be known to be poor, at least it does not prove disappointing.

Granting, then, that fatalism does not take away the zest of life, let us inquire how much it modifies our notions of right and wrong. It is plain that no possible answer to the problem of freewill can change the experience men have had of what is good for them. Such conduct as has proved useful in the past, cannot but be thought wise for the future. In so far, therefore, as our notion of right and wrong is founded on experience, it would not seem to be at all affected by fatalism; and we have seen that fatalism does not discourage us in working out our purposes. The case is different, however, if we reject experience as the sole test of right conduct. For if right conduct be that which is intrinsically consistent and harmonious with our nature and the nature of our relations to all things, then any change in our idea of these relations will change our idea of right and wrong. In this way fatalism may have an influence on conduct such as is exercised by all religious and philosophical beliefs. It may sanction certain acts and practices and condemn others; it may encourage certain states of mind. Thus we can conceive that if all the world turned fatalist, we might see our good people face life with a little more calmness and intrepidity; we might expect to find less self-accusation and less of what is called righteous indignation. For if we came to regard wickedness as misfortune and monstrosity rather than sin, we should not find it necessary to be so vehement in our condemnation of wrong doing, since we should not feel so much secret sympathy with it. Even now, who of us in his heart would not be a rake rather than a hunchback, a villain rather than a fool? In spite of all the moralists, we cannot admire desert or merit as much as the gifts of nature and fortune. There is nothing of which we are so proud as of a good family, a handsome face, a strong body, a ready wit,—of all those things, indeed, for which we are not responsible; but no one is ever proud of trying hard. We may decree as much as we like that trying hard is the sum total of virtue, yet no one will ever want a prize for faithful endeavor. To be able to do easily what other people do with difficulty, or what they cannot do at all, that is what we are proud of and what we admire.

Apart, then, from these considerations, fatalism does not change our notion of what things are right and what wrong. But what it does change completely is our notion of the nature of right and wrong, of the nature of sin. We sometimes feel that we have thoughts and desires which are profoundly shameful; we have moments and seasons in which we feel very wretched and guilty. There is an anarchy in our souls which seems somehow to accuse us of treason and rebellion. But what does all this become in the scheme of fatalism? A delusion, a disease. Guilt cannot slip in through the network of necessary causation. If my ancestors were vicious, if my bringing up was bad, if my temptations were strong, why should I upbraid myself? Yet how am I to account for this consciousness of sin, which is wholly different from the consciousness of folly or misfortune? I may have done myself all the harm imaginable through mere folly and stupidity; but however mortified or sullen I may be, I can never feel guilty or penitent. It is as hard to argue us out of the consciousness of guilt, as it is to argue us into the consciousness of real desert: for while virtue is too wise and humble to claim any merit, sin is so proud and foolish that it will be always bragging.

Let us go back now and see if the theory of free will can help us out of our difficulty. If a man, solicited by given motives in a given emergency, may act in various ways; if a new force, springing uncaused into existence, becomes an agent or factor in his choice; will not the consciousness of guilt be explained? I think not. For if the same man in the same circumstances can make various decisions, how does his decision tell us anything about the true, permanent nature of the man? Whence the significance of his choice if, without being other than he is, he might choose differently? If a new force, springing uncaused into existence, becomes an agent or factor in his choice, is he not thereby relieved of all responsibility? Surely, this new force, if such there be, must not be uncaused; not only is such a supposition contrary to reason, but it defeats the very object for which it was framed. We want to prove that the man himself is the cause of his acts: this supposed new force must therefore be evolved, according to some law, out of the man's inmost nature, if it is to be the true expression of the man or if the man is to be held responsible for its decisions.

The old difficulty, however, recurs here. If the will is evolved out of the man's nature and this nature is necessarily what it is, how does he choose his act, how is he free? A man's acts depend on his character, which includes his will, reacting on his circumstances. His character is itself the result of circumstances and of the characters of his parents. The question now arises: if we carry our inquiry back far enough, shall we arrive at a point where intellect and will are swallowed up in mechanical forces of which they are the slowly evolved product? If so, I know not how we can explain responsibility. But if we say that intellect and will are the ultimate elements, the way lies open for an explanation. Let us suppose a will solicited by no motives, and therefore free as a stream is free when it flows unobstructed, yet whose essence, like the essence of the stream, is motion and action. Now this will, by its free activity might enslave itself to passion or ambition, somewhat as the stream, by the force of its own current, might heap up obstacles in its way; yet with this difference, that the stream gathers these obstacles from its bed, while the will finds its dangers only in the intellect of which it is the expression. And as the stream, choked by what it has collected, is stemmed and blocked, until the rains swell its torrent and burst the barrier; so the will, enslaved by its own surrender, frets impotently in its captivity, until the rain of grace from heaven floods the heart and sets it at liberty. For a free man, because he is free, may make himself a slave; but once a slave, because he is a slave, he cannot make himself free. Perhaps in this way we may be able to reconcile individual liberty with universal law. For if the will, being a spiritual activity, can attach itself, by virtue of its native strength and energy, to any of the things presented to it by the intellect, before any of these things has power to draw or to coerce it at all,—then is the will free and answerable for its choice: then may we understand why we should feel guilty when we fall and grateful when we are saved.

Whether this explanation be a good one or not, the facts remain the same. No theory about free will can alter the teaching of experience or take from us our energies and desires. But if we believe that our actions and characters are wholly determined by physical causation, we must regard sin as a disease or deformity, which may make us dangerous and disgusting, but cannot make us guilty. If we believe, on the contrary, that the law of our being is a spiritual law whose essence is freedom; if we believe that this natural freedom is abdicated when it is abused (and would that be freedom which could not be abused and abdicated?)—if we believe this, not only do we save our conscience by showing a rational ground for our consciousness of guilt; but we save our dignity as well, by showing that the soul's protest against being the sport and plaything of every accident and passion, is not the petulant fretting of a born slave, but the noble lamentation of a captive king.

PLATO PRATER'S
DIALOGUE ON PLEASURE

Plato: By Jove, dear Percy, this world cannot boast
A spot more charming nor a kinder host;
In your big chair, beside your leaping fire,
The flagon ready, what can man desire,
While he may see, in your accustomed place,
The smile of welcome on a handsome face?
Here friendship melts to love's diviner form,
And while the soul is free, the heart is warm.

Percy: It's not the flagon, nor the fire, nor I
That make your pleasure, but philosophy;

George Santayana, "Plato Prater's Dialogue on Pleasure," *Columbia Manuscript Collection.* © 1969 Daniel Cory. The manuscript bears the date 1885.

There's William smoking in his favorite nook,
Yet see the great Philistine's angry look.

William: Changing at Lisbon dollars into *reis*
You grow no richer, though the sum amaze,
And Plato thinks all this so great a pleasure
Because he reckons in a little measure.
I know not if he thinks, he's so well schooled,
There is philosophy in being fooled;
But as for me, the pleasure feels the same,
Called by a cynical or fulsome name,
And what philosophy I yet have heard
Changed nothing for me when it changed a word.

Percy: Perhaps there's something in the words we use;
Were Plato William, what a name he'd lose!
In giving you that name, your sainted dad,
Was, I am sure, prophetically mad.
In his priest's office, 'twas your father's turn
Incense in Hingham Meeting House to burn;
Behold, an angel of the Lord appeared,
Standing upon the night. "Be not afeared,"
Answered and said the angel, "Mr. Prater,
For thou shalt have a son to call thee pater;
And neither wine nor strong drink shall he drink,
But shall be filled with wisdom as with ink—
Great shall he be, and great shall be his fame,
And Plato Prater thou shalt call his name."
Then said your father, "Whereby shall I know
That I should call my Christian offspring so?
No Platos in the Holy Bible be,
And ne'er a Plato on my family tree."
At this proud bigotry the angel grieved;
"Because," he answered, "thou hast not believed,
Even as I have said it shall be done,
And thou shalt have a heathen for a son."
They would have called you, when the christening came,
Nebuchadnezzar from your father's name;
But you, to that fond parent's consternation,
With kicks and screams refused regeneration.

Then he confessed, and he did not deny;
"Yea, verily, the angel told no lie,
And let my heathen son be Plato till he die."

Plato: My parents lived in transcendental days
When Plato for a name could not amaze;
And, spite of all the texts at your command,
Who's not a pagan in this Christian land?
Imagine how a heathen Stoic's head
Would bristle at what Christian William said;
A Stoic, who believed that he could still
Pain's evil, by not thinking pain an ill,
And whose strong heart, by ceasing to complain,
Turned to a virtue what it found a pain.
But how much easier to fashion joy
Than present pangs with reasons to destroy!
And yet it seems to me there must be cause
For all opinions in our nature's laws,
And if for such discussion you have leisure,
I would propose the question: What is pleasure?

William: Pleasure is pleasure: All that you will say
Can but repeat it in another way,
Till from the maze of artificial doubt
The clue of common sense can bring you out;
And when you have retraced your twisted track,
You'll thank your wits you got your knowledge back.
Pleasure is doing anything we like:
If loved to love again, if struck to strike,
To eat when hungry, to be cooled when hot,
To drink when thirsty and, in fact, when not,
To smoke a merschaum [sic], and to live at ease,
And above all things, pleasure is to please.

Percy: To hold your own up and to say "It's that!"
Is not to show the nature of a hat.
One costs five dollars, and of these, you know,
Two go for comfort and the rest for show;
And may we not believe our pleasures share
The hybrid nature of the hats we wear?

Some keep us sane and healthy on the way,
And some we value for the price we pay.

William: How can that be? "The way" must lead us still
To other pleasures or away from ill;
And talk of health or virtue, wealth or fame,
The thing you seek is pleasure all the same.

Percy: Think you Van Vooler chose his room this year
For being pleasant or for being dear?
Such fools will take—I know what you will say—
More pleasure in a thing the more they pay;
But if he gets his pleasure, by your rule
You shouldn't call Van Vooler still a fool.

William: See how you quibble! Since Van Vooler thought
That he was valued for the things he bought,
The nincumpoop is proved an arrant fool,
And boasts of that which brings him ridicule.

Percy: For half the world, your wisdom can't deny,
A man is worth the things that he can buy;
And something more than ridicule it brings
To flaunt a fortune and a lot of rings.
These make a milkmaid think the fool a god,
And from the footlights bring a smile and nod;
For these at last some reigning belle will stoop
To tempt the shyness of the nincumpoop;
And little compensations of this sort
Console Van Vooler for your ill report.

Plato: But let us say, if Percy quibbles still,
For future pleasures I have reckoned ill,
And though I think I am the first of men,
All others flout me,—am I foolish then?
What difference in pleasure does it make
Whether the pleasure rest on a mistake?
If it is foolish to be pleased with lies,
Truth and not pleasure is the highest prize,
And an ideal of the fit and fair
Turns into shame the pleasure that is there.

William: No: fit and fair are such because they please,
And pleasure rests on truth to be at ease.
A baseless pleasure pleases us in vain
Since it is followed by a greater pain,
But wisdom serves to render pleasure sure,
And truth to make it as herself endure.

Percy: What taints our pleasures, then, is not the lie,
But the discovery that makes them die;
And since a falsehood, if it gain belief,
Can turn well-founded pleasure into grief,
Conceit and wise delight alike must cower
Before the whim of the succeeding hour.
The wise are wretched if they change their mind,
The blind are blest if they continue blind,
And safest, truest pleasure can be had
Only by men irreparably mad.

Plato: Life's pleasure makes its value, William thinks;
But if it be so, how that value shrinks,
And what a blunderer must nature be
For pleasure to devise the world we see!
Is it for pleasure that the planets run
In patient circles round a burning sun?
Is it for pleasure that the lichens grow
Close to the edges of the chilling snow?
Is it for pleasure that the insects breed,
And pile their booty for another's need?
No: even we, in love's mysterious rage,
Rave greater thirsts than loving can assuage;
Love is no longing of the single man,
But giant nature rushing to her plan,
Rousing her spirit to complete her task
And working witchcraft in a woman's mask.
No thought of self impels the valiant man
To seize a standard and to lead the van,
But nature, as she bids the swiftest guide
The herd of deer along the mountain side,
Commands her slave, with weapons all her own,
To save a people or to build a throne.

'Tis for their country soldiers think they fight,
Not for their pleasure, and their soul is right,
For nature does not tremble at their pain,
Too bent on victory to count the slain;
She conquers not alone with them that win,
Her glory is the slaughter and the din;
The loss and triumph are alike her deed,
And fate enacted is her labor's meed.
Suppose a thirsty boy, some summer day,
Drank of an icy spring, and went his way.
Long after he returns and sees the brook
And stoops for that delicious draught he took,
But thirst has left him on this winter day
And silent and perplexed he turns away.
So far his nature led him by the hand
And those quick thoughts he could not understand
Are no more selfish than the eagle's flight
Or the birds' welcome of the morning light.
But if some devil, cunning in deceit,
Offers a poisoned leaf and whispers, "Eat,
And thou shalt feel the pleasing thirst once more
And taste the fountain's sweetness as before;"
Then has young Adam made the great mistake
And has begun to live for pleasure's sake.
Yet men can so forget their happy days
And so far wander from their simple ways,
As to believe that they have ever wrought
As now, when prompted by a crooked thought.
They eat, but think not that they eat to live;
They give, but fancy that they do not give,
But that for heaven or some selfish good,
They lend their children and their neighbor food.
Thus the unnatural and puny mind
Feigns a mean motive to debase mankind;
Thus the shrill-voiced philosophers of vice
Say all men love and labor for a price,
Liken the ether to the Paris slime,
And think the eighteenth century is Time.
But never did a simple, noble heart

Devise a pleasure, or enjoy with art.
That he may live, a mother tends her son,
And brave men labor that the work be done,
Lift their devotion heavenward in stone,
And build their thought, as nature builds her own.
She, like the grim Egyptian, is intent
On raising her eternal monument,
And, as she lays each stone upon the pile,
Smiles for a moment—pleasure is that smile—
But till her total purpose be expressed,
She toils forever, and she cannot rest.
Within those stones the past world buried lies;
Her they will cover, when the future dies;
She knows not why she labors, such is doom,
Yet loves the beauty of her rising tomb.

William: Who says that pleasure keeps the stars in motion?
It's not from me you got that silly notion.
Like all philosophers I ever saw
You're simply knocking down a man of straw.
We have our instincts, leading us one way,
Which it involves a pain to disobey,
And to escape the pain, we do a thing
Before we know the pleasure it will bring.
I do not say that instincts ever lead
Through knowledge of delight that will succeed,
But that the pleasure added to an act
Gives it the value which it else had lacked,
And though the cause of living none can give,
Pleasure's the reason why we ought to live.
It's better not to live than live in pain,
And life has prizes that we live to gain.
You seem to think that prudence is the root
Of evil and that man should be a brute;
That it is wrong one's happiness to win,
And that to live by reason is a sin.
For reason's work is to keep pain away
And conquer as much pleasure as it may;
To bend blind nature to our human ends

And teach her forces to become our friends.
What nobler object can we have in life
Than to be victors in the unequal strife,
To build the world upon a better plan
And to promote the happiness of man?
For as to nature's purpose, by this time
To talk mythology should be a crime,
And in asylums all should be confined
Who know what gravitation has in mind.

Plato: Was it not nature gave your reason birth?
And yet this lever that would move the earth
Rests on a fulcrum which is but a part
Of palpitating earth, a mortal heart.
Reason is weaker than what makes it be
And wise men's wisdom is humility;
They build their happiness on self-surrender,
And seek to follow nature, not to mend her.

Percy: When men imagine life is made to please
And hardship's object is to be at ease,
By that sweet paradox their wit's abused,
And they begin to toil to be amused.
It is their solemn duty to be glad,
But conscientious gladness makes them sad;
Pursuing pleasure they enjoy it not,
And fan themselves so hard, it makes them hot;
They lose their dollar gaming for a dime,
And suffer tortures for a pleasant time;
Yet for their folly the excuse is this,
That they have quite forgot what pleasure is.
When Adam sinned, and the immortals said
That henceforth every man should sweat for bread,
Against this sect they passed a special measure:
"The pleasurists shall also sweat for pleasure;
The more they sweat, the less fun they shall get,
The less they have, the harder they will sweat."
So, my good William, if your faith is true,
I'll tell you what two things you ought to do;

First, to forbid that it be taught the poor,
Who have enough already to endure;
Second, to give it up yourself for good,
And find the secret of a merry mood.
What, are you going? but I want to know
What real pleasure is, before you go.
Let us clear up the muddle we are in,
And Plato, who began it, shall begin.

Plato: Pleasure is peace. Whenever sharp desire
Enslaves the eyes and fans the bosom's fire,
If she has mercy whom the soul addressed,
The longing lulls, and pleasure is to rest.
When misers in a whispered dream behold
A gliding villain carry off their gold,
They waken with a pang, but breathing deep
They clutch their keys, and pleasure is to sleep.
When a wise man defends a righteous law
And sees the world is listening in awe,
Finding how weak are his astonished foes,
He feels his strength, and pleasure is repose.
And at the summit of the hill of life,
When all is beauty which below is strife,
Man feels his passions and his sorrows cease;
He has his all, and pleasure is but peace.

William: Pleasure is wealth: to hold within your hand
The reins of nature, and to give command;
'Tis not to stifle but to feed the fire,
Not to abandon but fulfil desire;
To heap the riches of abundant life
And but in victory to cease from strife.
Pleasure is growth: to feel the rising tide
Of vital energy and noble pride,
To grow forever to a larger need
And on a richer harvest ever feed,
The deep recesses of the world to scan
And make all nature the domain of man.
Labor with hope gives soul and body health,
And all our pleasure is in growth and wealth.

Percy: Pleasure is mirth: forever on the wing,
A quick, pert, merry, giddy little thing.
Where fashion dances, pleasure only skips;
Where folly swims, swift pleasure only dips;
Vice drinks the dregs, where pleasure only sips;
Where passion falls, sweet pleasure only slips.
'Tis but a spark, struck out as we are whirled
In this ridiculous and tedious world.
Go build a pretty castle in the air,
Laugh when it fades, and build one yet more fair;
Go kiss a little maiden glad and meek,
But kiss her once and kiss her on the cheek;
Go have your wine, your story, and your song,
Then leave the bawling fools, and come along.
So may you taste true pleasure, for on earth
The only pleasure that is sweet is mirth.

II

Causation and Flux

CAUSATION

Cause, like substance, is a notion much criticised by modern philosophers and sometimes discarded by them. The most usual and flimsy of their criticisms are psychological. When facts have been reduced to human perceptions, that is, to illusions, it is easy to reduce the pregnancy of facts to human superstition, namely, to the expectation of any sequence once observed among them. But this whole psychological web is artificial; it is the literary dress given by half-hearted critics to a subjectivism not nakedly presentable. The actual perceptions of any individual are few and not exactly repeated: those he can remember are even fewer, and most confused and distorted. Far from the identity of objects being imagined by mankind to express the similarity of their repeated perceptions, these repeated perceptions, though actually very diverse, are assimilated by the cursory psychologist when he knows that they are directed upon the same object. Moreover, even if the psychology of these critics had been frank and sound, they could never have made a good physics out of it.

A supposed rule, such as the natural philosophy of psychologists is based on, that the same phenomena follow upon one another is futile: there are no "same" phenomena. It is only natural objects and the ways of nature that endure after a fashion and may be recognised; but nature is not composed, like the "minds" known to philosophers, of a series of discrete ideas, succeeding and repeating one another. Nature is an infinite irrevocable flux of matter, never falling into precisely the same conjunction twice, never arresting its phases absolutely, nor halting between them: a material flux involving another, equally continuous, of the relations that are predicable from time to time among its parts; while this morphological flux in turn carries a third discontinuous

George Santayana, "Causation," Columbia Manuscript Collection. © 1969 Daniel Cory. Santayana meant this as Chapter III of *The Realm of Matter* (London: Constable, 1930). The book, as published, contains no chapter on causation.

flux upon it, that of the interests and ideas belonging to such of those morphological units as are fitfully conscious and troubled about their destiny. When this incidental play of consciousness, the most superficial stratum of nature, is taken for the whole of it, we need not wonder if the natural sense for that force is perplexed which secretly propels the world.

It is only in the flux of matter, or in reference to this flux, that there are any laws; and when the existence of matter is denied and laws are sought among the random pictures in sense, it is no marvel that laws are not found; for the alleged inductions based on repetitions in experience are either pathological—a single striking instance leading a helpless mind to fear or hope it shall be repeated—or else they are not inductions but shrewd discoveries of some part of the mechanism of nature. If the psychological critics of causation have sometimes retained their hold on natural laws (as Mill usually did) it has been only by an inconsequence. They have availed themselves of such convenient equivocations as the one contained in the word "phenomenon" which when they are psychological critics, means some essence momentarily given in sense, but when they are naturalists means some part of the material world, conceived in its natural setting. The rainbow, for instance, is a "phenomenon"; but between the apparition of that aesthetic essence in the sensibility of Noah and its reapparition in that of the Lake Poets there is no psychological connection.—Such apparitions, even if all mankind were counted in, would have no continuity, derivation, regularity, or proportion. Mill, however, having dutifully called the rainbow a phenomenon, to salve his subjectivist conscience, would at once have begun to discuss the substances that produced it, vapours and refracted light, and the rest; and forgetting he was an idealist he might have given us some instruction about the constitution of nature and the causes of our perceptions.

Nearer to the heart of the subject come those criticisms of causation which are based on the temporal relation of cause to effect. It would seem that when the cause is given, the effect, if it be one, should *immediately* ensue, or rather should have ensued already. If, to avoid this, we suppose an interval between the maturity of the cause and the production of the effect, another cause must determine the length of this interval; and the same difficulty would recur about the operation of this ancillary cause, which pulls the trigger.

Like most honest difficulties in philosophy, this arises from a too human view of nature. Nature is the realm of derivation; it is all process and genesis, and in this sense everything in nature has a cause—everything flows from something else. Niagara shows but an infinitesimal part of the force, persistence, and volume of that universal cataract. But this voluminous stream is undivided; its operation is equable, pervasive, mechanical. The units which we are apt to call causes, on the contrary, as well as those we call effects, are phenomenal, verbal, moral units; they are concretions in discourse. They violate the lines of cleavage in nature, substituting others made from a human point of view, and in a violent moral perspective. They couple directly things disparate and remote in their real genealogy. As astrology referred human dispositions to stellar conjunctions, so human wit still astrologises in its daily business, in its reading of personal and moral forces. Thus we may say, not without a certain feminine shrewdness, that the cause of this indigestion was lobster and the cause of that suicide was love. But lobster is usually digestible and love curable; and all that comes of such casual divinations is a true sense for the *general place* of the cause and a propensity to haste and passion in specifying that cause precisely. Every doctor has his special bug-bears and nostrums; every religion has its particular narrow path. In morals and even in knowledge of the world much is hotheaded and fanciful. The diagnosis of society is hopelessly difficult, because the terms in which we are forced to make it are captious: which is not to say that nature has not a precise constitution or life no general direction in which alone it may be lived with safety. Reality has a bias, an unequivocal order, which may be roughly but substantially indicated by popular wisdom.

To come to close quarters with causes, however, it would be necessary to penetrate to the mechanism of matter. There we should see what in the lobster deranged the stomach and in what way, and what physiological complications made love violent and ineradicable, ultimately diverting the impulse to embrace a particular lovely creature into an impulse to drown one's miserable self: for these revulsions and expedients of passion invade consciousness in a kaleidoscopic way, fatally or spontaneously, i.e., physiologically brought about, like the shifts in dreams. The ideal dramatic machinery of motives, passions, and reasons by which such shifts may be expressed or justified is a fiction after the fact, a rhetorical embroidery in which deep-lying natural propensities and crises are clothed in the actor's fancy.

If we consider events discretely, like statues in a park, we may well say that if they do not touch there must be a void space between them. The cause must either have produced the effect already or does not suffice to produce it at all. Or if, marching on bravely in the path of subjectivism, we try to frame a law that events shall produce their effects telepathically, at the exact distance, let us say, of nine months, we may perhaps be overlooking some discoverable intermediaries, and we shall arrive in the end at a savage caricature of nature. Idealism is indeed, in many ways, the expression of primitive bewilderment, returning after long acquaintance with nature, and therefore possessed of articulate ideas to criticise and of habits of thought and presumptions by which to criticise them. It is mere superstition to attribute one event to the magic influence of another, however constant the conjunction may be reputed to be between them. Were such a coincidence established by ten thousand instances, it would remain a conjunction of appearances, to be explained by some continuous flux of substance beneath. The breaking of innumerable waves in similar fashion one after another does not establish a causal influence of each upon the next. It invites the naturalist to study the origin of each wave out of the constant properties of water, the steady force of the wind, and the conformation of the shore; for if these true causes varied, the previous successive breaking of an infinite number of waves would have no tendency to provoke the swelling and breaking of one wave more. The generations of animals, and their habits, have no magic tendency to mirror themselves on the principle that what has been shall be. Such a way of thinking is not science but omen-reading and slack gnomic wisdom. Generations resemble one another so long as they are supported and compacted by the same equilibrium of material forces. This material equilibrium is not absolutely constant; therefore the types and habits of animals change more or less quickly, and all the now observable phenomena of nature, by the very force of nature, are destined to disappear. We have meagre reports of what life has been like on earth for a few thousand years, and many of them have already become almost unintelligible; yet our empirical philosophers pretend to demonstrate the uniformity of nature on that evidence, while other philosophers prove to their own satisfaction that experience must always have the same character, and marches towards a goal which they can discern. In truth, if we could look again into the world in some million years, if we found an earth at all, we should no more find the present animals in it than we should find the present languages: for words too, like other natural facts, do not repeat themselves magically *ad infinitum* in the same sequences, but are formed and combined afresh on each occasion. Experience is like literature, a superficial highly qualified, quite unreproducible outcome of very complex processes in matter. There are no more constant sequences in experience than there are constant sequences in words. Certain phrases, certain idioms, recur often in certain circles for a certain time: then that eddy in the stream of life is obliterated and nature continues her steady, unmindful career. Not long ago what we call language and what we call experience did not exist; soon both will have disappeared; and we cannot tell what similar or dissimilar expressions the movement of nature may bring with it subsequently, as we cannot tell what expressions she found in earlier times.

The psychological habit of regarding sensations as fundamental facts has created a special puzzle about the relations of body and mind. If the constant antecedents of a phenomenon are its causes, it would seem that any constant accompaniment of the antecedent is a part of it, and therefore, of the cause: so that a feeling of relief, if it always accompanied the rise of temperature above the freezing-point, would be a part of the cause of the melting of snow that would ensue. Absurdity in the attribution of causes is so habitual to mortals, that to attribute causal influence to feelings hardly seems a paradox to them. They may not always say that a feeling of relief can help to melt snow; but they commonly say that mind influences body, which is the same thing put more vaguely.

An ancient and rooted fallacy lies at the basis of all this confusion about causes. People who might not say that snow can be melted by a feeling of relief say with conviction that a feeling of pain will draw the hand away from the fire. Why this diverse appreciation of cases perfectly similar materially? Simply because they are not similar morally. By the operation of mind, ever since Anaxagoras and Socrates, people have understood a moral or useful direction impressed obviously though miraculously on things. They do not take mind in the psychological sense of an actual evanescent consciousness of anything. The power of reason, the obedience of nature to the excellences it should produce is what impresses them. They have not the key to this harmony: and the certitude they live in that their minds move the world is rooted in the fact that, they know not how, the world so largely serves their minds. How their minds themselves come to be or to have such interests as they have is a point left unconsidered: how, having somehow taken shape, these minds provoke corresponding changes in matter, without in the least conceiving the means or mechanism of those changes, is unconsidered too; but the miracle of an ultimate harmony becomes its own excuse for being, and habit and language make the magic of it familiar and therefore unquestioned.

Eventual values are called final causes: and the name of cause is not misused, although the cause here precedes its effect in time, if by that word we understand, like the ancients, any principle of explanation, any circumstance that may help the human mind to find its quietus in the presence of facts. Value is such a circumstance. An initial failure to understand the relation of values to natural existence has led mankind into two by-paths without issue: one the attribution of final causes, by which nature is explained by the supposed power of the good; the other the problem of evil, in which, seeing that the good does not prevail, an explanation is sought for that fact on the principle that, somehow, the good prevails notwithstanding.

The ingrained habit of attributing power to wishes and thoughts has contributed to the notion, not countenanced at all by the actual methods of nature, that a cause is a detached fact with a concrete message or behest, which its effect will presently fulfil. Nature has been conceived as a sort of demoniac society in which a thousand incantations and bewitchments crossed each other, each a motive, a virtue, an influence, and to understand anything was to distribute the responsibility for it among these various magical agents. Existence was a battle-field of actions and passions, in which nothing was more normally efficacious than wish, word, and prayer. In this Neo-Platonic Babel we have been reared, and it is no marvel if we cannot readily learn the language of nature. By causes we ordinarily understand such particular things of discourse, endowed with specific aerial powers; and it is against this remnant of magic that the criticism of causation, when scientific, has been directed; and hence too the ill-repute that has fallen on the word cause among scientific people.

The flux of matter is the ground of the morphological and of the psychic flux; but even here the propriety of calling the material flux the cause of the other two is dubious. Each posture of matter does not precede the truths or the consciousness which may express it, nor does it pass into them, nor spend any part of its energy in giving them birth. They arise and vanish with its self-contained transformations, as unanimity may arise and vanish with the successive phases of a friendship. That the relations embodied in flux are embodied in it inevitably, without exhausting or appropriating the least part of its matter or energy, is perhaps already obvious to the reader: it is impossible to imagine a more direct dependence of one thing on another, and yet the word cause seems out of place to describe the relation between a closed mechanism and the perfectly ideal forms which it realises from moment to moment. The relation of the material flux to consciousness is more difficult to understand, since it is a natural and contingent relation, and the second term of it is not implied in the mere existence of the first: that a consciousness which may lapse altogether should accompany some of the figures in the morphological flux, raising them to an actual and living expression, and clothing them in a new and variegated plumage, is a quite unexpected redundancy in nature: matter happens to have this sort of fertility, when it has fallen into certain shapes.

The consciousness of animals hypostasises into psychic acts some of the morphological relations into which matter falls as it flows—pleasures, ideas, meanings, emotions. These facts are actual and self-existent; their number and order—unlike the number and order of morphological units—is fixed and unambiguous. This psychic lightning, since it flashes out of certain motions in the cloud of matter, might well be said to depend upon them and be an extraneous effect which has them for its cause. But if we adopted this language we should have to remove from the notion of causation the suggestion of an identical substance or force passing from an earlier to a later arrangement: the psychic expression of life is contemporary with its material phases, and it is in itself perfectly unsubstantial, evanescent, inconsequential, and impotent. It is no continuation of the same process that goes on in body, no transformation of the same energy. It is a spirit brooding over the waters; and the principle on which it arises here and not there, and reveals this sensuous quality and not that, is a mysterious corollary to the morphology of animal life. The vital spark flies when flint and steel strike together; and its colour and heat correspond precisely, though in heterogeneous terms, to certain circumstances in the world of friction.

This spiritual radiation of material life might be called, in some senses, an effect of it: it is a discrete fact always attached to a different discrete fact; but the relation is not one of succession, but of simultaneity, so that philosophers to whom time seems substantial might be rather inclined to say that the bodily movement and its psychic expression were parts of the same event, and not causally related. Only it would then have to be admitted that only a part, the material part, of such an event showed any qualitative or quantitative continuity with what came before or after, the continuations of mental life being spasmodic, precarious, and imperfect; as is the brightness of an arc light, which does not follow with historical propriety on its previous brightness, but spurts or goes out most inconsequentially according to the state of the batteries and the wires.

There is much justification in calling the constellation of matter which any form of animation accompanies the cause of this animation: for the dependence is complete and unilateral. Yet the element of succession is absent, the terms being simultaneous; and it is consequently more proper to name the feelings that arise the expression or entelechy or hypostasis of the bodily situation, and this the organ or instrument of the actual consciousness. For we must remember that while in the order of genesis consciousness is the last, most unsubstantial, and most fugitive of beings, it is first in the order of discovery, and in its intensity of being; so much so that, from its point of view, the whole realm of matter may be called merely potential, until actualised, discovered, and brought to a head in experience. This situation is incompatible with another implication, besides that of succession, which is involved in the word cause. The cause is often thought to possess a greater dignity or comprehensiveness than the effect, to be the elder and nobler possessor of all that flows from it, at once a father and a model. Now mind, while simpler structurally than its ground (which could not otherwise be the ground of everything in it) by its very concision and symbolism adds a new wealth to nature, the warmth of life, and the vicissitudes of good and evil: while the infinite complexities of matter are without intrinsic value, and can be called good only for the mind's sake, when they produce or entertain it worthily.

Within the mechanical flux, again, to speak of causes and effects is beside the point. All the elements of the material world are original, its laws constant, and the possibility of calculating any posture of it is equal in any direction. No part or phase of substance is responsible for any other, or nearer to the ground of things. Causes are not assigned in those parts of nature, like the solar system, where the mechanism lies revealed. The laws of motion are not causes but descriptions; and the earlier motions are not causes of the latter, but other parts of the same continuum of motions. Motion would be impossible if there had to be a static cause for it; it simply exists. And as the most infinitesimal motion is already a transition, so the most elaborate evolution is only one movement; its earlier parts are not the cause, but only the beginning, of the later ones. There is a sort of dynamic democracy in nature, where influence and obedience are alike pervasive.

It is only when we veil and divide the mechanism of nature in terms of our senses and interests, that causes and effects become distinguishable; but then we have passed from the realm of matter and of science to that of appearance and discourse. When we consider the fate of animals, or of political and moral units, the steady and passionless flux of matter comes to be divided in our apprehension into propitious or fatal influences, into preparatory and hereditary strains. We discern dramatic forces, defining them by their relation to the moral realities they support. Thus the turns and twists of life become referable to causes, as malaria is referable to mosquitoes or the fall of one country to the rise of another. These are conventional or rhetorical units; and the whole sense, of which history is full, of competing possibilities, interests, and forces, has only a poetic sort of truth.

In this way the thought of writing a letter, writing it accordingly, and a friend receiving it in Australia may be called each the cause of the other, but not seriously: for the thought does not assure the writing, save on the hypothesis that the physiological mechanism works in an exemplary manner, so that no intention arises which is not prophetic of an operation actually to take place. This effect would not ensue if the man was scatter-brained, or if some change had occurred in his environment or in his body to "change his mind," or if he had died or lost his memory, both being primarily chance turns in his material organism. Nor would the letter if written have reached its destination and the cognisance of that Australian, if the ship that carried it had sunk or pitch from the hand of malicious persons had defiled it in the post-box. So that these social events—the thought, the writing, and the receiving—though in a given state of society usually ensuing upon one another, have no power, and have even no tendency, to produce each other directly. They are mere signs or omens indicating that, if the mechanism of the world continues to operate in a certain way, these events will emerge from it, not from each other, at the customary intervals.

Ideal units, such as a man's country, are always being conceived or felt without ever existing naturally; what is covered by them is a mass of matter, loosely deliminated [sic], and offering to the imagination an always different but somewhat continuous series of beauties, facilities, and comforts. Moral geography is compacted of myths. Consciousness, though almost entirely ignorant of the material reactions and issues of which it is the voice, is not ignorant that it bears some message, that it is burdened with a mighty announcement: and it finds terms of its own, like the prophet and the poet that it is, for this oracular communication. These terms are the secondary and the tertiary qualities of things. Like colours, or like the gods of Olympus, they clothe, vivify, and hide the mechanism for which they stand, in so far as they have a natural signification at all. They thereby reveal the world and its ways with a vague, redundant, practical truth shrouded in symbols. On this level the attribution of causes properly flourishes; it is necessarily somewhat arbitrary, and the same field may be traversed with equal discernment by a great number of these shrewd philosophies. We cannot say, for instance, that the attribution of motives to men is always inapt; the motives attributed are sometimes those which these men would attribute to themselves and think they were governed by. But even when avowed, motives are only symbols; what gives a man these motives, and these motives their skill and power, is something deeper and undistinguished. So the feminine art of assigning causes is not wholly fallacious, if we take it for what it is worth. It never reaches the true basis and generative motion of anything; but it often suggests what has occurred on the social level with which it deals and it describes the possible vicissitudes of destiny in a rapid and dramatic way.

The "causes" of things which a cursory observer can assign are accordingly mere arbitrary and exchangeable units, of a literary sort, behind which the flux of substance is going on, altogether too minute, complex, and voluminous for sense or language to trace it. Mankind accordingly live and talk in a sort of dream. All our familiar terms and images are masks; and the personage behind them all is always the same, an infinite, ceaseless, infinitesimal flux of matter, grounding and imposing these interesting appearances on us for a while with a treacherous monotony. They are not the units of its own movement; the morphological accident which supported them may therefore suddenly lapse; the appearance will collapse with it, into a disconcerting and almost incredible nothingness; but the flux of matter will go on unperturbed, ready to dance elsewhere to some other tune.

The interdependence of facts, by which one may be inferred from another, is of three sorts, to none of which the term causation can be applied without qualification. First, there is the coherence of the universal material mechanism, which, wherever it is sufficiently known, enables us to calculate past, future, or unknown parts of a system from those that are given. Second, there is the extraneous and unilateral dependence on this mechanism of psychic life, translating certain conjunctions in this mechanism into picturesque and dramatic intuitions, but without any transmission of substance or motion into that apparition. Third, there is a superficial, imputed, and apparently magical connection between units of discourse, when the course of nature happens to have brought them to light in somewhat similar couples several times in succession. The critics of causation have therefore, in each of these regions, plenty to occupy them and to justify their enlightened scepticism: but the terrible propulsion, the infinite pregnancy, of nature is not thereby removed.

What the formulas of mechanism describe is a method of transition —like motion in a straight line. The terms of this calculation already contain in them the miracle of change, the fact of universal unrest, the portent of destiny: and if this fatality is calculable, if it is a beautifully mathematical flux, that circumstance cannot arrest it, or hasten or delay a single one of the perhaps momentous things it must bring to light. The sense of dependence, therefore, and the sense of connection between past and future, are amply justified. When men look for causes, they are wisely studying the ways of nature, and fortifying their minds with all possible arts and all necessary resignation. These causes can never be truly found, however, so long as appearances are not first reduced to the terms of substance, and the mechanism of this substance is not disclosed. For this reason only the exact physical and mathematical sciences can make any solid progress: in the others, the superficial plane of the enquiry forbids all thorough understanding of the actual methods of change. In Darwinism, for instance, natural history seemed to take a great step forward: and so, indeed, it did, in that it conceived the possibility of reducing the superficial fact of diverse species, and the adaptation of their organs to one another and to the environment, to the mechanical influence of selection by death. Nevertheless, as the exact method of this selection was not traced, so as to become calculable mathematically, and as the exact origin of variations also remained unexplored, the positive gain and even the scientific tendency of Darwinism could come to be doubted: and it has not prevented a relapse into vitalism in some half-scientific quarters. The argument has even been heard that the "sciences of life" required a different method, because the mechanical method had not succeeded in dealing with them. These "sciences of life," however, are only the vague impressions and dreams of people unable to understand what occurs in nature: astronomy was once a "science of life," of that of the beasts of the Zodiac, or of the divine children of Heaven. Natural history, psychology, and all other fields where observation remains superficial, can be distributed only into impressionist units and described in rhetorical terms, so long as the substantial movement and inner connection of their objects is not discovered. If that should occur, however, the sciences of life would really begin to exist, because the mechanism of life would begin to be clear. Such understanding of nature everywhere on the material plane, with its universal order and consecutiveness, would not destroy, of course, the appearances from which human investigation must start. Astronomical appearances endure, and so vital appearances always will; but if they were understood they would cease to be confused with powers or causes, and to the great gain of the spirit, they would be recognised as that coinage of the brain which fancy is very cunning in; and as the ghosts disappeared, poetry would come into its own.

The notion that events have causes is inevitable and very true— *felix qui potuit rerum cognoscere causas.* The proof lies in the possibility of art and prophecy: e.g., by bringing logs together and setting them up with due precautions a hut can be built. In time, a fire or a storm may destroy that shelter. The operation of building is a mode in the flux of substance, which as it passes leaves as a sort of sediment another mode of substance called the hut, in which change, although not really absent, has another and much less obvious rhythm for human observation. Building is not (what psychologism would make of it) one phenomenon—a set of muscular and optical sensations—followed by other phenomena, occasional vistas of a hut; building is a system of conspiring motions in matter which in themselves set up the hut and leave it standing; the substance of the hut being a part of the substance concerned in those previous motions. When the fire or the flood comes, which is another stream of matter endowed with a different motion, it engages in its own rhythm the substance of the hut, which had attained such a placid equilibrium, either carrying it away in great fragments, or subtly transforming its molecular motion into what is called flame. The hut has become smoke and ashes, or rubbish and rotting wood; and the fire and the storm also vanish, the substance which had danced to those rhythms taking on other forms. For these events, selected and named by human anxiety, are imbedded in a thousand others, and contain a thousand others, not distinguished by such scant and biassed observation: and even such a homely and trivial event could not be described adequately without tracing the entire movement of the substances concerned in it—something impossible to human wit.

The act of building is a form of motion just as material as the rush of wind or of fire: if there are architects so contemplative that they never make drawings, give orders, or otherwise move in the field of action, it is certain that they build nothing. Even sacraments and miracles cannot work without some material vehicle; and when God said "Let there be light," this word must somehow have been an event in the material world; otherwise the light, bidden to be by an eternal will, would have always existed, and no event would have occurred. The subtle instinctive impulses of eye and hand, and the pursuit of safety and comfort by which the architect is led to build, or to plan or to conceive building, are even more unimaginable to him, and more out of scale with his gross images, than the mysterious energies of wind and fire: and his own work of building is represented in his mind by some vague symbol, perhaps only by the bitter word "labour"; as if the fire were represented only by the fire-fiend, or the wind by the god Notus. Certainly such mythical or verbal symbols mark an advance in knowledge over merely enduring those events and those sensations: important moral units have at least been discriminated and somehow named. But of the process in nature and the conditions of art such myths and names give no knowledge: they form a poetic physics which, even when grown trite and prosaic, remains merely pictorial and entirely specious, composed of images and words.

Eventually, this lazy humanism in science may give place to mathematical accuracy, which is not less human for being more austere. The Sciences cannot re-enact nature in her own person: they are descriptions, artificial even if conscientious, of some part [of] her conduct.

There is no better way of pointing to the most recondite truth than giving it a fair name: science and mythology are both justified by this necessity, and are not enemies, though they may be rivals; because the names they give to things are appropriate in different directions. All that a critic can ask is that both myth and science should retain the modesty of names, denoting facts without pretending to resemble them.

CAUSATION

Cause, like substance, has been in modern times a favourite mark for psychological criticism, which has plausibly analysed the idea men have formed of it and suggested its origin, without pointing out any evidence whatever to show whether causation, like substance, does or does not obtain in the natural world. We have seen that the human idea of substance has often been empty, verbal and perversely metaphysical, but that nevertheless there surely is a substance within actual things and events, and that in the sense in which substance means simply any self-existent thing there could not fail to be some substance if anything was to exist at all. Similarly, the human idea of cause has often been coloured by subjective illusions, such as the illusion of activity and the illusion of necessity; nevertheless there is a derivation in nature of thing from thing, and methods of generation and evolution are discoverable and discovered. All Art and shrewd understanding relies on known ways of working, but as the evidence for generative power is empirical it can never be exhaustive of all instances or widely extensible over unknown parts of the world. "Practically" we may say that grapes do not grow on thistles, and that virgins have no children; yet new fruits by gradual transformation or sudden grafting may really grow up on old stocks, and parthenogenesis is no less practicable than sexual reproduction. If we find our safest preconceptions betraying us in this way even in regions within our observation, how completely might they not be falsified in remoter parts of a world which perhaps is infinite? Moreover, empirical laws can cover even the events in which they are realised only in a loose or in an abstract fashion; loosely, when events are regarded as repeating themselves, since no concrete event is repeated; and abstractly when it is not detached events that are observed but rather certain constant relations, obtaining throughout a certain field, like those between mass, time and velocity in a mechanical system. These constant and precise methods of movement are, however, beyond the region of causation; they assign no causes why they exist or continue but are merely the actual character of such movement as is sustained and calculable. The only explanation of anything that is final and satisfying has accordingly no reference to causes at all, but only to constant and groundless characteristics of existence; and this, though it may seem a paradox, is a plain necessity in the case. Causes, if they required other causes to explain them, would lead to a vain regress, at no stage of it would there be any advance towards the ultimate. The ground of expectation is not the means of production. Mechanism, i.e., sustained and calculable uniformities in change, is the only possible ground for anything that is to be explained at all; and, in the nature of things, this ground is itself groundless and this explanation for those observed groupings which we call facts is an ultimate fact without explanation. The abstractness of this ultimate fact, however, is involved in its very pervasiveness and perpetuity: it is not the picturesque surface of nature, or the individual essences deployed before a dreamful superficial observer, that can be the units of an ultimate, substantial order; either there is no order at all, or these appearances may be dissolved into constituents among which a mechanical order is discoverable. The mechanism of the substance then becomes in a pregnant and fair sense the "cause" of the various appearances it wears: and causation is not a relation between obvious events repeated over and over, for there are no such events, but a relation between the mechanism of nature, proceeding perpetually, and the successive supervening groupings, individualities, and appearances which that mechanism brings about by the way. For we have seen that a mechanism cannot help embodying countless essences besides those which constitute it mechanically, or which figure among the constants in the equation which defines it.

The life of the world, the dramatic intensity with which events prepare and succeed one another, the bursting pregnancy of things, is thus unrolled before us in its intimate constitution. There is no uniformity or repetition of superficial particulars; yet there is an underlying uniformity throughout of an abstract mechanical sort, and this mechanism reproduces particulars endlessly, monotonously, where the mechanical formation involves similar redundant unities not varying insensibly or suddenly, where those formations fall into novel incidental shapes. Hence the infinite individual variety, this perpetual youth, the fatal incompleteness, the constant self-interruption, frequent disasters, and the profound monotony which we observe in nature.

CAUSATION

In what sense can one fact be said to produce another? In answering this question let me at once set aside an absurd but insidious suggestion. I must never look to essence to explain genesis. Even when an appearance remains unchanged the inertia which keeps it in being is not its own or a magic privilege of the essence manifested; it is either a precarious absolute accident, like the existing universe, or else is due to some sustained balance of forces hidden beneath, as a man's food and vital bodily functions keep his name upon the list of tax-payers, not any mystic virtue in his name itself. So when any appearance is interrupted but recurrent. A son may resemble his father in each corresponding phase of their two lives; but the characters common to the two can never be the ground of the fact they are repeated, much less of the fact that they are varied or exhibited in new associations, or at such desultory or rhythmical intervals. The distribution of essences (and causation is a principle of distribution) is always irrelevant to them. This fact is perhaps more striking, though not more certain, when successive appearances are disparate in kind. When the bite of a mosquito is followed by a fever, it cannot have been the ugliness of

George Santayana, "Causation," *Columbia Manuscript Collection.* © 1969 Daniel Cory. Another attempt at the projected Chapter III of *The Realm of Matter.*

that insect or his hum or my feeling of a prick that did the mischief: the connection, if any, must be traceable to some unsuspected germ meantime deposited in my blood. The flux of substance is generative, not the flux of phenomena. To attribute one phenomenon to the influence of another phenomenon is superstition or, when defended by philosophers, empiricism. The arts, even magic and prestidigitation, must work through substance. No essence has any proclivities or powers; none implies any other, except perhaps by containing it; and even then the inclusive essence does not demand that any feature of it shall be detached and shall appear separately. The realm of essence is an eternal democracy and precludes any passage of being from one essence to another or any fusion. Therefore derivation can never be dialectical and no change is explicable or even describable by the essential relations between its terms.

Here, I may say in passing, is a consideration fit to support or console the lovers of freedom. Laws, if there are laws, are themselves accidents, essences by chance embodied in appearances by virtue of their arrangement. Whatever uniformities or sequences may be noted in the perspectives of nature or history or moral experience are desultory rhymes not needing to be repeated beyond the instances in which they have been actually detected. The driving force, if anywhere, is not in them but beneath them, in the automatism of substance. For this reason empiricists, who deny or ignore substance, are constrained to regard causation as illusion. Irresistible succession in thought is mistaken, they say, for necessary succession in things. It is true that empiricists, in saying so, repeat the mistake which they denounce, since they regard the association of ideas as far from groundless, being caused by the previous order of impressions: but this slip might be amended and the notion that phenomena must recur in the order in which they first appear might be dismissed as gratuitous, especially as it is notoriously false. Freedom and indetermination accordingly reign everywhere on the surface of experience, and those whose logic forbids them to peep beneath the surface may rejoice for ever, like the angler, in the expectation of novelty.

Indeterminism, however, makes a fool's paradise, and the moment study and industry delve beneath the glassy surface, they discover some continuity of substance linking the odd phenomena and determining their quantity, quality, and distribution. But before science can trace genesis through substance (which it can do only by inventing fresh technical symbols) memory and dramatic fancy may find certain rhymes in striking events, and take them for reasons. This is the source of superstitions, expectations, and laws. That a match will light when struck is an expectation, that to light three cigarettes with it is unlucky is a superstition and that it will go out when dipped in water is a law. So long as the material derivations involved are not traced out in detail, law differs from superstition only in the degree of expectation which it inspires; when once this ceases to be instinctive and unquestioned it may be fortified or discredited by appeals to memory or to fresh experiment, until the superstition is accepted as law or the law discarded as a superstition.

The actual derivation of each event is singular, by the flowing together of the events immediately preceding in that place and substance; and this derivation is equally adequate and propulsive if the conjunction is novel and the issue unprecedented, as if the event is elementary and perpetually repeated in the routine of nature. The empirical notion that causation is a question of law or of uniform sequence, is purely sophistical, substituting connection in reflection for genesis in fact. A particular movement in nature cannot be due to the fact that a similar movement has occurred before; familiarity may create presumption, and a tendency to fill in mentally what is unobservable in one instance with what is retained of another; but this assimilation of different events is helpless and pathological; their identity is only verbal or formal; and even if the repetitions were exact and the universality of such sequences under such consequences were somehow established, that external circumstance would be perfectly irrelevant to the understanding of genesis in each particular case, by tracing the inner processes of change to their ultimate streams and elements. If, on a superficial identification of instances, the one is felt to be necessitated by the other, the feeling is superstitious; while if the intention is rather to deny that there is any continuity of genesis or derivation beneath appearances, and that these are juxtaposed in empty time, the view is sceptical or rather ignorant; because in fact appearances have origins. No doubt recurrences wear out surprise in a man, however inexplicable the recurring fact may remain, and a law, by establishing a habit, gains a right of citizenship in the conventional mind. Being an element of permanence, however abstract, it flatters that intellectual instinct, half laziness, half love of domination, which watches events with a superior smile, ready to say: I told you so. It is in this way that we appropriate our own powers in reflection: and any presumption of ours which events justify seems to extend these powers vicariously: for after all, even in our personal faculty of lifting weights or making jokes, we hardly know how we do it. In nature we possess our powers, as things bring about their consequences, by virtue of an enormously complex structure reacting mechanically on specific stimulations, when these arrive; but the growth and decay of such structure and the coming of such stimulations are either unsuspected or else impossible or unpleasant to trace; we take the risk, assume the god, and if we do not shake the spheres, at least affect to regulate them. So long as rules hold, all is well, and we may execute our plans and see our prophecies fulfilled in their outline; and although no prophecy or plan is ever fulfilled exactly, where the routine of nature remains constant our omens, however far-fetched, need not betray us. But causation is crawling work, it operates in partly impermanent conditions and insensibly transforms them; and any uniformities or constancies observed in events—or rather in the ideal measures or forms imposed upon them—elude precisely the point of chief interest; namely, Whence these instances, here and now, of these particular essences and laws? The number of desultory instances only multiplies the number of mysteries; if each event is groundless each time it occurs, it does not become well-grounded by occurring often; its ground, taken as a unitary event, must be sought in the ambient flux of substance generating at this point the occasion for that sort of incident; and the cause of its inward character, the secret of its own movement, cannot be the formula that describes it, but the meeting and fusion in it of material processes that, in each instance, lend that essence existence.

That appearances cannot be derived from one another follows also from their relation to time. Specious times, internal to appearances, are undatable and incommensurable except emotionally; no appearance reveals a time in which it can be related to other appearances. Now sequence is essential to derivation, and if appearances are not intrinsically consecutive they cannot be, intrinsically, the cause of one another. Before they can be regarded as consecutive they must be grafted on a physical time other than the temporal perspectives internal to them. This grafting of imaginative views upon the flux of matter is done by the action which, in the life of animals, vitalicises [sic] those views. Just as pictorial spaces, if they are to have positions, even by imputation, in physical space, must be attributed to some material being, as being the perspectives open then and there to his senses, or must be painted on canvas and hung on a wall, in order [that] their pictorial essence, through the substance which supports it, may acquire a temporary home in nature; just so memories and expectations would be homeless sentiments, belonging to no man's life, like the heads of cherubs floating through space on two little wings, if they were not proper to some material psyche, and could be identified with datable moments in her modifications and reactions amid the flux of nature. It is only by virtue of their material basis that the feelings of youth precede those of old age, or one man's life is earlier than another man's, or later, or contemporary. Nor are his own experiences continuous or successive on any other principle; because the conscious continuities or perspectives in his mind are sentimental views, existing only speciously by virtue of an actual undatable synthesis; and any accumulating memory or self-fulfilling purpose of which he may be aware is, for that very reason, proper to one of these views and internal to it. The mind could not grow or exchange its vistas or be one mind throughout these changes if it were not the mind of one body in one world. It suffices, therefore, to determine the derivation of material facts in order that the derivation of mental facts may be determined also; nor is there any other means of anchoring a particular feeling in one particular personal history, even one's own, or of discovering a feeling in others, dating it in history, or attributing a function to it in the development of art or conduct.

So far, then, I have found that the derivation of fact from fact is never dialectical, that appearances are never causes, and that the specious aspects of will, expectation, or intention, being appearances, are at best signs of the direction in which the material action of the agent will influence events, in so far as he possesses the requisite arts or instincts. Having thus explicitly confined causation to the realm of matter I may hope to discern more clearly the nature of genesis and derivation, both within that realm and in reference to such other dimensions of being as may be involved in its movement. Since within the other realms there is no causation, no derivation, and no physical time, the points at which nature touches them will be determined by her automatic progress on the material plane, without either solicitation or resistance on their part, or intervention from any other sphere.[1]

1. This is the end of page 11 of the manuscript. The next paragraph is on a page marked "17."—Editors.

All forms of derivation lie between two extremes, total novelty and perfect persistence. At either of these extremes derivation would vanish, since perfect persistence would contain no distinction of times or phases and would dip into eternity, while a total novelty would constitute a new world without attachment to the old or any neighbourhood in nature. The novel must appear in a frame of the relatively persistent; it must come as a shock or a variation to some previous being; and of course this previous being must suffer some change if anything is to arise requiring a derivation. Nor can the cause be a persistent state of this previous being, for a stable antecedent would already have produced its consequent; if it takes time to do so, something in it or round it must be maturing and counting the moments, until the explosion comes. In other words, the cause of any change must be itself a change. But from this pole, dialectic is at once driven back upon the other pole, which is the impossibility of change save in some permanent substance or medium. Take the most unsubstantial and loosest sequence conceivable, a dream in which each successive vision is entirely new and irrelevant, or a set of universes, utterly diverse, kindled and extinguished like sparks. In order that, in the realm of truth, these visions or universes may be successive rather than simultaneous, nay, in order that they may belong to existence at all and be more than eternal essences, there must be a dreamer to whom each transformation scene is observable and unexpected; else the apparitions would not belong to one dream, or be rivals and alternatives for one another; nor would the disparate universes be substitutes or rivals, if the substance or field of each was not needed to constitute its successor. The experience of change requires the continuity of a psyche, preceding and underlying each moment of intuition, and keeping the first term in the offing while the second term sails into port, and the fact of change requires at least an enduring place where the transformation occurs and an enveloping physical time (with all that that implies) in whose pulses it may be numbered.

Persistence amid change may be conceived as metamorphosis or as rearrangement; and rearrangement may often, or always in some measure, be the ground of metamorphosis. Atomism offers the clearest picture of this: changeless elements changing their relative positions in an unchanging medium, which even if called not-Being is avowedly as "real" and indispensable as the substances that float in it, since it enables their forms, which would otherwise be mere essences, to ac-

quire existence by figuring in time amid variable relations and assuming
relative positions and sizes. Rearrangement thus entirely suffices to
produce metamorphosis of structure and pattern, and this inevitably,
although the patterns and structures so created are entirely fresh units;
so that rationalistic minds are inclined to explain all novelties, if possible, on this principle. With the atoms of Democritus, however, such
an explanation breaks down at the very threshold of appearance, seeing that his atoms are inwardly endowed only with pure Being hypostatised, and packed into geometrical solids; although the void between
them is a hypostasis of pure Being too: purer, indeed, since its reality,
while infinitely intense and indestructible, is not qualified by any limits
or figure. These difficulties induced Anaxagoras to endow the atoms
with pure quality of every sort, so that sensible bodies and objects of
fancy might be compounded of them by mere juxtaposition, as a mo-
saic out of coloured bits: and this expedient has been tried again in
later times with atoms conceived psychologically and called ideas or
data of sense—also hypostatised essences to which some position and
career was assigned in an existential medium not otherwise specified,
space, time, consciousness, or experience. Mere rearrangements (or
reappearances) of such atoms might plausibly be deputed to constitute
the universe; but either the atoms remain always simple and indivisible,
in which case the actual unities of appearance arise by metamorphosis
and are superposed upon those rearrangements of imperceptible elements; or else every given essence however complex is an eternal atom
(as all essences are in their own realm) and the proposed explanation
of appearances becomes a modest naming of them in all their diversity,
without the least clue to any principle of distribution or genesis. Atoms
of pain, for instance, or of audible sound, even if somehow juxtaposed, would not *be* the feeling of change, growth, and tension which
is of the essence of actual pain or actual music. Actual music and pain
are therefore, at any rate, products of metamorphosis; unless, indeed,
they are not produced at all, but merely revealed in their given totality,
like the ideas sent ready-made by the Creator into the mind of Berkeley
or of Malebranche. Qualitative atoms, then, are as incompetent to
generate appearance by juxtaposition as are the atoms of Democritus;
and since metamorphosis has to be invoked in any case, it might as
well be a frank transformation of the material processes traceable by
science, although not imaginable, rather than an imaginary redistribution of specious essences hypostatised.

The movement of nature as a whole must be automatic, since there is nothing outside, in the same plane of being, by which it could be constrained. But this automatism cannot be mechanical in the same sense as an artificial machine, which is not automatic but requires a natural automaton, man, to make, tend, and reproduce it. Machines are incomplete mechanisms; and the universe, though automatic, is not in that sense a machine. This may be said safely without prejudice to a theology which might maintain that nature was an engine constructed and controlled by a divine engineer standing outside; because if any creative agency were to be at work on the same plane of being as its products, it would be simply a part of nature, as a human engineer is on the same material plane as his machinery: for if he were a disembodied thought, he would be indiscoverable, and his claim to have designed his engines, or to control them, would be fantastic and easily derided. So if on the contrary the creative agency were not on the same plane as its products, but a pure spirit, it could be manifested in these products only as a harmony, not as a force. Thus the automatism of nature, by definition, covers all her life and miracles. The only question which the study of nature might serve to answer for the theologian would be a question not of causes, but of results. Does the automatism of nature conspire to a moral end? What sort of moral lesson does she teach? Do her marvels, normal or exceptional, when conceived as expressions of spirit, seem to manifest a kindly providence, or an inscrutable fate, or an evil and insane magic? And is it possible for the human spirit to welcome or defy or exorcise her influence?

What are the least constituent steps in material processes and what are the primary forms of fusion between them? Let those answer who dare: but there is no warrant for assuming that any event, observed or conceived by man, is truly ultimate rather than a resultant of many factors; nor is it certain that uniformities apparently ultimate, like the elementary laws of motion, are more than rough views and specious unities on the human scale, covering temporary average resultants of a multitude of wild events. All the habits of matter may be variable and its substance may be subject to chance increments or dissolution. Everything might collapse at once, or any part might collapse separately. Meantime we must reason, as we must live, by animal faith; and if we imagine ourselves in the presence of some isolated rudimentary system, like three particles in empty space, we must presume that whatever they do once, if they ever revert to the same conjunction by a similar approach from similar directions, they will do the same thing again. This presumption is justified by various considerations: unanimous experiment; the absence of any grounds to the contrary; the suasion of experience, embodied in instinct, which leads us to repeat reactions as if things, too, would be faithful to their old habits; also the very arbitrariness of fact which being deaf originally to all other possibilities, need not be expected ever to awake to them or to rescind itself. Stupidity is at the root of existence, and stupidity is stubborn. Nor would any more sprightly habit be at all more rational, not even the alternative of pervasive variations and no habits at all. The analogies of nature might well lead us to suppose that if the paths of blockheads ever change, it is by blind percussion of one blockhead with another. Habits, once diverted, however, run on in their new courses and rhythms with the same inertia as the old, without sentimental reluctance or any tendency to atavism. A diffused uniformity, or faithful stupidity, may thus be safely assumed in nature, but only in her elementary habits, without excluding modifications of these on contact with one another, or the emergence of new resultant habits at any new juncture. We must still assume, however, that if such a juncture were repeated, the same new habit would emerge again. This measure of uniformity is postulated in the arts; and the present existence of animals, with their preformed organs and instincts, gives proof that, on their scale and in their habitat, a rough constancy has actually prevailed in nature for many ages.

GENESIS

Pictorial space and sentimental time form together an airy canvas on which dramatic fancy has always painted the world. If these media

George Santayana, "Genesis," *Columbia Manuscript Collection.* © 1969 Daniel Cory. This essay was clearly intended for *The Realm of Matter.* Santayana was probably undecided where it might fit: he wrote "Chapter" at the top of the first page and left a blank space for the number.

of distribution are visionary, is there some better principle of relation on which I may conceive existence to be distributed? For intuition, there is no better principle; because if I sought to discard those familiar perspectives in favour of any logical harmony or tragic law, I might devise some nobler form of poetry, but certainly not a more accurate or a deeper science. Pictorial space and sentimental time after all yield images of nature; a conceptual law, a *Begriff*, would be only a death-mask of discourse. Yet although radically the terms of science must remain visionary, there are methods of using and discounting them which can render them wonderfully pliant to the truth of things. Just as language cannot find any initial terms other than sounds, yet by inflection and syntax may compel them to designate unmistakably almost any physical or moral object; so the symbols of sense and the emotional perspectives of life may be made to declare the movement of substance and its secret ways. However private and singular may be the note by which observation marks the conjunctions of events, this mark, being a product of those occasions, an integral part of those loaded moments, cannot fall out of step with them, nor can it mis-represent their order if it registers its own. A common contingency unites any perception with its instant object; so that memory, if true to experience, reports the true order of those natural events which it records at all, no matter how abstract or poetical may be its view of them. Nor is this order immaterial to those events; on the con-trary, the contingent distribution of things is precisely what dis-tinguishes them from their essences and lends them existence; so that the most heteroclite observation can retain just the element in facts which matters for animal life, namely, the distribution of those facts and their effect on the observer implicated in their movement. A prag-matic mind may accordingly cultivate a double economy: it may ignore at once the internal aesthetic character of its perceptions and the in-ternal substantial character of things, and it may attend solely to their common march and external mutual relation. But a difficulty arises here; a fatal vagueness hangs about this abstract notation of events. For where are they occurring? In what medium shall they be deployed? If it be only (as it commonly is with pragmatists) in sentimental time, natural philosophy would be eliminated altogether, and nothing would remain but a limping autobiography, or a romantic social dream.

There is, however, another method by which the reform of spec-tacular physics may be attempted; namely, to substitute mathematical

for sensuous essences in the description of nature. The triumphs of
this method are notorious; by its internal elaboration, and by its application in astronomy and in the arts, it has made modern science
and life essentially modern—complex, aimless, and ugly no doubt,
but also rich and wonderfully agile. The mathematical method, however, if pursued alone, could never have reformed physics; it would
have been an exploration in the realm of essence, irrelevant to the
description of nature and to the arts. In order to be relevant to fact
mathematics must somewhere impinge upon it. But where? All ideas
impinge upon fact initially, in that they are images bred by the senses
and passions in contact with things: but this is not enough. Every
lie, every fancy, every dream rises out of contact with fact initially:
so do all systems of dialectical metaphysics; and mathematics, for all
its rigour, would be, like them, only an attenuated phenomenon if,
like them, it was attached to nature only because nature once suggested it to the mind. In fact, mathematics is the most practical of
sciences, indispensable and never misleading to the merchant, the
architect, and the navigator. It has abstracted from things just that
aspect of them by which they interact and grow out of one another;
in other words, their substantial aspect, the aspect by which human
action (which works with material instruments) can itself control them.
Thus mathematics impinges upon fact at a second point, at the crux
of action. It is applicable in the arts, rendering them exact and economical; it thereby proves its validity not merely as a dialectical dream
emanating from things but as a measure of their intrinsic operation.
It joins hands here with the pragmatic method which studied in things
only the practical significance which they might have for one another;
and at the same time it rescues this pragmatic method from the dreadful predicament to which it led while it remained empirical. For now
experience is not condemned any longer to designate events merely
by the notes which memory may keep of them, nor to deploy them
vaguely by virtue of some blind expectation or social instinct; now
the whole distribution of things, to any depth or distance to which
calculation may be carried, can be determined scientifically and veri-
fied step by step as occasion arises; and if the universe so deployed is
conceived abstractly—for how else should it be conceived by a local
animal mind?—at least it is conceived in sympathy with its fundamental order: its curve is plotted, its framework is distinguished, its
nerve is traced; and if the varied life and music that may play about it

remain unknown, or are imagined but partially in some myth, half self-indulgence and half sympathy, at least no fair thing is denied its occasion, and no false lights are dangled before the idle or super-stitious humours of mankind.

The arithmetic and geometry of commerce, learned by the manipu-lation of things, are naturally applicable to these things in rough ex-periment, prophecy, and industry: they are perhaps not applicable without variation at depths or heights in nature remote from the human scale; and they are not at all applicable directly to psychologi-cal or moral subjects. But they are not irrelevant to anything existent, because they are methods of noting its distribution; so that even where appearances elude scientific measure by their essence, they do not escape it by their occasions: it still applies to the causes that sub-tend them. In proportion as these causes are discerned, medicine and politics become true arts and the ancient incubus of unimaginable power, to be exorcised only by magic, is lifted from the soul.

To discern the causes of things—that is, to penetrate to that level on which their movement is connected and calculable—is an immense task, which will still beckon the last of mortals. It demands of man that he abandon the human scale, which he can do only in intent by an acrobatic intellectual art which is very fatiguing and jejune; he can practise it only occasionally, and he hardly brings back from those abstract flights any warm conviction to his animal spirit. He must remain to the end a passionate polyglot incoherent poet. This fatality will appear even in those threads of science which he may weave about his heart; they will be various, tangled, and often broken short; and their texture, as distinguished from the intellectual func-tion which they are intended to have, will still be his own, that is, it will still be visionary.

For example, there is the notion of natural law. This is a name for certain tropes—certain rhythms or typical repetitions—discernible in certain abstracted aspects of things: a law has nothing to do with the actual genesis of anything. Particulars are never repeated; they are always new and somewhat different; and their family likenesses or family habits, while they leave on the observer a certain common trace and a single image, cannot have arisen in the first instance be-cause they were destined to arise in many another instance later; nor can these later instances be due to the specious unitary aspect which the earlier instances were to the mind. Presumably the repetition of a trope must be due to the same sort of causes by which its first appearance was produced. A law is accordingly a device in discourse, not a principle in nature. Why do men (of some races) have thick beards, and women none? Because, says the sapient discerner of law, males always have them. This answer satisfies the wondering mind and domesticates it in the home circle of appearances; but if beards have an origin at all and are not detachable phenomena sprinkled by providence over experience, the origin of each beard must lie within each man; and their common characters, which are not exactly repeated, must be due to a generic resemblance between prior structure of one body and that of another in the male[s] of that race. Cross-breeding, or spontaneous variation, or castration may at any moment so modify that structure that no beard grows: and this not by virtue of a new law (which of course might be propounded by generalising from the new instances) but by a traceable derivation in each body from its germ, its food, and its particular fortunes in the environment. In the notion of law, accordingly, an empirical abstraction, a single image or formula, like a name, is clapped impulsively on such things as recall it to the mind: it does not penetrate anywhere to the origin of anything; it applies only to those things from which it has been or may be abstracted; and if any power is attributed to law to bring about its own exemplification, belief in law is simple superstition; for then the sheer force with which the form of some event may have struck the mind becomes an assurance that such events must be repeated.

But repeated when? Not every law applies everywhere; and whether a particular case contains the particular features which are the premisses for a particular law is a point often discoverable only by waiting to see whether the required conclusion is realised: if I die, I prove that I must have suffered from a mortal accident, sentence or disease; a mortal ill being one from which death follows by law: but if the actual disease or accident or sentence had been noted independently, it would still be uncertain whether it was mortal. So if a ray is refracted more than the accepted laws of physics allow, the "true" laws of physics are discovered, requiring this greater degree of refraction. Natural law is a matter of more or less summary notation—a matter of words; and yet, by the discovery of law and by the intelligent expectation based upon it, civilisation has been built up. Civilisation is a new organisation of habits, when these come to be controlled by institutions, external instruments, and maxims, instead of by instinct. Though a natural law be nothing but a specious essence and a mental symbol, the conception of it may mark an important progress in the domination of things by human intelligence and art.

The one great natural law, at once the charter of freedom and of necessity, is this: that similar things under similar circumstances change in the same ways. This conditional uniformity in nature is a fact: it appears in the revolution of the heavens, in the generation of plants and animals, in political change, and in all the arts. This fact is also necessary; because if two exactly similar things, under identical circumstances, acted differently, it would not be the nature of either thing that controlled the issue, but (in so far as it was variable) chance or a fresh creation. Chances and fresh creations may occur for all we know; the groundless is everywhere the ground of everything; the radical facts and habits in nature are perfectly arbitrary, and everything might originally have been different; why, then, should it not become different little by little, or all at once? Believers in miracles, in metamorphoses, in enormous unknown worlds, and in final cataclysms think of nature as she deserves. If their view betrays any human weakness, it is only in the reasons or flattering functions which they assign to these thunderbolts. But where chance enters, chaos begins; if a thing should behave, under identical conditions, now in one way and now in another, it would prove itself to that extent impotent and non-existent; neither result would be its work or its child, but an alien something would have arisen wantonly in its place. A specific manner of reacting under given conditions is the very nature of a specific thing. Such a fixed native propensity defines the various atoms, it defines a soul, it defines the world itself.

Therefore this necessity is identical with freedom and life. Propensities to change cannot be deduced from the essence illustrated in anything at any one moment: an essence has no propensities, and indicates none: it has only affinities, such as blue may have to red, the cherubs to the seraphs, or the circle to the spiral. When an essence is caught or found under irrelevant circumstances—since there are no circumstances in the realm of essence—it is shown to be the essence of a thing. This thing will disclose tendencies to specific transformation due not to its essence, but to the substance now beneath that essence and in the world beyond. A thing has a heart, as well as a face, and its heart is set either on preserving its actual essence as long and as well as it may, or else on running through and exhibiting a chosen series of phases, a trope, which shall manifest its secret nature. In the first case the thing is inert or inanimate, in the second it is animate and alive. If an inanimate thing did not persevere stolidly in its being, only crumbling or exploding at random, as other things may dictate, or if an animate thing did not hasten, as soon as allowed, to unfold its particular innate burden, that inanimate thing would have no nature, and this animate thing no soul.

Thus predetermination, a profound inveterate bias in will and effort, is the very condition of existence; a creature without it would be a nothing. Not that many an animal is not loosely put together and scatter-brained, a wayward spirit, or several warring spirits, moving within him; he then acts on one principle or on another, according as external influences for the moment perfect his various impulses. In adults this seems a contemptible weakness, but in children it renders education possible: by systematically stimulating one habit and inhibiting another, the trainer may consolidate a tender nature and instil the national virtues into any waif. Circumstances create character; and although this fact is disguised, and may seem to be contradicted, where inherited qualities are many and determinate, it is confirmed when we look deeper, to the origin of all inheritance. How should nuclei first arise in substance at all, except by the distinction which position and surroundings bestow on one aggregate and not on others? Spontaneous variation in seeds is a change externally caused; it comes from some accident of temperature, nutrition, or pressure upon a germ; the same influences which cause the seed to grow and to develop somewhat individually, after it is formed, cause it to be formed somewhat individually in the first instance. The adoption of a new trope in nature can never be the work of a soul, herself the trope previously instituted and hereditary; alien circumstances must shift her balance in the night, without her consent or knowledge. At every stage in life, some actual heritage is compelled by circumstances to unfold itself not as it would, but as it may; by the warping or accretion involved that heritage itself is modified; so that the more plastic and long-lived a creature is, the more it becomes the image of its fortunes, and other than its original dowry and instinct required. Nor will the seed of the next generation issue unchanged from such a battered or accomplished parent; a modification will ensue, not such as to transmit the aged features or acquired gifts of the father to his offspring, but some random change due to nutrition or other circumstances affecting the formation of the seed mechanically. Thus life will be transmitted with a slightly different twist; only the event will show whether for the advantage or disadvantage of the young in their future environment, itself not identical with that of their ancestors. Life is a burden laid on the living, a terrible compulsion to be and to be after a certain arbitrary fashion; hence early tears, when the will may not have its way; hence alacrity in youth in trying its powers and peace in old age at having released them.

When bodies are very similar, and their environment of the same sort (as homogeneous atoms would be in a void or stars in the heavens) each and all will always keep doing the same thing; the history of each may then be erected into a law for all. This common trope will be called mechanism or natural necessity. But when the environment is divers[if]ied or when the bodies in it are dissimilar, each at each moment will do something unprecedented in that society. This unprecedented movement will be exactly that which any similar body would have performed under like circumstances; but since in this system this situation has never arisen before, this sort of movement will be novel in it; it could not have been anticipated by an observer of that world so far; it will therefore be called spontaneous, emergent, and free. That under such circumstances such a substance would always undergo just such a change, is not merely a guess or a postulate: it is an analytic truth and a matter of definition. If two eggs looked exactly alike even under the microscope, but one produced a chicken and the other a duckling, this result would of itself prove that the eggs were of different species; and this would be certain even without appealing to the concomitant fact (doubtless discoverable) that one had been laid by a hen, and the other by a duck. Even if this diverse origin could not be traced, and the presumable difference in structure in the two eggs were imperceptible, they would not be perfectly similar except graphically; that is, they would present for the moment an identical essence to human observation, without on that account being identical substances. For genetically and dynamically, as substances actually exist and are inwardly distinguished, these similar moments would not be separate units at all, but parts of a trope including now one context and now another; as a word in one sentence is not graphically or audibly different from the same word in another sentence, yet has a different efficacy and sequel in discourse, in as much as it is an integral part of a different phrase; and discourse, in its substance and genetic principle, is not a juxtaposition of separate syllables, but a series of vocal gestures and explosions, which come to the surface, by force of habit, in words more or less trite and familiar to lexicographers. These separable words are but the shells and husks of that expressive movement, by which discourse bursts from moment to moment into flower, like a miraculous tree. So the eggs hatching into different fowls, even supposing (what is incredible) that they were graphically identical, in the flux of substance would not be units separable from their different sequels. Not that a trope has any mysterious material unity, and cannot be cut in half or nipped in the bud; but at whatever point it is cut short, it lapses into tropes of some other order; tropes of some kind being the minimal units of a flux, and a flux being indispensable to existence. An event is the transit of an essence across the background of substance, diversifying its pervasive properties, and immeasurable extent. This incidence summons the substance itself into existence, which otherwise would have remained a sleeping monster, the essence of a substance and not a substance in act; and at the same time that incidence introduces some particular trope into the context of matter, and makes it the form of an actual fact. The execution of some particular movement, however slight and brief, is requisite to mark a moment in the life of nature. It is also requisite in order that nature may live at all, or exist: because if she exhibited one or more essences, however complex, without transitions between them, she would not be nature, there would be no genesis in her, no maternity, and nothing would exist. Tropes, the assuming and dropping of essences in sequence, are the minimal facts. Essences, not so taken up and surrendered by a substance, would have no preeminence over the infinitude of other essences, not even such relative eminence as to compose a realm of truth: nothing would emphasize them or extract them from the realm of essence—a function which only an irrational principle can perform, which is at once lasting and changeful.

The units of natural being are accordingly tropes, the simplest as well as the most complicated of them being original; the elements in any trope (and a trope is a recognisable sequence of distinguishable elements) taken separately neither imply nor create its total movement. If arrested ideally, or by material accident, at any point, the trope would not show, at that segment, any evidence of its dynamic destiny: nothing would marry that segment ostensibly to its origin or its sequel, but it would be merged indiscriminately in the total constellation of the universe at that moment, which is geometrically and graphically infinitely complex and chaotic. If a projectile be arrested ideally or accidentally at a single point in its path, it will not offer to inspection any evidence of its velocity; nevertheless, it would have a particular velocity in reference to any system of surrounding bodies. The instants of geometrical time are not units of physical being; they can contain and exhibit essences only, whereas the units of physical being are definable by tropes, and are measured and multiplied by superposing tropes on one another. The analysis of existence is the resolution of tropes into minor tropes or the composition of wider tropes out of them. The issue will in each case be novel, compared either with the constitutive elements engaged, or with the large fact dissolved into its components: but the genesis traced, whether forward or backwards, will always be natural: that is, it would always occur under like circumstances. All hangs on the direction of the observer's eye: looking backward from what to him is a culmination, he finds elements in which it is not contained; looking forward from the elements to any sequel which they may have, he finds nothing but those elements engaged in producing it. There is no further difference between mechanism and vital initiative, necessity and free will, events predictable and events unpredictable: and quarrels on the subject are a sad waste of moral heat.

THE FLUX OF EXISTENCE

External relations are those which at once unite and separate accidental neighbours, making possible a shock between them, an exchange of place or even a substitution. External relations are perilous; and if any

George Santayana, "The Flux of Existence," *Columbia Manuscript Collection.* © 1969 Daniel Cory. A version of Chapter V of *The Realm of Matter.* The presence of Santayana's usual marginal notations suggests that he might have thought of this essay as very near to being ready for press.

Existence: its logical and moral status.

of the terms is an animate being, the other terms must remain dark and merely presumptive to its mind, vehicles of fate, never safe possessions either for the head or the heart. But such external relations are precisely those which define existence and distinguish it from essence; so that a profound monition lies in this analysis. To hug anything existent as if it were thoroughly fathomed or possessed must be the beginning of a tragedy. Existing things are to be feared: only their gifts can be loved, which they make to the spirit.

Its natural locus is not specious space or time.

Now external relations might seem to be relations in space and time; yet this cannot be the case, if the space and time in question are given images possessing a specious unity and essence. Neither pictorial space nor mathematical extension (which is an abstraction from pictorial space and its internal measure) can establish or contain truly external relations. The same is true of sentimental and of mathematical time. The parts of these essences are always parts of an inclusive whole, homogeneous with them, implied by them, and thoroughly perspicuous in its infinity. We need but recede for a few paces to render internal to the picture any parts of it which at first might have been out of range. No existence is involved either in the variety of these parts (if they are variegated) or in their union in the whole; none of them is ever cut off from the others by variable and hazardous relations. Everything fills its place and date, embedded in its continuous surroundings; the whole prospect being an image which existence generates, not a medium in which existence lives. The existence, as always when a mere essence is studied, lies in the subject, not in the object: it belongs to the act of intuition, and to its necessary unknown organs. It is this act that, by a quick glance, lights up so much and no more of the picture and momentarily divides it into arbitrary parts; it is this act that lives precariously amid external relations, and is being continually generated, redefined, and obliterated under their pressure. If I stop to admire and analyse space and time as they appear, existence has fled from those ghostly presences into my inquisitive person. It is in me, or behind my back; in the spirit thinking or in the hidden forces that make it think.

What this spirit may be to itself, in its spiritual categories and dimensions, does not here concern me; I am now pursuing the butterfly of existence, which an innocent philosophy thinks it can catch in the

There are enacted transitions from one concrete centre to another.

net of intuition, and pin down in some graphic image: but existence is not there. I am enacting it, however, in this sad discovery, as those philosophers are in their light chase. It lodges precisely in our irrational encounter with some influence external to us, which causes us to select this or that winged appearance to fill our respective foregrounds; they and I coexist in our separation, as the speculative systems which we conceive cannot coexist in their contradiction. Doubtless on the same plane with our substantial selves, many other things exist, which we are endeavouring to survey and to synthesise in our systems: but when the mind strains to apprehend those existences, drawing their outlines and retaining their names and forms, it has turned from them to ideas; those plodded miles have become a landscape; existence and flux have fled from this new and clarified object, which is only an essence, and

These centres are self-existent particulars.

have taken refuge in the agencies and in the process employed in evoking it. Existence was seated in the particular, and intuition has found only the universal. In my search for existence, then, I must look away from all these objects, these flowers of intuition, and must dig at its roots. Every fact is planted somewhere in the soil of nature, where it sets up a sort of boundary-stone, a self-posited centre, a point of meeting and transit for all such influences as help to produce it. If, as in the case from which I must start, this centre is a seat of intuition, it supplies a point of view, an origin for perspectives; these perspectives will be essences expressing the highly selective responsiveness of that centre to surrounding things of various sorts at various removes; and since the centre and its intuition exist by an instant concretion and self-isolation those outlying facts will remain alien and problematical from its point of view. They, too, if they exist, must exist each for itself, and be particular. The concretion which creates them, making the point they occupy a distinguishable centre for action and reaction, need not carry any intuition with it; but an intuition could have no existence and no meaning unless it arose in such a concretion and adopted its point of view. Thus all existences exist by mutual exclusion, either in total ignorance of one another's being, or eyeing one another with suspicion and probably without understanding. Alternative positions, alternative characters are alone possible to them; if they cohabited and formed a placid whole they would lapse into fragments of a picture: and if this picture itself was to exist, and not be a mere essence, it must in turn find lodgement in some concretion in the midst of flux, among things external to itself.

If all existence is seated in some particular, and in that sense occupies a point (though not one in specious time or space) and posits that point as a centre for the universe, how can a universe effectively surround or condition this particular, to which it is expressly foreign? It might seem as if an existent particular, self-posited and not merely a specious element in some image, was condemned to perpetual isolation; so the points of an existing space, if they have individuality, would be monads rooted for ever in solitary safety; and if they had an inner history and dreamt of a world, that world would be specious and internal to their dream, not the world at all in which they actually existed. This consequence has been loyally accepted by at least two great systems, in the Sankya system and that of Leibniz [*sic*]. But the plurality of monads, in such a case, is precarious: why more than one dreamer or one substance? If we revert now to our original conception of a universe in which the particular was to be an element, how shall we say that this particular hedges itself in, so as to become concrete, and the sole seat of existence? What substance or forces dwell in this node or centre which does not dwell in the medium in which it is placed and knotted? It will not help us to conceive the particulars packed close and continuous: if this continuity is betrayed only by the internal state of each centre, we revert to monadism; if it is an arrangement of particulars, a truth about them, not affecting their inner states, the medium of relation and the truth about the arrangement of units become more important than the units themselves; if these exist at all, they cannot be the sole existents.

Dialectical difficulties in conceiving a flux.

To combine continuity with discreteness is easy enough in mathematics, as it is in the images of sense, because no actual existence is seated either in the parts or in the whole, and all is a play of terms and definitions: but to combine them in act, to display them separately and yet together, is no task for thought: there must be an exchange of substance between form and form, an actual metamorphosis. Existence can lodge solely in particulars, and yet can form a world out of them, if the particulars are in flux, so that one may become another, not by taking its place in a specious medium, but by transmitting its substance or its motion to another particular, which to that extent and degree is its natural neighbour, the partner and rival of its life. Substance thus

exists only in particulars, each standing on its own feet and adding itself to the universe without being included in any other particular, or
empty medium, or observing mind; but these particulars could not exist
or become parts of a universe without possessing an exchangeable
substance, called matter, within or beneath them, which puts them in
quantitative, genetic, dynamic, perilous relations with the other particulars in that universe. Flux and metamorphosis are therefore im-
minent, if not actual, in all existing things.

Existence, like change (which is virtually contained in it) cannot be
defined or contemplated adequately, because it is more and less than
any essence which it may manifest; more, because it enacts the character depicted; less, because it enacts it blindly,
since to possess existence or to execute change is by
no means identical with feeling an incubus or seeing a motion. Of course, it is impossible to attribute
existence without having it: but this attribution is
itself an act of animal faith, a disposition to action. Its meaning would
vanish to a pure spirit, devoid of self-consciousness and of fear. Even
motion, perhaps, would lose its specious character, its flicker and
precipitation, without the contrary impulses which successive stimulations arouse in the body, and the signs of which overtake one another
in apprehension, giving us the feeling or intuition of change. In actual
change, on the contrary, there is no such overlapping of contraries, but
a pure succession of differences; so that the essence which reveals
change to intuition, the essence of confusion and haste, is expressly
absent from the true nature of change.

Observation and language may nevertheless indicate sufficiently
what existence is, as I am endeavouring to do here; its nature is well
expressed in the classical categories of substance
and essence, matter and form, *prakriti* and *purusha*.
Yet when we ask, as we are inclined to do in dialectic, what is the intrinsic essence of this substance,
or the inherent form of this matter, apart or beneath
all essences and forms, we are evidently in a hole; and yet it would
be fatal to discard that elusive term and retain form only, because if we
did so we should be banishing the very existence which we were pursuing.

Consider, for instance, the case of geometrical atoms, which offers

Solvuntur ambulando, but cognitively things ulterior remain postulates of animal faith.

Discourse, since its terms are essences, must always miss the nerve of existence.

the clearest possible picture of permanence combined with perpetual change. The atoms are absolutely solid and hard, the void perfectly

Example of atoms, in which solid extension is ideally identical with empty extension outside.

motionless; yet in it the changeless atoms keep up an incessant dance, forming endlessly new patterns. But how is matter within each atom distinguished from the space surrounding it? What sort of being or position has this dividing surface, with soft ex-

tension on one side of it and hard extension on the other? These notions of position and impenetrability dissolve on inspection; they can be nothing intrinsic; they hark back to specious effects, like colours and visible motions, or else to massed encounters with gross bodies in action; they require a centre of reference in an agent or observer to lend them substance, scale, and position—a substance, scale and position which will remain absolutely relative to his person. But from his point of view the atoms, far from monopolising existence, are its most ideal and notional limits. Indeed the atoms of Democritus seem once to have been called "ideas," and to have had the same Eleatic and Pythagorean origin as the Ideas of Plato; but so taken they would be pure essences, terms in a dialectical construction which only the most reckless metaphysics could confuse with the existing world or regard as its substance. The effective constituents of nature must be things, not ideas: they must be posited, not defined. Perhaps at bottom Democritus still obeyed the mythological impulse of his nation; his philosophy may have been to him a sublime poetical transposition of this world, rather than an analysis of explanation of it; a means of quitting and scorning it in rapt union with eternal Being. Otherwise, in relation to nature on the human scale, the atoms and the void would both seem less substantial than the temporary bodies formed out of them: since it is not the separate atoms, nor the void, but the arrangement and motion of them which have sensible effects, so that the vicissitudes of experience, which alone compel us to posit substance at all, would be due to collocations quite accidental to the substances posited. It is evidently to the breath of change, to some wind blowing through those dusty spaces, that we owe our existence, not to the space and the dust to which we and our world will perhaps return when we have ceased to exist. Metaphysical transports are legitimate, but they elude the facts, and leave them standing unexplained, for the natural philosopher to decipher.

Now atoms of a sort, not geometrical ideas hypostatised, have their place in natural philosophy, as we see in chemistry and physics; be-

Existing atoms are
small bodies found
in the larger ones
encountered in
action.

cause the structure of matter is granular, and existence is something initially dispersed and unequally distributed. But physical atoms are soft, and essentially divisible: they are concretions in existence, and nobody knows how long they may last, or what they may contain. They are called atoms only in a relative sense, like any natural individual or animal when it figures, like a microbe, in the structure of some individual on a larger scale. In this sense existence and flux always imply atoms, and are composed of them, since existence and change must begin at a point, in the part, and can never achieve wholeness; but these atoms themselves, being existent, have no absoluteness or immortality; they are knots, bubbles, stitches; patches in the quilt. The merit of the atomic theory, so understood, is that it is a physical, not a metaphysical, hypothesis; it does not divide things into dialectical elements, such as "form" and a *materia prima* which, being an essence, cannot exist by itself, but divides them into parts, such as they may be actually composed of; so that the atoms are not merely imagined but often counted and discovered.

In their presence, however, the philosopher is still at the beginning of his task, as he is in the presence of human society or of the heavenly

Practical intent
and faith, not
enlarged
intuitions, reveal
existence.

bodies. He sees that existence is dispersed into many centres; he himself, with his whole present being and opinions, occupies one of them; and he must ask himself how these centres arise and dissolve, and how they are connected or transformed into one another. It will not help him at all, if he merely becomes more learned, or travels farther afield, thereby enlarging the picture which he has of the world. Memory, prophecy, and history, as well as science and spiritual insight, live in moments or series of moments, even as matter lives. Intuitions are generated and lost like all other existences, happy if in their day they frame some symbolic image of their sources and destiny, in so far as destiny and the causes of things must needs preoccupy a living animal; yet happier if they are suffered to ignore those predicaments, and existence itself, and can fulfil simply their intrinsic spiritual function, which is to express freely the spontaneous life of that centre at that moment, in terms of such essences as may be native to it, as song is to the birds. There existence would be at its best, but forgetful of existence; and all this ecstasy will only mislead the natural philosopher if he adopts its deliverance, and imagines that, because it is so fine a thing, it must convey a miraculous understanding of its own nature and origin. On the contrary, its very dignity lies in not needing to do so; and for the naturalist it is merely one more fact, one more moment of existence to be collated with all others. His own sensations and ideas, though less ecstatic, are in the same case; they too are spontaneous; he must discount them, if he would recover his sanity and his scientific intent, by interpreting them in action, and treating them as conventional signs for his external relations. Thus when I define existence as Being in flux or in those external relations which make flux possible and likely, the meaning would elude me if these phrases did not prompt me to rehearse some actual transition, perhaps to abandon dialectic, like Hume, for backgammon. Since in talking about existence I actually exist, the fact appealed to is always at hand; my very perplexities in describing it exemplify it perfectly; and in slipping away and mocking me, existence perpetually surrenders to me its inmost secret.

In one sense my own existence is the only key to existence that is supplied to me; when I attribute existence to other things, hypostatising

The self, for the philosopher, is the typical and central existence.

a given essence or dodging a flying missile, without knowing what it may be, I in some measure personify the object and assimilate it dramatically to my own form of being. The element in me, however, which I project in conceiving existence is not my spirit nor my human character, nor my discourse; it is not even the given essence which I use to describe my object and which I identify with it for the moment; for this essence is no element of myself; it appears to me only in the act of turning to the supposed object and taking it in; or if having become self-conscious I supposed the given essence to be something in myself, like a dream, I should not be attributing existence to it in its specious medium, but to myself and my labouring spirit. This spirit would not be pure intuition (which can never determine what theme it shall choose) but some particular nucleus of massed images and intents, a life sundered from all else and from itself in its lapsing moments, something existent and in heavy flux. It is in fact this sort of dumb being within me, this material ballast, which assimilates me to the things which I believe to exist about me. I too, to my own feeling and belief, am a weighted atom, an irrational substance, full of stubborn habits and hidden springs. So that before assimilating other things to myself, I have assimilated myself to them; and I must exist, and feel myself to exist, by participating in material being and flux, before I can conceive their existence as a participation on their part in the force of this particular precarious existence which I enjoy.

In a manner, indeed, all existence may be called personal; it is all enacted by particular beings, in a particular context and occasion, and

Existence a tragicomedy.

under the mask of a particular essence. But these personages may be dumb; they are willing to play in the dark without an audience. Soliloquies and shows supervene but rarely. The world is a pantomine which each clown plays sadly to himself; his silly material antics are necessary if he is ever to supply an entertainment either for himself or for others. Only bodies can have a place for a heart; and their private automatisms are the source of the public drama. Its moral passions merely re-echo on another plane the comic and tragic constitution of existence on the material level. Everywhere there is this fleeting concentration of substance in spheres and cells and bubbles, comparable to persons; everywhere the same excellent actor, Matter, playing every part in its day; everywhere these exits and entrances of poetic characters coming from nowhere and disappearing into nothing. Existence is multifarious, inexhaustible; it is essentially sporting, and bobs up with the bravado and gaiety of youth; but its destiny is sad. The types it exemplifies, down to the least detail, are indeed eternal, and the substance which manifests them is no doubt perpetual; put the particular persons exult and triumph for an hour in an untenable position upon untenable claims.

The flux of existence, in which I am carried along with such slight courtesy, cannot be dominated by my mind; I know it only as that

Spirit may draw the moral.

opaque sea, filled with more or less amiable monsters, in which I am swimming. Much less can I define the inner nature of the matter thus indefinitely diffused; but in respect to the experiences and appearances within my ken, I may say that matter has the privilege of continuity and ambivalence; at any point it may become a nucleus, self-limited and concrete, with a character contrasted with the characters assumed by matter elsewhere; yet even here it may presently surrender that character and assume another. Meantime each concrete point is a centre for a universe, and a fighting unit within it; not fighting for victory, though it may profess that purpose, but fighting in a common immeasurable and endless battle; for in a flux victory is impossible, except to a spirit that views that flux tangentially, and lays up its achievements in the realms of truth and of essence; seeing that existence, in its very instability, continually takes some specific form and lends a historical individuality to each crisis through which it passes.

SENTIMENTAL TIME

The chief characteristic of existence, as distinguished from any essence which it manifests, is that it arises and lapses continually; so that an actual world never embodies the complete essence of that world, and no event at any instant realizes the whole essence of that event. Existence, both in long and in short stretches, exemplifies its ideal phases only bit by bit, and in an irreversible order. This irreversible order in lapsing events I call physical time. Physical time is a method of change which may be measured by its own stages, it is not a series of dates in an absolute duration. So long as no change occurs durations and dates are inapplicable ideas; existence itself is then in abeyance and lost in eternity. Until a break comes, Being, whatever its character, remains a pure essence or the pure intuition of that essence, then indistinguishable from it; and the interval may as truly be called null as infinite.

Actual duration is measured by events not, like specious duration, by the absence of events. These events have no measure save their parts and their limits, and no date save their relative positions in the order of succession; nor is it possible to say that events, taken intrinsically, are simultaneous or successive, as if they occupied distinguishable instants in an absolute time. In an absolute time all instants would be indistinguishable and, so to speak, of the same date. If the universe is divided into distinct series of events, each a complete story (as implied in monadism and psychologism), there can be no sense

George Santayana, "Sentimental Time," *Columbia Manuscript Collection.* © 1969 Daniel Cory. Above the original title "Sentimental Time," Santayana wrote "Chapter VII." His ideas about the organization of *The Realm of Matter* were at this time obviously different from those embodied in the published version. The title was later crossed out and "Flux" written in its place.

in asking which story is enacted first, or whether one lasts longer than another. A series might be called longer if it contained a greater number of distinguishable events, as an epic is called longer for containing more verses; but not for occupying a greater length of empty time in spinning itself out. When two series unite, so that the same event appears in both, they are simultaneous at that point; and the supposition that all actual series unite at the creation and at the last day would reduce them, in that respect, to a common physical time, and their various internal rates and relative positions might be determined in reference to that total event, in which they would all inhere by their extremities. In that case chronology would borrow its ultimate measures and points of reference from eschatology.

On a small scale, this actually happens continually in the field of action, in so far as it supplies any foothold for faith or art. Actions are measured by things accomplished. Art has works which are its ends or goods, the tests of its existence and success. Without works achieved there would be no history but only a flux of substance through an infinity of total phases; and this flux, having no culminating points or morphological waves, would have no measure or rate of speed. The difference between such a flux and nature is precisely that nature produces works; little systems like paper boats swimming in the flood, whose bobbings and pulses serve like heart-beats to measure their own duration and that of other things in the same field: what science now-a-days calls "clocks." If nature made no clocks she could strike no hours; but she is actually a most indefatigable watch-maker, all tickings and chimes; and it is only in her clocks that she is nature at all. The animal body is such a clock, becoming conscious of its tensions and more or less vaguely of its revolutions; and the specious durations of which this dreaming clock is aware intimately report to it the flux of nature and the direction and rough measures of physical time. These specious durations, with the perspectives forward and backward taken within the specious present of each living moment, I call sentimental time.

Sentimental time is a dramatic category, a specious private perspective, as remote as possible both from physical time, which is inherent in events, and from the truth of history, seen under the form of eternity, as omniscience would see it, and as the human mind strives to see it in epic poetry and philosophy. Nevertheless sentimental time is the first witness in experience to the existence of physical time; and its private emotion and momentary vistas supply the only model available for conceiving history at large; in which, though it be raised to the plane of eternal truth, the image of transition and the breathlessness of action must be retained; for otherwise history would not be a picture of *events*, but some reversible pattern of essences in which there would be no genesis. The specious perspectives of living fancy are accordingly requisite if ever speculation is to be rendered relevant to the flux of existence. In sentimental time, as in all discourse, honest testimony to hard facts is mingled with spontaneous fable and with merely rhetorical mists. A fact, an overpoweringly real fact, is indicated there: namely, that existence is in flux, that at every point, as at the crest of a wave, there is a rising, a bursting, and a lapsing stress; not to recognise somehow this transition with the radical contrast it establishes between what is no longer and what is not yet, would be not to report existence at all. The world is an engine at work; things are arising; and the sentimental distinction between "now" and "then," between a fading past and an uncertain future, somehow does justice to that portentous fact, though it be in childish and pathetic terms. How else should a living animal become aware of that inexorable mutation in nature, which is everywhere substituting on essence for another, and like a capricious nurse now forcing a fresh toy upon the placid mind, now filching it away? In order to understand what mutation is in itself and how events can be successive, the mind would need to fathom the intrinsic nature of substance—an impossible achievement, and an unnatural one, seeing that mind is the last product, the most ethereal aroma, of that substance in its travail. The only approach to the truth possible to a mind is through the criticism and correction of its symbols. These symbols must be accepted, but they may be discounted, and recognised to be symbols only; and then the truth, not as an object of intuition, but as a goal of intent, on which many symbols converge, may be humbly adumbrated and honoured.

Not much reflection is required to prove that sentimental time (though there are sentimentalists who would make a substance of it) is an animal illusion. Every season of life, every age of history, every day of the year thinks itself alone truly alive and alone basking in the noon of reality; all other times seem uncertain and crepuscular. Existence seems to be existence only "now"; and it is with great reluctance and without conviction, that any living creature admits existence throughout the past and future; so emphatic is each successive "now," yet so unseizable; for it is a moving "now." Evidently the animal mind is the voice of the passing moment; and while in nature passage and process are normal, and endow every part with an equal reality and emphasis, the mind is like a flower that must fade where it springs, leaving it for other flowers to spring elsewhere; and from that shifting bit of earth where it is treacherously rooted, it must at once feel and endeavour to transcend the mutation of things and its own mortality. The false colours, the double aërial perspectives, which render events in one direction faded and in the other uncertain, in falsifying the outlying facts render them knowable at this centre; they become present in their absence, and the distortion imposed upon them announces their absence, while here revealing their remote existence. Certainly the past is not faded, except to the eye of the present, and the future is not indefinite, except to present ignorance; but by selfishly naming them so, the present is able to acknowledge their independent existence and to indicate the different directions in which they lie. So to name one man father and another man son is to designate them relatively, because every man is himself, and each must be a son, and may be a father; but the names are true, because generation has a single direction, and the man who is both son and father cannot be both to the same person. So to call one event past and another future, though the names are poetical and selfish, is true, because derivation is not reciprocal; much truer than it would be to say, as a disembodied spirit would, that all the parts of time exist at once. They exist equally but successively; and the fatality which places each event and each intuition at one point in this process and at no other, is expressed honestly, if blindly, by calling each point in turn alone present and alone actual. Physical time is not at all sentimental: every event in it dances its round bravely, holding antecedent and consequent firmly by the hand, without absurdly pronouncing the one a ghost and the other a nonentity; but sentimental time, which does so pronounce them, is the natural dramatic symbol in the minds of animals for that steady flow of substance which is creating and destroying them, and in which their action is imbedded.

The least sentimental term in sentimental time is the term "now," because it marks the junction of fancy with action. "Now" is often a word of command; it leans rather towards the future, and seems to be the voice of the present summoning the next moment to arise, and pouncing upon it when it does so. But all this exciting experience, in which "now" keeps ringing like a bell, forms a sort of wider now, the temporal landscape open to intuition, which psychologists call the specious present. This landscape, when action does not concentrate attention on some particular feature in it, is more sentimental than "now," and leans towards the past. It is the field open to reverie, and may show almost infinite vistas. The most multitudinous and the most systematic objects which thought can conceive must be framed in by some specious present. In less meditative moods, the specious present usually covers the immediate physical past, bringing to intuition the chief events on the human scale which imagination can distinguish in the environment.

Even when action or scientific observation is uppermost, the specious present is accordingly a poetic unit. Action and scientific observation, though framed within it, ignore it; but arts like music and eloquence are directed (without knowing it) to enriching this specious present and rendering it, in some climax, so overwhelmingly brilliant and pregnant, that scientific observation and action become impossible, and all is merged in the spell of enthusiasm. It is the tension under such a specious present that, after a moment, bursts into irrelevant action, such as tears or applause or laughter or contortions; because the artist, by his magic, has cut off the normal reactions of the practical man, and the blocked currents, after producing that momentary fulness in the realm of spirit, must produce some convulsion in their own realm of matter, until the normal outlets are reopened. The *new feeling* that accompanies the act of crying, laughing or dancing is entirely irrelevant to the ideas which preceded; it breaks in unaccountably, irresponsibly, and often to our serious annoyance; it is the passive sensation of those convulsions in which the gathered tensions are relieved.

Although the images in the specious present are largely drawn from past impressions not yet exhausted, interest in the specious present is usually turned towards its living edge, to the novel features coming into view, to the bow, not to the wake. Expectation is usually keener than perception, because unless a shock is very severe, perception is peripheral and allows the greater volume of the mind to vegetate undisturbed; whereas expectation engages the centre of the man, perhaps all his faculties, in readiness to meet the unknown at a moment not predictable.

Why should the mind expect a future at all? Why does such a

romantic category dominate the practical man? A genuine empiricist would be incapable of conceiving anything but the past; a true positivist would realise the ideal of the Cyrenaics and the sceptics, and live lost in the feeling of the present. If philosophers had meditated more on the logical enormity of expecting a future, and living intent upon it, I think they would have formed a humbler and truer idea of what the mind is; they would have seen that its whole ground is animal life, and its whole texture imagination.

The compulsion to expect a future cannot be either empirical or logical: it is clearly physiological. A hungry and watchful animal is prophetically organised, he is ready for more. This physical readiness, opening the eye and the mouth on nothingness, in case something should turn up, is translated into the forward intent of the mind, into an attention which has expectation in it. I can easily conceive that some animal should have expectation without memory; the machinery requisite for perception and retentiveness has a beginning, but it cannot exist, even at its first moment, without being ready to go on: instinct and intent are accordingly deeper than memory and underly it: the projection of memory into the past, by which it becomes a sentimental perspective, is itself a sort of inverted expectation; we remember by imagining what we should find if we could travel backwards.

The picture we framed of the future, when expectation is filled out in pictures, is not a copy of memory; nor does the eventual future, on the level of human experience, ever reproduce the past. The only future an animal can conceive or believe in is one peopled with images bred by his present spontaneous faculties. If this expected future resembles his past either generically, or in some details, it does so because that past was cast in the mould of his special senses and intellect, the very faculties which now in their simmering readiness, prompt his expectations. Apart from this inevitable family likeness between dreams or prophesies and images of the past, there is no reason and no truth in the empirical "law" that the future must repeat the past. If the flux of nature contains repetition (as it does in all mechanisms and in such organisms as reproduce their kind) it does so only in places and presumably for limited times. . . .[1]

1. The remainder of the manuscript is missing.—Editors.

PICTORIAL SPACE AND
SENTIMENTAL TIME

Pictorial space and sentimental time are sensuous presences. Like other essences they belong in themselves to the sphere of poetry, or (when analysed) of dialectic; they are not natural existences, but like idle sounds turned into words, symbolise the occasion on which they appear. So we speak of a *real* time and a *real* space, leaving it for science to determine gradually in what respects we may attribute the characteristics of sentimental time and pictorial space to those physical facts or relations. The general tendency of science is to reduce the literalness originally ascribed to the ideas of poetry, and to declare in the end that they do not at all resemble the objects for which they stand: in this case that physical space is not at all pictorial, and physical time not at all sentimental.

A radical suggestion in this direction has lately startled the somnolence of the thinking world. So little, the mathematicians tell us, need physical space and time resemble the aesthetic essences that display space and time to human sensibility, that they need not differ in kind from each other, but that time may be really (i.e., physically) a fourth dimension of space. Space at the same time need not conform at all to the pattern which pictorial space supplies: and just as common sense and the arts of building and navigation discount lineal and aerial perspective, and gives us a ground plan of things terrestrial and things celestial, so pure physics may discount what is still pictorial in that ground plan, and give us a formula for the method of all existence in which the distribution of facts in what we call time and space may be expressed in quantities of a single quality.

If physical time can be called a fourth dimension of physical space, and if in this manifold the aesthetic essence of space is as little to be found as the aesthetic essence of time, there might be no objection

George Santayana, "Pictorial Space and Sentimental Time," *Columbia Manuscript Collection.* © 1969 Daniel Cory. An early alternative to Chapter IV of *The Realm of Matter.* In the upper left corner of the first page Santayana penned, "This earlier version contains good things." The text suggests that the essay was written in 1920.

to stating the matter conversely, and saying that physical space was three more dimensions of time. This, for a philosopher accustomed to think in psychological and historical terms, has some advantages; certain forms of idealism have prepared the way for it. A mind has been conceived as a series of ideas; and many such series of ideas, many minds, have been supposed to proceed simultaneously; so that the single dimension of time has been multiplied perhaps infinitely, as if from a single spring—say the mind of the Creator—many rills had flowed and continued to subdivide themselves into a labyrinth of channels, until all flowed again into some sea of death or of apparent nothingness; a gulf from which by a secret evaporation they might float back, perhaps, to replenish their source. The stream of time would thus have many forks and many meanderings, through which life would flow at different rates and in different volumes: and whilst no doubt common tangents, running across all the streams, might be conceived to divide history into equal days and years, yet it is plain that the length of sentimental time in each life, or each reach of life, would be independent of these external divisions: life would be short measured in heart-beats, themselves the measure, for that life, of all duration; and art would be long measured by the stages to be traversed in learning to live: but the shortest life sentimentally might last infinitely longer, measured by the conventional common scale, than the life sentimentally the longest, most wearisome, most crowded with little actions and little thoughts. If psychological idealists had been men of freer and more speculative mind, they might have been led to dwell more on the pure relativity of time: because taken vitally and sentimentally, lives have no common measure and no possible date. Aesthetic time is a private perspective: and it is impossible that these perspectives taken each as a whole, in its transcendental unity, should be an element, having a specious date, in any other perspective. Nevertheless, by a surreptitious appeal to physical time (and even to physical space and the distribution of men in it) idealists have continued to regard some lives as simultaneous and others as successive; and they have continued to regard the respective lengths of these lives as comparable externally, imagining, for instance, that a dog's life came to an end on a certain day, but that the life of his master stretched on through the morrow, and through an infinite number of subsequent days. Evidently, on the hypothesis of idealism or biographism, the only sense in which lives can be contemporary, or comparable in date or duration, is this: that the *objects* imagined in one life are the same, part of the same, or the same in different temporal perspectives as those imagined in another. If nothing whatever present to one mind were present to another mind, they could not *in any sense whatever* lie in the same time; whilst if exactly the same events in the same order were observable by each, the two would be simultaneous virtually, though not literally; because still there would be no common stretch of physical time under them, but only a common theme. As two persons, centuries apart, may read the same book, so two lives, two if we allow ourselves to distinguish the time in which lives occur from the specious time which they survey, although ages apart, might be one life on the hypothesis of idealism, and have numerically the same experiences. We should say, then, that two persons reading the same book *ipso facto* are contemporary and the somewhat figurative or mystical talk, as it might seem, about the identity of our thoughts with those who think like us, would be absolutely and literally accurate: since identity of object would bring with it and would establish identity of date and place for the observers. It would be impossible that two minds, absolutely absorbed in reading the same book, should exist at different times or should belong to different persons.

In recoiling from this paradox, as even idealists do in the applications of their system, we should enter the path of scientific construction. Beginning by positing physical time, we should be led to posit multiplications, dispersions, and coordinations of various streams of events in it. To posit such forkings in time is equivalent to saying that events occur also in space: in other words, that physical time has other dimensions, signified to animal apprehension by aesthetic space. It will not take long for scientific observation, tracing the complexities and order of experiences in sentimental time, to recover those conceptions of the natural world which common-sense has long accepted; the old man in his study will merely repeat judicially that education of the senses which he first acquired in the cradle. It will presently appear that the space in which the objects given in time are distributed is a Euclidean space of three dimensions, and that these objects themselves have a continuous spatial history and a perpetual mechanical equivalence throughout their transformations. In a word, the life of reason in us will reveal to us the life of nature at large.

If our geometrical understanding of nature, however, should lead us later to separate the material world from its temporal dimension and from the successive appearances from which our notion of that material world had been drawn, we should find ourselves in difficulties. There would remain no point of attachment in the spatial world, as we then should conceive it, for that temporal world in which, in the first instance, we seem to live. Events would be multiplied beyond the power of apprehension, and concentrated into instants in which there could be no event: and it would be hard to say whether our intuitions of time and change arose at each of these instants—infinitely close together and infinitely multiplied, with no possibility of establishing a scale among them—or at some interval embracing an infinite number of instants, an interval spatially neither of a greater nor of a lesser plurality of phases than any other interval. I think nothing could be made out of this problem: it would be necessary in the end to dismiss it, as having been wrongly conceived. We should never have allowed ourselves to treat the three dimensions of space as anything but three more dimensions of time: not only (as a transcendental critic of knowledge would urge) because *our notion* of the spatial order was derived from a temporal experience, but also, and more correctly, because the *objects* discovered in space were always more or less enduring objects, having an intuited persistence and end, a life for sentiment (*sunt lachrymae rerum, ac mentem mortalia tangunt!*); and even if occasionally the duration of any material fact was not appreciable, and it seemed instantaneous, yet it was always embedded in a series of other spatial facts—a background, an origin, a result—in which both relative persistence and general continuity were essential: so that the fact and the scale of change, like diversity of distribution and quality, was [*sic*] inseparable from spatial existence.

Critical analysis might thus have easily arrived at the conclusion, so laboriously and obscurely announced to us now by the mathematicians, that pure space (in which there could obviously be no changes, no rate of change of size, no scale, no divisions, and no variety) cannot exist; that change, or changing relations in a field of change must accompany material existence and should form part of its definition; and that therefore the nexus between the spatial and temporal dimensions of nature is not adventitious, but primitive; so that, further, when we understand the cosmic process for which sentimental time and pictorial space are our private symbols, we may as well say that its duration is a fourth dimension of its spatial constitution, or *vice versa* that its extension is a complex of three more dimensions added to its time.

Physical time is composed of natural moments or states of substance, not of mathematical instants. No instant can be next to any other, whereas the moments are contiguous. In the mathematical schema for time—which is what fancy pictures as infinite empty time—the moment is always a period, and contains other distinguishable moments: for in empty time there could be no reason for giving preeminence to any moment over those included moments into which the instants within it (always infinite in number) could divide it. But physical time is occupied by events; and it depends on the character of these whether the number of moments shall be infinite or not. At any instant which is physically distinguishable (in that it divides two natural moments) some event must come to an end, some other event must begin, and some third comprehensive event must be going on. I call an instant so marked a critical instant (it is one at which some material change occurs). A duration within which nothing comes to an end and nothing arises is a natural moment; and such moments must exist in nature unless the critical instants within every event are infinite in number. It would take an infinite number of critical instants to subdivide a moment *ad infinitum* into other moments. Only instants at which something comes to an end and something else begins can mark stages in that comprehensive event which endures and temporally embraces both: if during this extended event the number of critical moments is not infinite, the event will stretch over only a finite number of moments: and the length of none of these ultimate moments will be measurable. Each will be a unit of physical time, impossible to compare in duration with any other moment. A duration long or short may be imputed to it either sentimentally or historically: sentimentally when it is felt (in an exclamatory way) to be very long or very short; historically when it is a considerable or a negligible part of the period or the event in which the historian is interested. Astronomers, in this sense, are natural historians: if they choose the revolution of a planet or the period of a light-signal for their unit of time, it might well appear that in some parts of nature there were more moments covered by such a unit than in other parts of nature: and then the astronomer might call the moments of which fewer went into his unit long moments, and those of which many went into his unit short moments; but the appellation would be reversible, and it would be just as true to say that his unit was sometimes short and sometimes long: for comparable lengths are relative, and ultimate lengths are incomparable.

If we suppose the number of natural moments to be infinite within any duration, as well as the number of critical instants, specious time will not seem a very good symbol for the nature of physical time: because in specious time the number of felt changes is small, and the rhythm marked; whereas if in nature the number of events within every event [were] infinite, it would be difficult to see what relevance these intuited rhythms and these obvious units have to the flux of substance. They must in any case have *some* relevance, because it is the flux of substance that produces the intuition of specious time, and the whole battle of distinguishable things. If the number of contemporary events is infinite, it can therefore be only at infinite distances: in any local system of nature, in any cosmos, we must be able to reach ultimate moments, the end of each marking a critical instant, before and after which an infinite number of indifferent instants must be passed over before we come to another crisis, and the beginning of the next moment.

Physical time, if and when it is so divided into specific moments, within each of which all endures and nothing changes, may be called natural time. Natural time contains great rhythms and obvious crises, from day and night, the seasons, and life and death, down to heartbeats and the fractions of seconds measurable by clocks. It is braided together, like the flux of nature which fills and determines it, of strands of different duration; its periods cover and extend over one another; they may be measured in terms of one another; but when we descend to the ultimate moments, during which nothing new occurs, the durations become incomparable naturally, and even to call them equal is to impute to them a property to which nothing within them corresponds. They are similar, indeed, in being durations within which no crisis occurs. If for any reason anyone chose to say that such moments, in one part of the natural flux, were brief and crowded together, and in another part marched at a slow pace, like spondees after trochees, there would be nothing in the nature of the moments themselves to refute or to justify such a fancy: nor could it be done by carrying over into the perusal of such moments any subjective, physiological measure of duration; for what was physiological in such a measure—heart-beats or beats of attention—would be subject to the same subdivision into units ultimately immeasurable; whilst the *sentiment* of greater or lesser duration would not tell us at all how long it (the sentiment) lasted in physical time, but only what sentimental distances and perspectives, what precipitation or weary waiting, filled the specious time within it.

If natural time be so conceived, it may be said that specious time is an excellent expression of it. What is the best sort of relation between a fact and a perception which is to know it? The perception must be other than the fact in existence: it must lie in a tangential plane to the time and space of the fact: and it must envisage, as its immediate datum, an essence such that, when it is attributed to the fact and used to describe the fact, it may indicate the pertinent elements in the essence of that fact—pertinent, I mean, to the context in which that fact is viewed and to the interest that leads the percipient to attend to it and make it the theme of his assertions. Now specious time fulfils these requirements very well in relation to natural time, or the flux of nature. For the specious time is a landscape which has no position at all in the space or time of nature: but the event in the psyche which includes the intuition of that landscape has such a position; it is in the closest causal and temporal relations to natural time and to just those events in it which (since they affect the life of the psyche) are interesting and absorbing, and are sought for by the intellect; it is on them, precisely, that its questions turn, and on them that, in thinking, it looks for light. Moreover, specious time presents an excellent image of natural time in the following ways: (1) it is a total view of an incomplete object, an object that is felt to extend beyond the limits of present apprehension; this is possible because (2) within the datum there are successive divisions or rhythms[1] which carry the form or frame of apprehension decidedly beyond the points at which clear apprehension is focussed, and (3) the units distinguishable and the beats felt lie against a continuous background, like the nimble notes of a melody sustained by a prolonged note in the accompaniment. It is in just such ways (modified only as existence must modify merely ideal relations) that natural time is diversified; for every event in nature (cf. Whitehead) is included in a larger event, and beyond every event there are others (the whole universe can hardly be called event being an eternal fact) and in the march of events, amid much that, in its synthetic form, is novel, there is law and repetition of forms; so that not only the flux, but the character of the flux, the familiar round of things, extends beyond any assignable portion into an indefinite past and future.

If then we are absorbed in watching and studying the felt movement of things, we gather a very good notion of their real movement. This

1. These rhythms include a *direction of survey* which carries intent far out into the infinite, beyond the horizon of clear data. We expect more such things.

almost perfect fitness of specious time to describe natural time is confined to specious time intently and speculatively contemplated. The
psyche in whose life specious time is a vista is very far from being
radically contemplative: her animal quality makes her a participant, a
fighter in the flux, rather than an observer of it: her capacity to observe
is only a by-product of her eagerness to elude and to pursue a certain
circle of objects. These objects are chiefly those that are near, recent,
threatening, or magnetic. Specious time is therefore qualified by temporal perspectives wholly absent in natural time: earlier things are
therein called past, later things future; those earlier still are called
ancient, and dead; those later still are called uncertain, vague, non-
existent. This is sentimental time: the aerial perspective of the moral
world, by which, from every particular station, a fog of ignorance is
felt to cover the distance, a round horizon is drawn at the radius of
one's emotional tether, and a total difference of nature is attributed to
what happens to lie before and to what happens to lie behind, at every
point traversed in succession in the endless journey of the spirit.

In so far as specious time or any part of it is essentially past, future,
near, long, or slow—specious time is an animal falsification of natural
time, and a sheer contradiction to its own pronouncements elsewhere,
since every natural moment that is future is also present and past, every
moment that is remote is also at hand, and every rate that is fast or
slow is also, from some other point of view, the exact opposite. Nevertheless the perspectives of sentimental time are not arbitrary: false as
they are, if projected into natural time, they are not only perfectly real
in themselves, and emotionally momentous, but they are significant of
the natural relations in which the animal lies; for the animal creates
these perspectives in virtue of his readjustment and modification by
some events—(those past and near)—and its premonition of others,—
those which his instincts or habits are ready to meet. And the very
propensity of living beings to view time sentimentally is an appropriate
expression of their nature and of their relations in natural time: so that
sentimental time, like every moral and local perspective, expresses a
true, though relative, quality of events. It gives a picturesque or emotional rendering of a true situation.

The flux of nature has a direction, and though it may be surveyed
backwards, in memory and history, or in science when it investigates
origins, it is even then reconstituted in sympathy with its original forward march. Later and earlier are not like right and left, irrelevant to

the objects surveyed, because events flow, and could flow, only in one direction, as the sap of a tree; and although in nature every event is as much the root of the following event as the flower of the previous one, yet these relations are not interchangeable. Why, exactly, is natural time irreversible, and what does this property involve? Because it is not a mathematical order but a natural genesis involving inheritance: the radical power and compulsion of existence to pass from one phase to another.

The semitic languages are written from right to left; we might adopt this usage, and nothing would be changed or marred in our literature. But if we wrote a single word beginning with the last letter and ending with the first, "literature" would become "erutaretil," a new sound without sense. Any musical phrase illustrates the same fact: if reversed it would lose its whole essence. A life that should begin with the sentiments of a death-bed and end in the womb—a movement reversed as the cinematograph might reverse it—would create a monstrous event which, in spite of its strangeness, would still preserve the character of a progression in one direction; the new order would be no less essential and distinctive to the new story than the old order was to the old. The reason is that temporal transitions, when they are not merely geometrical, are cumulative: they are subject to the principle of acceleration and the summation of forces; and to slacken the pace is not the same as to quicken it; to divide is not the same thing as to unite.

Progress is not necessary to progression; in a temporal sense, decay is no less an advance than is growth. The forms of growth and decay might be reversed: both would remain progressions. If living beings passed from dispersion to organisation without a nucleus or seed, as Empedocles, for instance, seems to have believed that they did, nature would move forward by magical impulse; growth would seem a miracle of final causation, and decay (which would concentrate life in a unit summing up all its accidents) would create a sort of natural echo or material record of the past, instead of (as at present) obliterating its traces. Invert the history of the autumn leaf. Imagine the dust into which it dissolves, rushing together spontaneously from the four quarters of the heavens, like the scattered ashes of mortals at the sound of the last trump; first a little mould would gather in some sheltered nook of the earth; it would then crystallize into a few ribs and a little dry network of fibres connecting them; then this web would assume greater consistency (picking up other substances that would fly into it from the air) and show patches of a red and a green colour; finally, its outline having become symmetrical and its stem obvious, it would suddenly flutter upwards and attach itself to a twig, ready for it on some bough; there it would grow slowly smaller, fresher, and greener, until it shrunk into a sprout and into a drop of sap in a little swelling upon [the] surface of the branch which had supported it; and with this branch itself it would finally retreat into the trunk and into the earth, merged in an undistinguishable fashion in the common substance of its species. Obviously such a reversal of what we term growth and decay would illustrate succession no less conspicuously than does the present evolution of nature: indeed, it may not be wholly fanciful to say that, in mental and moral life, this reversal actually takes place: for the spirit advances by accepting every sort of accident, every image, and every experience that fortune may bring in its way, and concentrating them into a form, and then into a single principle or sentiment, giving a pure but pregnant expression to all its past vicissitudes. This progression, which reverses the order of vegetation, is progress in wisdom: and surely the life of reason is no less successive than that of nature, and the earlier parts are no less causal and needful in reaching the later ones. Concentration into the seed is as *desirable* an advance, as is growth from a seed outwards into diffuse manifestations: so that the eulogistic sense of progress is not only not presupposed in the movement of nature but exactly opposite and reversed processes—from concentration to dispersion and from dispersion to concentration—may be equally admired and felt to constitute a vital advance.

Life is no illusion, and no source of illusion, so long as we take it simply for what it is, and express its visions and its passions as a pure poet might express them: all this experience is actual experience, all this dream is an actual dream, all these rhetorical fictions and evanescent notions actually cross the stage of consciousness. In this sense the vistas of sentimental time are important realities: and nothing needs to be censured or corrected in the lyric poetry which in all ages has sung the triumphs of death and time, nor in the emphatic prophecies which, in order to hide and drown the painful uncertainty of men about the future, have announced eloquently what this future was bound to be. Those prophecies were ignorant and egotistical, and the actual future falsified them, of course: and even those elegiacal epitaphs on the past were impertinent, because the weak and transitory hold on existence which is there lamented is the essence of existence itself, and the dead souls mourned over are in truth as living as the present passion (now also past) which pitied their ghostly condition, forgetting its own no less slippery tenure of life. But falsehood and impertinence belong to the mind only when it risks assertions about outlying things: we need but to rescind this transitive ambition, this egotistical impudence in our judgements, for all our thoughts to become harmless pictures, very real facts, and perfect expressions of the nature and situation of our souls when we frame those visions.

Sentimental time—a moving present between a vanished past and an unborn future—is something altogether evident and important, taken lyrically and autobiographically: but its ineptitude is obvious and extreme, if we try to turn its perspectives into intrinsic properties of the experienced natural flux, which they express. The vanished past? Certainly all years prior to 1920 A. D. are past at the time when I write these words, and all later years are future; but the reader will know that one of the years subsequent to 1920 is as living a present as 1920 is to me now; my future will be his present, and both presently a third man's past. There is no moment in the whole history of nature that is not future for an infinity of moments, present for itself momentarily, and for an infinity of moments past: its imputed futurity and pastness accrue to it by virtue of the existence of other moments; and its presentness (taken absolutely) is a name for its existence and inalienable actuality, or (taken relatively) the same presentness is a name for its middle position between those things which, given its place forever in the realm of truth, in the perspectives which it itself contains, it occupies between what it calls past and what it calls future. Past and future are therefore denominations extrinsic, adventitious, relative, and compatible. It is true of every fact that it is past from one point of view and future from another, and both eternally; and that it is in itself eternally present, not merely because it might (somewhat loosely) be said to be present to itself, but rather because it is a station from which temporal vistas, forward and back, are open: so that in its transcendental timelessness it assigns to itself historical station between what it sees as past and what it sees as future; in the act of looking in both directions it seems to place itself at the centre between them. These attributions of past and future to perspectives are not the real determinants of position in the flux; for every event is [sic]. It is really before some events and after others, whether it knows it or not: but this position in the world of genesis does not make it partake either more or less than any other event either of pastness, presentness, or futurity: it merely designates the fact that the before and after both pervade it, and extend congruently beyond it over other events, the relative directions of which, in respect to it, are not reversible.

Past and future are like east and west: no place is essentially eastern nor western, but every place not on the same meridian is truly to the east or west of every other; and (except in the single case of places separated from it by 180° of longitude) it is not in both relations to anyone. Time does not allow such an exception, unless indeed natural time comes round in a circle, in which case every event would be both past and future in respect to every other.[2] Assuming that this is not the case, the direction of events in time, relatively to one another, is never ambiguous: and this truth is well symbolised in the sentimental distinction between past and future: past events are truly past and future events truly future from *this* point of time: and the quality of pastness and futurity truly belongs to them, respectively, in this vista, so that it would be an error to assert of any of them which lies in one direction that it lies in the other, as if I said that my death had already occurred, but my birth not yet: sentimental time, like pictorial space, gives us a true indication of the irreversible collocation of things in nature. At each moment a different emotion is justified towards different things; but everything justifies both emotions, from different quarters; and as every defeat is somebody's victory, every future is somebody's past, and every past somebody's future. The attempt to say that what is past now or for me is *intrinsically* past, and what is future now or for me is *intrinsically* future is simply a piece of stupid egotism; and it is a disgrace to a philosopher to succumb to it. The temptation to do so, in spite of the obvious double coefficient of every event, shows how slowly animal illusion can be shaken off by the human mind: especially where life requires a different attitude to things—past future, right wrong, native foreign—the most absurd absolutism lingers in judgement because it is still difficult for people to see that though what is actual is actual absolutely and in itself, what is important is important *only because it is relative to what requires it.*

---

2. A postulated repetition, which would make the future event numerically distinct from its past prototype, is self-contradictory: for not only the essence of the two, but their existence would be identical, since the external relations which introduce and define existence would be the same in both instances. Only circumstances can distinguish instances.

In the realm of essence the nature of "before" is not earlier than the nature of "after": both are eternal and, in that sense, always contemporary in their mutual implication. When deployed in existence, however—and this is a chief note of existence—something comes before and something comes after, in such a way that the essences are embodied in facts which, unlike their essences, may be divorced: each fact might have come without the other, and therefore without illustrating in respect to it this particular essence called "before" or "after." Each might indeed have illustrated the opposite essence and may do so in respect to something else; facts may change places, but essences never can. There is, accordingly, something more in each fact than the character of being earlier or later: and these predicates are indexes to these facts, pointing at them from outside in order to identify them through an external relation; they are not definitions of the individual facts, nor descriptions of anything intrinsic to them. Yet not altogether extrinsic: because unless each fact persisted (i.e., had the earlier and later exemplified within it) it could not exist or be a fact at all: nor could it lie in the same world of existence with other facts unless it was *either* before or after the rest, or (what involves lying in such relations to still other facts) were simultaneous with them—for in order to be simultaneous two facts must be parts of a third fact or must lie in parallel lines of derivation from some third fact.

When an object is absolutely simple, we have no means of correcting the attribution to it of the essence which we intuit in regarding it; this essence must stand in discourse for the character of that object, and be its proper description. So in the case of pure duration within a moment: the essence of pure duration—passage from a before to an after, without any *other* distinction between these two terms—must be accepted as the description of pure persistence, a passage whereby a fact is believed to change its date and remain *otherwise* identical. This degree of diversity, diversity in time, must be attributed to existences no matter how otherwise one and indistinguishable they may inwardly be. Pure flux must then be supposed to be adequately expressed in the sense of pure duration: for the given essence and the essence embodied in the object must be regarded as the same. We may indulge in a mental reservation on this point; we may suspect that the true form of persistence in existence is not *like* the aesthetic sentiment of waiting or watching: but it must be like it in its relations (otherwise the intuition would not be relevant to it, or even cognise it erroneously) and the only relations that are pertinent are these: one end of a duration *coincides* with or passes into one thing and the other end into another: in such a way that the duration (with its special polarity) extends over them severally without a break; in other words, flux extends over all *other* differences which may be introduced into existence, without being broken or reduplicated. It is the same *pure* relation of before and after beyond the point where a change occurs; and this necessarily. For if a break—in which no persistence persisted—occurred between the pure persistence of one existent and the pure persistence of another, the model or type of before and after would no longer cover their mutual relation; and they would not be (relatively to one another) in time at all. Whatever variations, therefore, occur in existence, persistence in time is invariable there: not the *rate* of variation (that is another and quite open question) but the *fact* of persistence without intermission or variation, extending over all changes at all rates.

The appropriate name for this inevitable persistence, the object which the sense of duration *must* express if it has any object at all, is *Substance*. Substance is the principle of persistence both in the absence of change and in the midst of change: a principle underlying all changes and giving them both their absolute direction and their relative position in time.

Substance,[3] then, embodies more than the essence of pure duration, or of the before and after; it is not a mere flux, but something changing. We could reach this conclusion also by a transcendental argument: if substance were mere flux (almost as emphatically as if it were pure Being) it would be irrelevant to all those revolutions and conflicts in nature which it is invoked to explain. Here, however, I am attempting to approach substance not transcendentally but scientifically: i.e., trusting the impulse of animal faith which regards experience as a discovery of fact. I am asking what *is* the fact which the experience of duration reveals. And I answer that, at least and as a beginning, it is the *existence* or fact of a change (much more than the essences of change, which are unchanging and non-existent); and this existence involves a passage from one condition to a different condition: therefore, more than a duration in which one and the same condition persists. Substance, then, is so far discovered to be persistent in natural time, and to suffer modifications. But is there anything that need per-

---

3. The manuscript carries the note, "Flux throughout, in lieu of 'substance'" here, but Santayana did not make the substitutions.—Editors.

sist throughout these modifications save the fact of change? In other words, are we justified in saying that substance is more than a name for the truth that one mode of existence or state of nature perpetually follows upon another?

Essences given in intuition are passive and inert, and the intuition may be taken, if we like, as a name correlative to that passive presence; in that sense intuition will be transparent, notional, and passive too, and also something non-existent. But in that case we must not confuse intuition with the wakefulness of animals or even with their sleep; consciousness, awareness, thought is (apart from selecting any particular essence) a very distinctive sign and expression of life: it has a pregnant nature; it is intelligence. Far from being an abstract correlative to a passive datum, it is a spirit of inquiry, a sweeping question addressed to things at large, a virtual positing of all nature to be ransacked, and of all essences to be chosen and used in describing nature. There is no paradox, to a philosopher who understands that mind is an expression of animal life, in this antecedent scope of awareness: it is not an *a priori* constitution imposed on experience to come: it is not a creative will or absolute power of positing or feigning objects. It is the cry of an animal tossed into an unknown world: it expresses the inner tension of the body, and its general sensibility to whatever may touch it. Experience always comes under the form of totality: intelligence is addressed, from the very beginning, because it is the moral life of a natural being, to the remotest quarters from which influences may shoot towards it, and to the whole of reality. What aspect or what limits the world may wear at any moment is an accident: the mind cannot invent or divine anything that the reactions of the body, or its inner vege[ta]tion, have not set before it: but it will take and understand the essences before it for a description of *all there is*; it will remain essentially addressed to everything; to all the rest, if there be more; to the world it lives in, whatever it may really be; to the true and unknown god. This attitude, for all its intellectual ambition, is simply a transcript of material responsiveness and material affections; all things touch, or may touch, the animal; all things are therefore the theme of his solicitude, the object of his watch. What essences rise before him are not his object, except by an ambiguity of language or a lapse on his part into a sort of idolatry: for the mind, being an animal function, may be deranged and stunned: it may be hypnotised by its images: it may mistake essences for things, and fall into an intellectual coma, or an

empirical idealism. For the mind, when awake and watchful, the object
—however near and circumscribed—is primarily something not given,
infinitely more obscure and formidable than the actual datum, with an
existence and a life of its own: it is a substance. Essences given in intuition and used by thought become objects on their own account only
in suspended, abstracted, ulterior moments, when aesthetic forms and
logical unities come to be separately considered. The intended object
of living perception is always not-given; it is pursued, studied, inquired
about, described; and the prior virtual knowledge or assumption that it
is there to be observed, the demonstrative gesture or searching look
by which it is indicated, are inevitable attitudes in an animal: if the
mind did not make this assumption, if it had not this *a priori* faculty of
directing itself on remote unknown things, it would be irrelevant to
the animal life which in truth it manifests: it would be some little strain
of disembodied ideation, without a meaning or intent, such as empirical philosophy actually reduces it to. In fact it is addressed to all
time and all existence by the mere fact that it itself exists: it is intelligence in its essence: and nothing is given to it save to be understood,
to be interpreted as a sign of all ambient existence, of all things past
and future. If philosophy asks these questions, it does so because these
are the questions that all life asks: if life did not ask them, philosophy
would not be able to do so.

The distinction current between sensation and thought is an external
one: sensation is thought in so far as it is awareness of an essence, and
(in active animals) assertion and belief in an existing thing: and
thought is sensation, in so far as it traces the contours, and darts about
amongst the obvious relations of terms present to intuition. Both sensation and thought, regarded transcendentally, are pure observation:
both, regarded biologically, are adjustments of an animal to the surrounding world, and possession on his part of symbols—more or less
fantastic and elusive in their own aspect—which he can use to mark
or name what most concerns him in things, or in their effects upon
himself. There is of course a difference of degree and of application
between sensation and thought, otherwise two words would hardly
have distinguished them: sensation is thought under the immediate and
exclusive influence of external or peripheral stimulation: thought is
sensation with its eyes closed; the play of attention over ancient images,
or the new images which they bred. This is figurative language: for
there is more, both in thought and in sensation, than attention to

images; there is synthesis, extensions such as formal expectation of new things determined as to the place and general nature they are to have, but not as to their particular moments and forms; there is also judgement and assertion; there is intent, because both are expressions of animal life, not the contemplation of absolute essences by disembodied spirits. But when all this is taken for granted, we may say, in order to mark the diversity which there really is between thinking and feeling, that sensation is intelligence applied to what is present to the body in space, and thought intelligence applied to what is, in that respect, absent. That is the biological difference: and the biographical or autobiographical difference, the one which literary psychology can discern, is that in sensation we perceive things vividly one by one and under external conditions, while in thought we perceive them faintly and together, and can retain and turn them over not indeed at will, but under the influence of our dominant mood, passion, or habit. Thoughts seem therefore more our own; other people are less able to share them than to share our sensations—although this, too, is a matter of degree only: and we settle our account in thought with things at large, and prepare for action at long range, whereas in sensation the suggested acts and choices are impulsive and terminate in present things. But there is no reason for supposing that sensation is *truer* than thought, or thought than sensation: both are relevant to things, both are our symbols and language for describing them: now these descriptive essences may hug the form or movement of a single thing, now rather the form and movement of many things in their order of succession, leaving their individual figures utterly vague; but these differences are differences of notation or of calculation, they are differences of language and method, not of applicability or truth. So that when one school of philosophers maintains that sense is knowledge but thought is fiction, whilst an opposite school replies that sense is not knowledge, but that knowledge is thought about the data of sense, both schools are wasting words. Sensation and thought are equally descriptive, equally transitive in intent, equally observant in intuiting their data; and as to the truth of the beliefs which they bring with them, both are dependent on the same external structure of facts, and on the degree to which what they assert of some part of the world is extant there, supposing the world has a part that, in that sensation or thought, has been discerned adequately enough to render assertions about it possible and relevant.

III

Fact and Essence

WHAT ARE DATA?

"Concerning the immediate objects in illusions, hallucinations, and dreams, it is meaningless to ask whether they 'exist' or are 'real'. There they are, and that ends the matter." This passage from Mr. Bertrand Russell's book on *Mysticism and Logic* (p. 176) tempts me to some belated comments: not in order to quarrel with a thinker who is so willing to [and so] well able to correct himself, and who makes so unmistakably for enlightenment; but rather, in order to take advantage of several openings he gives and to defend the distinction which I think necessary between the *ideal terms* in which experience comes (which I call essences) and *objects of intent,* such as things or events, which are reported in those terms and believed to exist.

Far from ending the matter, to say of appearances "There they are" only raises the question. It raises the question for the perplexed animal, whose task is to interpret his data, rather than to collect them; and it raises the question for the philosopher as well, who is trying to understand the relation which these data may bear to human belief and to its ordinary objects.

Let us ask, then, what is the force of this very ambiguous ejaculation, "There they are." "There" evidently does not mean anywhere in particular. If the appearance before us is extended and divisible, and if we limit ourselves to what it contains, we find a hint or type of the spatial —a landscape—but not space nor a part of space, since without being infinite the datum has no definite boundaries and no position. What we mean by saying it is *there* is rather that it is *here,* that is, that I see it. So the various parts or qualities that I may discern in this specious extension, as well as any other data, like sounds, that I may fuse with it,

George Santayana, "What Are Data?" Humanities Research Center, University of Texas. © 1969 Daniel Cory. Bertrand Russell's *Mysticism and Logic* was first published in 1918; the fact that Santayana calls these comments on the book "belated" suggests that they might have been composed several years later.

are all *here*. A moment ago they were absent, now they have come upon me. If "there" means anything, then, it refers to the objectivity of the whole field of data in respect to a self, thereby assumed and felt to be relatively permanent; it indicates their present relativity to the mind. But I will not press this point, because I heartily agree with Mr. Russell that the relation by which anything becomes a datum or an object is incidental to its proper being. Even when, as in the case of imputed thoughts or feelings, it is part of the conceived facts that they should be part of somebody's experience, it is no part of them that I should now conceive them. When data are said to be "there," the phrase is accordingly entirely irrelevant to what is given.

In the second place, what is the sense of this plural pronoun "they," and why not say instead, "Here is x, reality, God, or myself"? The sense is, presumably, that by attending closely I can distinguish certain features or characters in what solicits my attention, whatever its status may otherwise be; and these characters, in so far as I distinguish them, indeed become obvious. Any vagueness, obscurity, or vacillation which we may accuse them of is imputed to them extraneously, in view of some ulterior expectation or demand of ours; in itself, in its quality and degree of determination, a datum is precisely what it is. This precise quality is what I call an essence. Besides the obscure and questionable object before me, there are also traits (such as this obscurity itself) which, if arrested, are unquestionable and clear.

To call this clear object *the immediate datum* is justified from the observer's point of view, or from that of reflection, when we realise that after all the signal was given first, and that without it the thing signified could never have been suspected to exist: thus the term immediate is used transcendentally (and it is properly a term of transcendental philosophy). But if immediate meant first in time or in the development of experience, the clarified data or bare essences positively given are not the immediate: they may not be noticed at all at first. The assurance of an obscure fact or force is far more primitive, radical, and fundamental than the clarified terms which loom up when we arrest the attention. Belief may, in experience, precede all definitions of the object or of the belief itself: and the object, not the datum or vehicle, may be transcendentally the immediate presence.

Now Mr. Russell says that data are particulars, and seems to think that no one will question that assertion; yet it makes me very much doubt what he means by data, and how much he may be reading into the object of intuition (an essence given) which can be found only in the object of intent, the fact believed in. For all I find in a datum is a universal, an essence which is indeed particular in quality, perfectly self-sufficient and its own standard of definiteness, but which (as a part of its deliverance) has no place, no date, and no reference to me or to any other observer; so that it might be found, identically the same, anywhere, at any time, and by anybody.

As discourse selects its data from a wider field vaguely at hand to the senses, so attention might obviously be turned on the remainder also, and on its relation to the special datum at first selected; so that the entire field of latent sensibility (as much as any selected feature or quality) is a total theme and an essence. The entire character of any appearance (which is all than can be found in it) may evidently appear again, and is a universal. Emotion and poetry tend to recall such total data.

In calling an essence a datum reference is avowedly made to the attention or awareness falling upon it. This element can never be itself a datum; its introduction at this point seems dogmatic and obscure, and while I entirely agree with Mr. Russell that awareness is something over and above the essences we are aware of, the evidence for its existence must be drawn from the higher reaches of reflection, and is inadmissible to the pure empiricist. If we denied the necessary co-operation of this act of attention, to make an essence into a datum (as we might do without the least prejudice to its specious character) the chief temptation to call this essence a particular would disappear. On the other hand, if selective attention must be presupposed, as Mr. Russell admits, then (whilst the ideal identity of the datum would not be affected) its supposed absolute existence and fitness to be a constituent element of the physical world would be ruined; for its presence, taken to be ultimate and unambiguous in such an idealistic epistemology, would in fact be an expression and a sign of much deeper things at work, with which we could never have knowledge of acquaintance. I cannot resist the feeling that it is by some secret assimilation of the pure datum to these deeper things (which Mr. Russell either admits or does not deny) that so keen a logician is led to turn given universals into particulars. That very phrase "There they are" is evidence of this: for a critic that had thoroughly discriminated data from things on the one hand, and from latent sensibles on the other, would rather have said "Such they are," which is all that given essences, uninterpreted by instinctive intelligence, can justify us in saying.

It is in fact the third word in our text, the word "are" that is the most enigmatical. Certainly essences "are" what they are, and their ideal character or identity is what will seem to a pure logician to deserve preeminently the name of Being. But this Being proper to Platonic Ideas as to other essences is logical, immutable, immaterial, and altogether different from phenomenal or physical existence flowing through space and time. When Mr. Russell says his data obviously "are" he means that they are phenomena here and now and to him; their being, he tells us, is always particular, often physical, and probably as transitory as the movement of attention that falls upon them. True, he is not willing to say they exist; but this scruple is due to an altogether special and recondite use of the word existence, a use which he advocates, without always adhering to it in practice. To exist, in his logic, should mean to be true or to apply: the term should accordingly be used of descriptions, but would make nonsense if used of facts. We might ask, for instance, whether "perfect happiness" exists, meaning whether there is anything to which this description applies; but if perfect happiness were actually given it would be nonsense (according to the proposed use of words) to say it existed; because that would be saying that the perfect happiness actually felt was a mere description that applied to something else. Unfortunately the word existence is in common use and an effort so oddly to shift its meaning can only produce confusion, especially as Mr. Russell might very likely change his view before the public had had time to adopt it. Nevertheless the analysis which has led him to this proposal is very interesting. A logician may well hesitate to say of his ultimates that they exist. His ultimates are essences, which in fact do not exist, being only ideal terms, specific characters intrinsically possible, forms of being. In animal perception, given essences are normally descriptions, and apply to ulterior things and when these essences are said to exist at all it is precisely in the proposed new sense of the word existence. When we ask of an appearance whether it exists, we are asking whether an object exists of which it is a true description; the mere fact that such a datum appears seems to us (quite rightly) not to involve its existence: the only existence involved, when the datum is an illusion and describes no existing object, is that of our perception or delusion itself, with its presumable basis in bodily life. The datum is intrinsically logical or aesthetic and does not become mental when given; but something mental does then arise and exist, namely, the flash of awareness falling on that datum.

As to the meaning of the word existence, a thorough discussion would take us too far afield. Like most common and important words it has various shades of meaning in its various applications, since to the scandal of philosophers words were made to be used and not to be defined. But let me say this in passing: in considering existence, as in considering anything else, we need to distinguish the essence from the fact. The essence of existence, though indefinable like all simple essences, is familiar, being an object of continual intuition; but the fact of existence is an object of belief—a belief which is indeed inevitable in life, yet may be questioned by the determined sceptic and is actually denied by some mystics and logicians. All existents, even oneself, are things meant, not given, and the descriptions we possess of them always leave them in some degree of obscurity. Man, being a sensitive and contemplative spirit, has clear objects or data before him; but being at the same time, and more radically, a hunting and labouring animal, he has obscure objects about him, on which his attention is directed, although he does not know initially just *what* they are: and in this confusing situation—with clear appearances which he cares nothing for and obscure facts that are all important to him—his expedient is to assert that whatever appears to him is true of the facts—whence all the fictions and allegories of sense, rhetoric, religion and philosophy. Existence is a kind of stress (such as is attention or energy), a stress which actualises[1] some essences and not others, and thus affords occasion for change and for external relations—change and external relations being the great marks of what exists. The selected essences, though they do not forfeit their ideal nature when thought of or exemplified, define the existents to which or in which they appear. Thus a mind is defined by the circle of intelligible and sensible themes over which it ranges; and these mental existents, such as thoughts and feelings, are called after those essences given in them; as the word love is used to denote the waxing and waning event of loving quite as much as the ideal essence of the sentiment then felt, but previously well known to the poets. If we are tempted to think this distinction artificial or to doubt which of these two things we mean in a given case, we have only to ask ourselves: Is this love a quality of emotion or action that can recur and that can be shared, or is it a crisis, an *Erlebnis* in Lucinda now which nobody else can appropriate and which never can recur? The former is the essence given, the latter is the feeling that exists.

Nature too is defined by the forms and laws which it manifests and renders true. We may say that such forms and laws exist, because we

---

1. Santayana wrote in "falls upon" as an alternative to "actualises."—Editors.

find them illustrated in existence. In truth it is only the event that exists, bearing the name of the essence found in it. The difference between the two is manifest when we ask: Am I describing a fact by its given universal character, or am I noting this universal given character itself? The latter is the absolute datum; the fact is an object of intent and endeavour, a particular that I believe would exist whether it yields any datum to me or not.

Since existence involves external relations, it follows at once that existence can never be given. All given parts of a datum are internal and essential to it. When perfect happiness is the datum it cannot be a datum that perfect happiness exists; but the fact that it exists, which is true though not given, can be discovered when dropping for a moment out of absorption in perfect bliss, we reflect and say, "Here we are in heaven at last, and for all future time!" This discovery would be a belief only; the complex essence "Myself in heaven at last, and for all future time" would now be the datum: but obviously its truth and the existence of its past and future perspectives would remain hypothetical. Indeed, on returning to our pure ecstasy, the notions of ourselves, our past longings, present attainments and future safety, might be wholly obliterated: and if our ecstatic insight was the truer one (as we may piously believe) the essence given to our reflection when we discovered that we were in heaven for all future time would actually have been false. For we should only be in heaven in as much as we were not ourselves and had no past and no future. Thus the existence of a given essence is never given, existence being always one step above or one step below the datum. For this reason mystical logicians, who are out of humour with the tantalising and transitive nature of life and of the knowledge of fact, deny existence; and I think they are right if they only mean that it is irrelevant to logic and that when we contemplate the realm of essence, it can drop out of sight.

It is because Mr. Russell has come so very near to dispelling the confusion between essences and facts that I have been tempted to take his view for my text in these observations. And I think it is where he denies the distinction, and says that data are physical, or can be put together into things, or constitute a world in six dimensions, that we may best feel that he is really talking of universals and purely ideal essences. To say that some essences are physical is, in one sense, perfectly innocent and obvious. The idea of a house might be called a material idea, as other ideas are called musical or poetical, or as Mr. Russell maintains that pain is mental. The reason is that the essence of pain can be actualised only in a mind; just so the essence of a house can be actualised only in bricks and mortar. But of course the essences of both a pain and a house are possibles and universals only, not physical or mental beings; and such they remain intrinsically even while consciousness or matter lends them a temporary actuality.

Even the fact that Mr. Russell proceeds to construct a world out of these sensible essences, does not convince me that he really mistakes them for physical objects. His world has six dimensions, it has as an integral part every figment of fancy or reason, and in it the past is as much dependent on the future as the future on the past. Such a world does not seem objectionably real; I gladly accept it as a typical denizen of the realm of unbodied essences; no one is in serious danger of confounding it with living nature. It would be, if it could be worked out completely, an interesting symbolic description or algebraic shadow of this world—the only sort of object, I know, that its author has any respect for.

Mr. Russell seems to me less successful in disengaging essences from mental facts. Professedly no doubt, he distinguishes sensation from essences given in sense (which he calls *sensibilia*) and I suppose he would distinguish in the same way the human acts of perception, conception, and belief from the essences given through them. The laws of nature would certainly not be identified by him with knowledge of these laws. Yet it is ominous that the subsistence of these objects when not given is regarded by him as hypothetical; so that in their certain and given being they are, according to his own definition, mental facts —a mental fact being one in which awareness is an element.

Although Mr. Russell allows that things may subsist when not given, his ideal of scientific method is to regard data as the only facts, and all else as methodological fiction; sensibilia not given and things are to be introduced grudgingly and kept down to the narrowest possible limits. He would like to find solipsism scientifically satisfactory; and I fear, if he carried this principle out, that he would have to reduce his personal experience itself to a fiction resting on the single datum of the moment. The ideal of science, on this principle, would be to have no discursive science at all, but an imbecile certitude in the presence of the absolutely given. This realism is evidently a form of psychological idealism, and involves the same retractation of all knowledge. What would have to be retracted, if the claim to knowledge were to be frankly maintained, would be rather that first assumption of psychological criticism that whatever appears arises when given and is destroyed when lost sight of. It is this assumption, which Mr. Russell nominally rejects, that still inspires him in supposing that data are particulars, out of which essences would need to be drawn by abstraction and things by construction.

On the contrary, essences are the first data we have, and things the first objects we mean—animal sensation having initially this transitive and significative force. The alleged particular is simply the ill-conceived "idea" of Berkeley or "impression" of Hume—a hybrid which is neither the object of intent (which is the thing) nor the terms by which that object is indicated (which are essences) nor the mental experience (which is an event, a moment of living attention) in which both object and terms are surveyed. Instead it is that dead atom of psychological chemistry, the mental experience turned into its own object, and decked out in the colours of those signals by which the object is reported to us. Thus in fact—in spite of the revolutionary discoveries of Cantor and Dedekind, this philosophy of science is still that of John Stuart Mill. We have sensations—and he believes in permanent possibilities of sensation—and we assume—for no reason and without apology—the validity of expectation and memory, and the power of one sensation to know another. To feel it *safer* to suppose that data arise when perceived and lapse when forgotten, is virtually to regard them as "ideas in the mind." Essences, which is what they "are," cannot possibly suffer this fate, since they are universals, and their being is irrelevant to their instrumental and momentary presence in knowledge. The datum is the deliverance of the experience, not the experience that occurs. What is not *safe*, since it is in flux, is this experience: the deliverance is invulnerable. It is an eternally possible theme or *motif* glanced at by that experience in passing and incapable of being itself either created or destroyed. Of course the elements of the natural world, with which Mr. Russell tries to identify his data, may be as unstable as human experience, or infinitely more so, if the learned so discover them to be; but Mr. Russell's reason for making sensibles lapse with sensation is not drawn from chemistry or physics; it comes from the evident dependence of appearances on the play of animal organs, and their position. These appearances exist only as objects for subjects—which is the nature of "ideas"; they are perspective views; and the talk of perspectives taken from points occupied by nobody, perspectives no less actual than given views, is unintelligible to me. Material things deployed about any point might offer *possibilities* of perspectives; but, as according to these systems the elements which would appear in such a perspective, are not material things prior to the perspective, but are created by this perspective and with it, we have a so-called physical world of mere possibilities of sensation, resting on the perilous apex of my sensation now. In other words, we have empirical idealism.

Is this philosophy scientific? If the term scientific is taken as merely eulogistic, anything may be scientific that you please, for instance that pure mathematics in which, as he says "we never know what we are talking about, nor whether what we are saying is true." But perhaps this describes the future of scientific philosophy rather than its past: Mr. Russell calls Hume scientific, who certainly knew what he was talking about, and said very true things about it. Yet it seems odd to call his analytic reflections scientific. I should have thought they were playful critical [sic], psychological in the autobiographical sense in which psychology belongs to literature rather than to science. The natural sciences do not anatomise things into data; "in physics as ordinar[il]y set forth," says Mr. Russell, "sense-data appear as functions of physical things." Of course: because science is a sympathetic extension or refinement of public knowledge; it proceeds by observation of things, experiment with things, and hypothesis about things, suggested and controlled by those experiments or observations. It is not a reconstruction *de novo*, founded on a literary dissection of private experience— dissection and reconstruction likely to be (like Hume's) most partial and wayward. Science would never have made any progress if it had been condemned always to begin by ignoring what is already known concerning its subject-matter. Now it happens to be known to the public that human knowledge is incidental to *animal life*; and it is also known that it involves an exercise of *intelligence*. If you abstract, as Hume and Mr. Russell do, from animal life and from intelligence, your view of human knowledge is likely to become artificial and chimerical. Neither your units nor your processes will be those of any living mind. You may make a very ingenious construction out of your chosen essences, but it will be almost irrelevant to the facts. For your system of notation may ignore so capital a point as that nature is the environment of man, who is an animal endowed with material sense, and a sportsman's intelligence, so that he regards and knows his environment. The units in this interplay are not sense-data, but bodies with their movements and habits; and the mind, and what it can discover of the world are governed by this. Data are but signals; and they are signals *a priori*, because intelligence is an expression of adaptation in the past and of capacity for further adaptation. In view of this, a datum is a challenge; and animal intelligence does not cry "There it is," but "What is that?" It is but prudent of the intelligent animal to deal with things and events in the large (as science always begins by doing), without substituting his precise data for their felt presence and their call upon his instinctive reaction; I do mean not prudent practically (because the wildest thoughts do no practical harm if no erratic conduct accompanies them) but prudent theor[et]ically, in as much as it is not likely that his precise data should repeat the qualities which things have in themselves, whereas it *is* likely that his instinctive reactions and summary impressions should correspond to [the] total nature and movement of the things about him. Only in the pauses of perception, when action and spying are suspended, do the objects meant (which happen to be those that exist) recede into objects of conscious belief, and therefore of potential doubt, while the bare data come forward as the only direct and unchallengeable objects. I am far from denying the chastening force and speculative glory of such a retreat into pure contemplation of essence; but we must not expect, by that method, to learn anything about ourselves or about the world. Yet with those devitalised data, absolute, momentary, and unmeaning, Hume and Mr. Russell ask their epistemological homunculus to start in life.

ESSENCES NOT ABSTRACTIONS

That universals, which are the only possible data, should be called abstractions is perhaps the most radical of the many transformations

George Santayana, "Essences Not Abstractions," Humanities Research Center, University of Texas. © 1969 Daniel Cory. Another reflection motivated by reading Bertrand Russell's *Mysticism and Logic, and Other Essays* (New York: Longmans, Green, 1918), written probably at the same time as the preceding essay.

that immediate appearance suffers at the hands of intellectual faith. Intellectual faith, of which what we call knowledge is a variety, properly looks outward; it is a report, prophecy, or warning; it tells us of things not seen. These things, though our notions of them are aesthetic and symbolic, exist as a matter of fact, so that normal animal faith, if not pressed too literally, is substantially true, like normal speech or the mutual comprehension that men have of their meanings. This truth of intellectual faith is perfectly explicable; our bodies and minds are congenitally adapted to the world in which they flourish, and could not flourish otherwise. Hence our interests and presumptions are directed *a priori* upon such ulterior things as in fact are likely to surround us. When things assault our senses, we react upon the things; and when we say "There they are" we mean there are things we can eat or strike or be struck by; there are the outlying objects to which we are addressed. These things which we believe in, are what in our haste we say we see; but the actual visual data, being but signs to us, we jump over.

Our senses—if we mean by our senses the entire reaction of our body and intellect on the stimulation of some sentinel organs—our senses reveal particular things, which we necessarily clothe with such qualities as at the time appear to us, no matter whence we fetch these appearances or what their degree of elaboration. Comparing afterwards these qualities—our original signs or data—with the trusted things of nature, conventionally and rightly believed in, we say the data are *drawn from* the things or *abstracted* from them. Yet they are the original terms of our description of those things. The most "abstract" of these terms are the categories and distinctions of grammar, which nevertheless express the most rudimentary and momentous differences in our animal reactions: think of the difference between "I struck him" and "He struck me"! By these subtle but primitive movements of intent, playing on the universals given, our description of things is created: so that if we arrest the natural life of the intellect and, becoming psychological critics, turn back upon the materials of knowledge, we shall be compelled to confess that we are acquainted with nothing but "abstractions" and that what we have "abstracted" them from, since it was never a datum, must be unknowable. Yet since the essences of sensuous fancy and of grammar are unsubstantial, we are not comfortable (being at heart animals) in their ideal presence; and perhaps we are tempted to confuse them with ourselves

thinking them, or to assimilate them to the objects of intent we have
lost, and to call them particulars and turn them into things.

The truth is that the previous operation of abstraction or generalisa-
tion by which "concepts" are reached has nothing to do with the pre-
sentability of these essences: those which, for our faculties, happen to
be intelligible are given just as truly as those which happen to be
sensible; and as essences they differ only in complexity or quality,
not in status. The whole distinction between sense-data, percepts,
and concepts is psychological and historical. The abstract is what is
less familiar to the speaker than something less simple which includes
it; the general is whatever does not contain discriminations which we
are accustomed to make. The taste of water is abstract, if you expect
whisky with it; and my near-sighted vision of this mere bird is general, if you can plainly see it is a swallow; but even yours is general,
if you cannot tell me whether it is a female swallow or a male. The
most abstract possible term, Being, may be, and sometimes is, the
sole datum, while no essence given to man reaches an infinite degree
of internal elaboration. The straight line for our experience is no abstraction from seeing the actual sinuosities of rulers and rails; these
look straight from the beginning. The ideally straight line is one of the
first essences yielded by the inspection of many a thing or motion,
and it is precisely the same essence in them all. It is a constituent of
our descriptions, not an abstraction from our objects. When a child
has not yet learned to distinguish "father" from "strange gentleman,"
his simple notion of man is no abstraction from more detailed essences;
nor do we ever call generic our notion of an individual person, say ourselves, because it covers rather vaguely a changing and complex fact.
It is universal, but it is given.

A datum is the deliverance of an experience, not the fact or event
that the experience occurs. Until we distinguish one yellow from another all given yellows are one and the same. As all the leaves of a
buttercup may seem identical in colour, so several buttercups in one
field may seem too, though the clear perception of them is probably
successive. Yet if the interval is marked, as between the buttercups
of two seasons, we shall be told that the identical yellow we find in
them is an abstract and general quality, and that the data we really
saw were the different particular yellows. Why not say, then, that
each buttercup contains an infinite number of particular yellows, although we fail to distinguish them, and that the obvious colour of

any whole flower is infinitely abstract?[1] Surely, the notion that data are particular is a materialisation of ideal terms, which are at most signs or qualities of existing objects, never existing objects themselves. But because we conceive that the things called buttercups are particular we slip into the fallacy of supposing that the colour we see them by must be so too. Knowledge of things often reacts in this way to falsify data, which neither language nor instinct is so well fitted to envisage.

Thus Mr. Russell says that "common sense believes that what we see is physical, outside the mind, and continues to exist." But common sense believes it sees things; if you could make it admit that it saw only data and perspectives, it would at once deny that they were physical or outside or inside anything, or existed at all. For perspectives are not *what* we see in animal perception: data are not primary objects. To see in the pregnant sense is to feel ourselves, because we have eyes, in the presence of a thing, without conceiving that we are in full possession of its nature; for it startles us into looking again, and harder (which would be absurd if it were the datum already given) or to sniff at, or touch, or eat it. But convinced that it is not a datum, we proceed. This edible object, not its colour or taste or sound, is what common sense believes to last, and to live its own life. Seeing for a sane animal is believing; it is not beholding a series of essences as it may be for an idiot, or for a sceptic.

The supposition that any essence is in itself abstract or general or incapable of being an immediate datum is the hypostasis of a human accident. We are so made that we come upon some essences by mere feeling, some by perception, some by comparison or synthesis and others (like the syntax of words) in the instrumental form and flying act of thinking. Essences, when subjected to this adventitious classification, can the more easily be confused now with mental facts and now with physical things.

To discern essence is also necessary if we are to give any fair account of judgement. If knowledge of acquaintance regarded particulars, nothing past, future, or absent could ever be meant or described: for our only primary terms would perish as fast as we caught sight of them. If I judge that Desdemona loves Cassio I must have some acquaintance with the love I impute to her. If my acquaintance has been

---

1. In the margin, Santayana noted, "Look out for this oscillation between the contrast with *acts* and with *things*."—Editors.

only with a particular event in my own experience, neither this fact
nor its concrete accompaniments can be imputed to Desdemona. If
the love I have experienced has lasted more than one instant, it has
consisted (as I understand Mr. Russell) of an infinite number of particular loves: and which of these is to serve me now, if we admit, *per
impossible*, that any one of them could again appear? Or is the love
I impute to Desdemona a "concept" somehow taking the place, and
sharing and not sharing the quality, of those particulars? To know
what this "concept" means, must I recall one or more of those irrevocable particulars, and collate it with this concept, which nevertheless
has already taken their place? Or is it the "class" of my particular past
loves that Desdemona's love is to be included in? How, on these empirical and summational principles, could I ever gain the notion of a
love in Desdemona at all, so as to talk about it?

The fact is that the meaning and truth of my judgement, "Desdemona loves Cassio" has nothing to do with particulars in my past.
What is requisite is that somehow—no matter how—I should now
designate by the word love a given essence (with which I have present
acquaintance) also identically found in Desdemona. This essence will
be far from being that of any particular love I have had, or now feel,
or any summation or abstract of these. It will be called forth now, in
an unprecedented quality and perhaps with great distinctness, by the
stimulus which the story of Desdemona, or her words or aspect, exert
upon me: and I shall attribute my present ideal datum to her, for the
same reason fundamentally as I attribute green to the grass. It is not
inconceivable that at this moment, in the stress of dramatic fancy, I
may dream and know for the first time "what love is." The love that
now rises before me, the object of my intuition and the ideal term of
my judgement, is an essence as definite or as indeterminate as it
happens to be: it will be a *description* of Desdemona's supposed love,
not a literal copy or full model of it—for I am far from *suffering* the
emotions or performing the actions which I am assigning to her. They
are denoted only, they are objects of intent, like material objects; but
my present fancy furnished me with a description of these qualities
(love, not mere friendship) as well as a notion of their place (e.g. in
Desdemona's life.) But my description will be true if that very essence
(of course with further determinations and accompaniments) is present
in the intuition of Desdemona—or is present in her conduct, if it
should turn out to be her conduct rather than her emotions that I had
chiefly in mind.

I think this example, and the whole nature of judgement, shows very clearly that the datum is a universal essence, whether we call our intuition a sensation or a thought, and that therefore this essence is capable of being at once an immediate ideal object, and a term in a judgement or description, and a factor in any number of other experiences, and the quality of some material thing or event. Essences are therefore,—like the Platonic Ideas of which they are a sort of infinite democratic extension—the key to knowledge.

TWO IDOLATRIES

To worship existence, and to attribute existence to what is merely form are two opposite idolatries; both deeply intertwined with the growth of mind. Patience and prudence are requisite to disentangle them. The net result, when the work is done, seems to me to be this: that existence may as easily be a curse as a blessing, and that this moral issue depends on the fact that living beings possess, or may develop, feeling and imagination; in which lies the essence of mind, and the ultimate good of existence.

Now it is by not suspecting, or by denying the originality and inner fertility of mind that the two idolatries I have mentioned arise: and I will endeavour to retrace, in part, what may be the way of it.

Sensation is a luxury; but an animal once out of the womb or the egg-shell, seldom enjoys it pure: he is compelled to work and fight for it: and the fear of sensation, in its dreary or painful excess, often taints the whole flow of his life. He begins to work so as not to suffer and to play so as not to think. His imagination and feeling become for him mere omens of ulterior dangers; and he would despise his mind altogether if he did not think it an index to other things.

So far, though there is a certain servility of attitude, there is no positive error, no actual idolatry. Sensation *is* an index to other things, namely to its causes, organic or external; and thought may actually

George Santayana, "Two Idolatries," *Columbia Manuscript Collection*, © 1969 Daniel Cory. Probably meant for *Dominations and Powers: Reflections on Liberty, Society, and Government* (New York: Scribner's, 1951); date indeterminate.

be prophetic, if it expresses the habitual ways of the world or the tendency at work to preformed actions. But a constant preoccupation with circumstances may lead him to ignore himself altogether, and to empty his mind in order to dress up the material world in all his mental and moral riches. Sights and sounds, which are sensuous products of the organism, he will take to exist first, or to exist only, in the outer world. He will suppose that they always lie there, like flowers in a garden; so that the mind would have nothing to do but to inspect realities already existing, without adding anything to them, except perhaps its own limitations. Mind would be looking out of the window and naturally seeing whatever was going on in [the] street; but it wouldn't be able to see round the corner; and this limitation of the prospect would be the only contribution that mind would make to the riches of the universe.

On second thoughts, however, even this would be too much to say, and the very existence of such a thing as mind would become dubious. For not the observing spirit but only the window, by its shape and position, would limit the vista. Mind, if we still gave that name to anything, would have to be virtually all-seeing; it would become merely another name for the truth or the actuality of all things. But this universal truth or actuality would be cut into partial perspectives or refracted by local mirrors in such a way, that not every feature of the universe would lie in the same plane or be relevantly continuous with every other feature: somewhat as the prospects from different windows in different houses would command only portions of the street, and be only partially coincident. Even if we patched all the views together we should obtain but a broken and imperfect assemblage of the facts. There would be gaps, reduplications, and contradictions, contrasting with the consistent continuity of universal existence.

As to mind, on this hypothesis, there would be one pervasive divine apprehension, the seat and witness of all events: but among these facts so apprehended, there would be animal bodies, corresponding to the windows in our simile; and in so far as the universal mind looked through one or another of those bodies, it would obtain partial perspectives and reduplications of the same world which it beheld also directly, by virtue of an immediate and impartial presence in every part of it.

Moreover, animal bodies might not be merely windows, but like complete habitable houses they might contain hearths and fires. The universal mind might then warm itself familiarly at each of these fires, which we call our passions. And if the universal mind, when thus locally warmed and impassioned, might be called a private soul, we should after all re-discover the originality of animal minds and the fertility of spirits for the spirit; because in following the life and movement of our bodies, the universal mind would have experienced many a singular pang, not otherwise known to it.

Indeed, such is the evidence in the case, that even inspiration, as I have described it above, would have to be re-admitted into this system of the world, intended to reduce mind to a pure passivity, and to the self-evidence of prosaic and public facts. For it turns out that when not looking out of some private window or sitting at some private fireside, the All-knower would see the world not as we picture it, but as some sort of mathematics in automatic motion: and our bodies would be the organs which that All-knower must inhabit and employ, in order to know a colour, a sound, a pain, or a passion. It would be this special moral or aesthetic experience, mediated by animal bodies, that would, after all, deserve the name of mind, feeling, or thought. The mathematical automatism otherwise discoverable would be matter in motion, or the flux of physical existence. Thus the originality of mind and the fertility of spirit for the spirit, would be restored; and it would be in painting contrary perspectives and feeling contrary passions that mind would live, rather than in the mechanical vibrations of universal matter.

Such would be the summary conclusion: yet common sense has some difficulty in distinguishing clearly the elements original to mind from those native to the realm of matter, and in distributing them properly. The initial deliverance of consciousness—say in a sudden pain or in grasping something—contains both references: an animal cry is full of its own emotion, yet is keenly intent on the foreign force interrupting the placidity of vegetative life. That this force is foreign and that it works locally are sentiments implicit in the act of rebellion or pursuit; even the most general distress struggles against an incubus, and kicks in all directions, if too blind to know which way to kick. But the very intensity of this outward reference, to something essentially foreign and unknown, attaches to that object of expectant attention the sentiments or images which it awakens. Wrath at the object, for instance, curses the object: and the curse clothes it in all the characters of evil. The object becomes a devil. Or, in another mood, placid interest in the object, clarifying the image which it awakens in the senses, defines that object in terms of this image; and the essence given in intuition passes for the essence of the thing perceived. The object then becomes a pellucid phenomenon. Yet not for more than a moment, in a sort of aesthetic trance: because manifestly the essence given in intuition varies with each organ of sense and with every point of view; whereas the life of objects (objects that act and are therefore collateral with the active self) is one and continuous; it changes in secret rhythms and in undiscovered ways while observation plays at touch and go upon their surface.

In this predicament the human mind adopts a whole chain of expedients, grammatical, poetical, religious, scientific, by which to do justice at once to appearance and to reality. The assumption throughout is that there is a reality, which is other than immediate experience, and which may be misconceived; so that it takes cleverness or divination to discover the truth. Mere prolongation or variation of immediate experience is not intelligence: it is the helpless condition of infants, idiots, and dreamers. At the same time the terms in which intelligence conceives the object are themselves inevitably essences immediately given. A concept, a meaning, a belief, or an inspiration lives and moves in the immediate; there must be direct intuition of it, or it would never arise. The whole drama of knowledge therefore goes on in the imagination. It could not go on anywhere else; and we should not be irritated at the variety and fancifulness of the logics by which men actually think, seeing that their thinking must be bred within them, out of the resources of their animal life, and in such terms as fortune offers to their intuition.

A ready way of filling out appearances with something deeper, and conceiving a life going on beneath them apart from observation, is to fill out appearances with feeling or will: in a word, to personify them. Animism, as this form of imagination is called, imposes itself inevitably on the primitive mind, especially at moments of high tension; for then emotion and passion are in the ascendant; images are little more than signals for directing action on this or that object of hatred or lust; and it must be in terms of strain, of action and intention that the other party, the real object, is conceived. Not, indeed, with abstract or metaphysic clearness; because one's own action and intention cannot be conceived without images. It is the image of one's own body, already hypostatised into a material substance, that is seen engaged in the pictured action;

the enemy or quarry is also posited materialistically: and animism would be an impossible system if the whole pullulating substance of nature were not posited first, and felt to be animate. The fighting souls of winds and seas, of beasts and harvests, of gods and men are therefore conceived in part behaviouristically. All these imagined souls have bodies in which they live and act; and it would be impossible to disentangle the passions and intentions felt to animate the world from the imagery that reveals them. The direct sense for animation in nature remains irresistible when it remains violent and spasmodic: but in a steady civilised mind it recedes from the greater part of the universe, and becomes conscious myth or conventional psychology; in both cases observation of the material facts guiding the dramatic imagination.

CRIES AND NAMES

Words have a double virtue and express a double tension: they are first cries, and then they become names. Nor need this doubleness be exhibited as essentially a progress, as if words *ought* to be descriptive and not exclamatory. The progress in expression, if we insist on seeing one, is itself double; and the perfection of utterance lies as much in the direction of music as in that of accurate report. Music itself reports two kinds of reality: ideal relations or progressions of sound, and vital or moral dispositions of the soul. But music makes no attempt (except in crude mimicry or onomatopoeia) to report other realities in their own terms; rather it translates them radically and initially into its own vital medium of sound, and elaborates the patterns that offer themselves there, without minding the analogies and hidden vital connections that subsist between this ideal realm of sound and the realm of matter or of passion. Yet these analogies and connections guide the whole articulation of sound for the human voice and ear, and enrich utterance with all its moral suggestions.

George Santayana, "Cries and Names," *Columbia Manuscript Collection.* © 1969 Daniel Cory. Probably intended for *Dominations and Powers.*

Cries are caused by sudden changes or sharp tensions in the life of the organism. These changes or tensions normally produce emotion also, although the cry usually precedes the clear perception of the shock that caused it. We say, however, in current literary or autobiographical psychology, that the cry *expressed* the emotion: and this is true at least for the sympathetic bystander, who on hearing the cry dramatically imputes the emotion, or even actually feels it himself. Whether the person who cries out actually feels it, or in what form, is a question of the rate of diffusion in the impression received. If the diffusion is rapid, bad news may make a sensitive woman faint before she has mentally "realised" what has happened; while a man of well-knit stolid disposition but ready verbal intelligence may see in his mind's eye the whole disaster that threatens him, without saying a word or feeling any distinct emotion. Yet his demeanour, meantime, may prove that he has been profoundly affected, and perhaps the course of his whole life redirected by the news.

For current discourse, however, which is what concerns us in politics, cries are directly associated with tendencies to action: their conscious or spiritual accompaniment is little attended to or, if imputed, probably misunderstood. Cries have occasions; they also have prophetic value; and this double material bond not only exhausts their practical signifi-cance but also lends them their tendency to become names and to acquire a logical definition. Cries of surprise, fear, or warning call at-tention to definite objects: they are signs, and in memory may become names. So cries of endearment or abhorrence may supply names for their objects. Some sappy husbands and wives never call each other anything but "dear"; there are names, such as "cur," that may be used as exclamations; and profanity works this vein to exhaustion. But these are regressions from developed speech to an original indistinction between names and cries. The names of simple sensations are not names of individuals but of generic feelings, yet they are often called forth by particular objects and cause us to point to them. The cry, so used, becomes a name. And when in abuse or endearment expressions like *darling* or *scoundrel* become mere cries, they by no means lose their objective reference. On the contrary, the more passionate the cry, the more direct its application; so much so that a kiss or a blow readily goes with it.

Intrinsically, however, an image contains no emotion and an emotion no image. Feeling is its own world. For this reason we may remember the most dreadful experiences circumstantially with perfect calm, or with the quite different emotions of a moralist or a story-teller. Were it not for this, life would be continually arrested by the too adequate memory of life. Actually the cries die in being uttered and the names survive and lend things a hollow immortality.

The vaguest or the purest emotion must have a complicated physical ground; I might even risk the suggestion that the most heavenly emotion would have the deepest roots in the earth. But the emotion remains inarticulate; it does not know its own roots; and if its roots spread widely, it may be called forth on widely different occasions. In English, for instance, the exclamation *Oh!* conveys little but a wave of feeling washing over some impression or some thought. It may convey pain or pleasure, surprise, relief, or assurance. When we say *Ah!* the field of emotion is narrower. Whatever has struck us has then left us a bit wistful; feeling has passed into the minor key. Had we said *Splendid!* or *Too bad!* our emotion would have become a judgement, and a specific occasion would have been described, at least in its relation to ourselves. Where sense or imagination has supplied some clear image of this occasion, this image will be suffused with the moral colour of that emotion. Whatever we discern, be it something definite or something mysterious, will be welcomed or hated, pursued or fled from automatically; for emotion is quite capable of existing without any distinct object or revealed cause. Then this commotion itself, stirring the bewildered psyche into a panic, may well evoke a fantastic image of something superlative, as in a dream, to colour and to justify so strange a passion.

There is therefore an everpresent possibility that words, without being morally empty, m[a]y be about nothing. They may be mere sound and fury, or rhythms and mimicries; and when they begin to have significance, their meaning may peer vaguely at moments only behind a cloud of darkness or diffused light that scarcely awakens attention. Words are normally understood before they are distinguished.

That words are gestures before they are concepts is a fact of immense importance in politics and morals. Liberty, Country, Victory are mighty cries; so are Duty and Religion. Everybody feels which way they make; but the better the words are understood, the more their force diminishes.

Cries have a double career open before them: to become music or to convey knowledge. Their own virtue is that of music and lies in developing the intrinsic life of their organ; but this organ is itself double, since cries are both uttered and heard; and at the same time they form part of an animal life that involves many other and more pressing functions. While speech develops internally into articulation and prosody, it therefore becomes entangled in the general life of the psyche, its senses and passions. Words become names for the things to which action is directed: and prosody becames a grammar linked with the relations of things to one another.

Evidently the spontaneous organisation of cries by prosody and grammar will not render them a good means of conveying knowledge of physics or biology: yet it is only physics and biology that at all avail to trace the dynamic order of events in nature. Yet events in nature and the art of controlling them chiefly concern politics and morals; so that language is a great deceiver in this world. It would perhaps have been a blessing to mankind if cries had been developed only into music, not into words. Music is not irrelevant to the spiritual life: it is a most sympathetic expression and enhancement of it; and it does not distort the truth of anything else. But language inevitably distorts the truth of the natural order. Words, when attached to ideas, inevitably become the medium of discursive thought, and of logical reasoning: but logical reasoning and discursive thought are not knowledge: they are only ideation. Essentially they are nearer to music and poetry than to science; for that which language properly conveys is not knowledge but intuition. The idea communicated is only an essence, not possibly an adequate truth and very likely a pure fiction. Natural science and natural history detest rhetoric: and when rhetoric invades them they become the flatterers of human vanity and satisfied ignorance. Now vanity and satisfied ignorance are great snares in politics; we must build on the facts according to our powers: and then intuition and all the free arts may be led back to their due place at the head of the table. Images and words may then flow as abundantly and intricately as they like. They can never dry up. Even the slave may sing at his work.

Deception is sometimes voluntary in speech, and comic, as in the mimicry of animal sounds, in onomatopeia and, more delicately and subconsciously in alliteration. This last is indeed a reaction against representation or knowledge, as rhyme and meter are also: music is asserting itself. If not allowed to neglect the truth altogether, at least it says, clothe me clothe it decently [sic].

Besides euphony, speech has an immense internal development in inflexions and syntax. Here the voice modulates itself unemotionally in obedience to the variety of objects and their shifting relations. Words are themselves incidents in that flux of nature; and they find it fascinating to move in the same dance more nimbly than material things, catching them in unreal perspectives, and identifying them insultingly with one another.

Grammar catches things, or rather attempts to catch them, in a net entirely alien to their nature: for the terms of grammar are essences, definable ideas, meanings related logically to one another: whilst things are conventional material units constantly shifting their substance, qualities, and relations and presently dissolving altogether. Grammar consequently often misleads physics; yet it follows physics submissively enough in intention, like a dog out for a walk with his master, but running ahead and scooting down every side alley according to his canine nature, until he is whistled back.

In the path of knowledge, then, words are perpetual obstacles as well as necessary instruments, at once inadequate and redundant, false masks and true signs. In the paths of expression they are freer, yet even here they often run into vicious courses; because although in fiction they are not bound to conform to any alien model or prescribed object, as they are in the report of truth, yet they are still tied, as it were by an umbilical cord, to their parent world and cannot prosper if their organ becomes diseased or atrophied. So rhetoric and versification, euphuism and wit often grow stale or excessive: they become old-fashioned vanities, and good taste abandons them. Even logic may outrun its vital supports, and become ridiculous in its correctness; and I am not sure that mathematical speculation always remembers that it is but play with ideal terms and may become idle.

It is in its spiritual deliverence that language recovers its original vital function and becomes a cry again. Materially a word exists only as a sequence of vibrations; but the sequence excites as a whole a single and sustained intuition in the spirit—a feeling, an idea, the moral possession of a total far-spreading event. The *spirit* of a word is the intuition evoked in uttering or hearing it internally; and in that intuition the word crowns its physical career in human society and achieves its only ultimate value. In animal life it may have been sometimes useful and sometimes mendacious; now it is only more or less interesting, more or less joyful, more or less beautiful. For the spirit rests in the good actualised; all that was instrumental, once a burden and a care, becomes a memory now no longer disturbing, but merged in the poetry, spice, and truth of a living picture.

When a young man is carried away by his own eloquence, he feels enthusiastically rebellious, gloriously emancipated from the folly and stupidity of the world: yet every now and then the persistence of material ties, which cannot be escaped while life lasts, calls back the rolling sound, grammar, and poetry of his thoughts to some relevance to reality. The dice that rattle in his brain are still only essences, ideas, words in their mental echoes; yet he knows that he is actually gambling for hard money. Intoxicating as his ideal game may be in its play with marvellous possibilities, the urgency of it is really borrowed from the material alternatives that conventionally and disastrously underlie it. By this break the rush of images is brought to a stand-still. The enthusiast had forgotten that his cries had become names: that terrible things, not in the ideal picture, might come trooping up in answer to them.

NOTIONS OF SUBSTANCE

The causes of the belief in substance common among mankind do not coincide altogether with the reasons that might justify it. A quantitative and local continuity in things is indeed obvious to primitive man in what he manufactures, but it eludes him in all else; for whence, he will ask, the matter that forms the clouds, or the dreams of the night? Attentive physics and speculative physiology are requisite to show us that the basis of these things also is a continuous redistribution of matter. Consequently the notions of substance that have prevailed in philosophy—the right one having established itself only in practical life and in the arts—have been generally inapt. Sometimes substance

George Santayana, "Notions of Substance," Humanities Research Center, University of Texas. © 1969 Daniel Cory. The title was supplied by the editors. Santayana's note in the upper left corner of the first page reads, "Much of this is good both in form and substance. (A few omissions, and revision of terms.)"

has been placed in pure being, sometimes in Platonic Ideas, sometimes in the laws of nature, and always in something metaphysical, that is, in a kind of existence or fatality other than that of discoverable nature things. It was not a substance to be found within obvious objects, and gradually to be brought to light by a closer examination of them: it was rather a different substance supplied by logic or by dramatic analogy, something imagined to exist behind things and, so to speak, in their stead. So, notably, the mystical notion of pure being, an abyss, simple and single, into which things sink and out of which they come. This is a most poetic phantom, and as such profoundly significant; for all natural objects of experience and love, being contingent, exist miraculously, momentarily, and, for the heart, deceptively only; yet (says the poet) that night which swallows them up cannot be mere nothingness, since it continually yields them up again, or objects like them. This Cronos that devours his children, this limbo of infinite but neutral potentiality, may thus be felt to have a most intensive reality; it is called the substance of all things, being a sort of fertile death pregnant with them all, yet changeless and one, since in its bosom they are not divided.

This mystic substance, however, is something visionary: it is a negative after-image of the flux of natural things, in which their differences are blurred and their energies added together. It would be incapable of exercising any of the functions of a true substance. I will not repeat the sophism of Hegel that pure being is pure nothing. The essence of being (or of existence, which is probably what is meant) is an essence as positive and particular as any other. It may even be an object of intuition by itself (as many mystics know, and doubtless many animals) and far from being identical with the essence of nothing, it is the very opposite of it. But pure being, by definition is without change, parts, or articulation; it can therefore offer no ground for any particular event, either in time, or in space, or in moral opportuneness. The ground of every particular existence must therefore be sought in some other particular existence, or group of existences, not in a mystic substance; and if no continuous quantitative substance has been discovered running through events and by its movement determining theirs, it will be necessary not to refer these events to any ground at all, and to make a substance of each of them, as is done in empirical idealism; or else, somewhat verbally, to refer them to the general system or order which they constitute, as is done in idealism of the absolute or cosmic sort. But in this last we should pass to the modern notion that substance is a schema or law; of which more presently.

Closely allied to the absolute substance of the mystics is the God of monotheism, when free and speculative theologians explain his nature. In Hebraic tradition and in the faith of the people God is a particular spirit living through time, renewing his thoughts on occasion, and watching the spontaneous operations of nature and of the human mind, so that the latter, at least, may be sometimes displeasing to him. He is, however, an invincible magician, and as the world arose at his command and can be extinguished at his nod, he is certainly the cause, if not the substance, of its being. Such a God, however, would find an experimental world in his own person; and the question about substance would recur in respect to the movement of his thoughts, will, and actions. Theology, however, has eluded the thorny problems that would thus arise, by attributing immutability to the thoughts, will and actions of God, to which these names, therefore, can only be applied figuratively. He is to be conceived as an eternal mind to which all essence and the whole course of existence are present at once. The divine idea of the universe and the divine judgement that it is very good (which is what the divine will would amount to, I suppose, *sub specie aeternitatis*) might then be called the substance of things in the transcendental sense, or even in the Platonic sense, if the divine idea and will were but imperfectly fulfilled in existence. Matter, which may perfectly well be admitted too into this system, would have been created by God and set in motion at the beginning of the world, to be, in the scientific sense, the substance of nature. This theological system would be consistent and clear, if theologians could only stick to it; but many of them, and those the most inspired, are haunted by the mystic notion of substance as well. Their God must be an unutterable abyss of being, and perfectly simple, in which case, of course, the moving world has no relation to him, and is an inexplicable accident and a scandal, doubtless an unreality. Others, mystical in a more plastic and Platonic fashion, think of God rather as the ultimate *goal* of the universe, or as the moral order which it *ought* to embody, or more particularly as the focus of their personal aspiration, as the Perfect Beloved of their dreams; but, as happened to the pagan Platonists also, they easily slip from this moral religion into the blank mysticism that worships the unutterable abyss of pure being; for if personal aspirations, what ought to be, and the goal of the universe were honestly consulted and expressed in the concrete, they would be found to lie at the opposite pole from substance, namely in civilisation or the life of reason—a diversified, profane, natural, artful, and even amusing play of experience. To escape such an issue, which to the mystic would seem frivolous and distressful, the ideal of natural life must be suppressed and in its place a very special and quite decadent passion, the love of the Absolute, must be allowed to legislate in morals; and then indeed the good and substance would come to have some affinity to each other, or even to be identical.

If we define substance as a self-existing, persistent term in change,[1] we see at once that the first property can hardly fail to be assigned to something or other. If there is existence at all, something has to be self-existing in the end, if only my present thought. But persistency and continuity are more problematical attributes; to posit them comes in practice to positing yet another attribute of substance (the one most offensive to skeptics) that of being *occult* on occasion. This most suspected quality, however, is the most conspicuous in metaphysical substitutes for matter. There are two such worthy of special mention. I do not mean historically (for I am not attempting a history of the subject) but because each in its way discloses a hidden, unsuspected reality behind nature, more permanent and intelligible than the flux of immediate appearance. These appearances, according to one view, are instances of a type; according to the other, they are realisation of a law. The latter is a notion on which modern philosophy prides itself, thinking that Platonic Ideas and material substance are alike exploded; and when we have discounted the illusion and frivolity of such a boast, there remains the fact that laws are permanent moulds of change, and that like Platonic Ideas (permanent moulds of existence) they help us to classify and mentally to appropriate the flux of nature. If we admit evolution, laws seem more permanent than types, and more intimately woven into the texture of the world. They are not, perhaps, quite everlasting. The range of time we survey (the prehistoric past and all the future being conceived only by assuming the permanence of laws and being therefore incapable of corroborating them) is but an instant compared with eternity. All well-attested laws—that of gravity, for instance, might be special case[s] of others not yet clearly discerned—

1. Santayana's original, later revised, read, "If we define substance a something self-existing, persistent, and continuous. . . ."—Editors.

such as those of electric atoms. Nor is it, of course, a safe assumption that the possible variations in natural laws would in turn be found to express some law of variation in laws. The total aspect of evolution might present no consecutive method at all, but some meandering and inconsequent contingency: there might be a sort of chaos in time, if not in space, and nature, like a living language, might gradually change its grammar and become unintelligible in its own house.

The notion of types or Platonic Ideas being the reality behind things is not now prevalent in physics, and never should have been so. It is an interpretation of discourse, not of nature; it belongs to moral philosophy, not to natural science, since it clarifies the goals and meanings of human life, but never discloses the causes or origin of anything. Displaced and treated as natural powers, Platonic Ideas at once turn into metaphysical substances; they are undiscoverable and incongruous with material things, the real substance of which is simply what is to be found inside of them. Nevertheless in discourse, in art, and in morals, the Platonic method is and must remain the sole method of reason. They are the essences, fixed by intent or hinted at by growth and inspiration, in which the spirit might find its congenial objects, and the counters of its game. They are not substances behind things, nor fixed patterns in nature, nor forces, nor prescribed forms, outside which it would be deformity to fall; they are essences above things, to which things have chosen to aspire, or ideals with which we have chosen to compare them.

CAUSATION OR TROPES

That existence is in flux is (as I use these words) axiomatic, since it was by observing that I changed in surveying some essence at different

George Santayana, "Causation or Tropes," Humanities Research Center, University of Texas. © 1969 Daniel Cory. A fragment of indeterminate origin; the title is a provisional one Santayana wrote in pencil in the margin. The first sentence suggests a connection with *Scepticism and Animal Faith: Introduction to a System of Philosophy* (New York: Scribner's, 1923).

moments and in different lights, in order to identify it or to analyse it, that I first discovered my own existence. But the flux of existence is not absolute; I mean, it does not pass from one instant of being to the next in such a manner that anything may follow upon anything, without these successive existences having a continuing relation to one another in sequence, place, quantity, and quality. Were this not so, and were the flux absolute, it could not properly be called a flux, because it would be impossible to define even the succession of its instants. Every state of the world would be one state of it, and would have no relation of before and after to the others. Indeed, the very condition of existence would be abolished, because there would be no change, either in each instant or from one to another. They would lie in no common field, and no substance would flow through them. That the flux is not absolute is another way of saying that nature is not chaos; there is order in it. Knowledge of one part can lead to true presumption about the character of other parts. Change, then, although perhaps pervasive, is not absolute: there are elements, material or formal, in it which endure through the change.

The various notions of substance which I can frame are hypotheses about the character of this permanent element in the flux of existence. I may conceive it as a quantum of matter, or as a law of change absolutely obeyed everywhere, or as a guiding idea never perfectly realised, or as a purpose to be realised only at the end, or as a persistent effort to establish a particular order, never actually established at all, or as a persistent effort merely to destroy whatever order is established for the moment. Even this last, the most negative and romantic of connecting principles, would be something constant in the flux, enabling it to flow by subtending and linking its various phases. The universal No, the rebellion of the metaphysical Will against each thing that it found, would at least relate them all to a common principle of self-hatred and instability: and perhaps it might establish an order of succession among them, if each successive state really eluded the evil conspicuous in its predecessor, before proving evil in its turn, and stimulating the Will to destroy it also. Existence would be the art of jumping perpetually from the frying-pan into the fire; and this tragic law would be the connecting principle of the world, otherwise sheer chaos. It would be a true bond, however fantastically named or conceived; because it would ensure that the requisite sort of illusion, and the requisite sort of distaste for it, should never fail: that successive illusions should always have this relation of affording illusory relief; and that no other accident, no merciful hand, should interfere with this monotonous fatality. So metaphysical, so falsely substantial, is this evil deity, that ways of dethroning it may be devised, and may succeed: it is so real that it may be destroyed. This would not be the case with a mere form, a passive description of what appearance happens to be. Such a fatality, which the Buddhists call Karma, is a principle at work in appearance, and producing it: so that if by some underhand or magic art I can dislodge the tyrant, the torments I suffer will cease.

That some dominant principle, even if only the magic decree that change shall be perpetual, governs appearance, is a conviction common to all systems of nature, to all systems that can hope to institute an art of life. Without such a subtending principle, no general proposition could be framed about the methods of nature. The most superstitious and fantastic magic recognises a sort of legality, proportion, and meticulous order to which its miracles must conform: one word gone wrong, or one rite omitted, defeats the whole incantation. There is accordingly a ground presumed for everything, if only we could discover it. The systems of nature that call themselves critical and that think they discard substance, merely revert to belief in magic: only instead of embodying this magic, as primitive men do, in material things or in the sound of words, they attribute it to disembodied laws. These laws are, in function, the substance of nature in their view: but they are not called substance because they are not distributed materially among things, nor internal to events. But their externality and their brooding over events from a higher sphere would properly cause them to receive the name of substance, as did the platonic ideas, when once their individuality and authority were clearly established: for they would live forever in their own realm, and on their own occasions would call nether facts into existence, or cause them to disappear. There can be nothing more substantial than a superior principle that governs existence against its will.

The conception of substance as a formal principle, a law or platonic idea, belongs both to superstition and to criticism: in the one case it is regarded as a magic fate, in the other case as a habit of events, regarded as phenomena in experience, not as events in nature. That the substance of things is their platonic ideas is a wonderful conception, a sort of philosophic rendering of polytheism. It is a view of substance proper to a lover or a poet. It does not exclude, indeed ultimately it implies, that there is also another substance in things, namely matter; but it overlooks this internal substance, the principle of their temporal, local, and changing existence, in order to place behind and above them, as the true principle of their being, the essence which they suggest to the mind, without fully or constantly embodying it. It is as if I asked things what they are, and they replied: "We cannot tell thee what we are, and we do not know nor care: but we will tell thee what we wish to be. What we wish to be is the origin and goal of our being: it is like the meaning which words are invented to convey, and which remains when they have been uttered. The breath and the few noises that carry a winged word lapse as it is uttered, and we will not identify ourselves with things so frail and ephemeral, and so hard to seize or to define: but we will identify ourselves with the meaning of that word, with the message it lived to give: and that is a part for ever of the meaning of things, or the divine mind and intention. From that mind and intention we came like a half-articulated cry: in that we also end, and find our eternal rest and perfection."

Apart from the need of supplementing this higher substance above things with a material substance within them (which would ultimately account for their whole being and fortunes) there is one difficulty with this platonic metaphysics, which renders it impossible seriously to regard the ideals of things as their principle. This difficulty is that the flux of things is far more radical than the Greeks supposed: it is not an oscillation about a few types, but a profound and irrevocable transformation of types, and goods, and meanings, and ideals. Undoubtedly each of these types, taken as an essence, is eternal: but so are the essences of all monsters and changelings and hybrids. There is not in nature any constancy to particular types. To suppose such constancy is an illusion like that proper to persons who speak only one language or have heard only of one religion, and suppose that they are universal, unchangeable, and alone consonant with the nature of things. Platonic ideas do not govern nature, but nature, in falling into this or that form, suggests for a while some Platonic idea or other to the contemplative mind: the ideality of this idea, I mean the perfection which it expresses over against the imperfection of the facts, being supplied by the poetic mind of the observer: either because it is easier or pleasanter for him to conceive it so transformed, or because he is led by sympathy with the movement of the actual thing to divine and to prefigure what it would grow into if it could. But these goals of thought or of life change with the changes in earthly circumstances, and in animal structure: and a new set of ideas, like a new elective government, is called by the self-governing world to rule over it in name, but never to be obeyed, unless they are careful to command only what the people are bent on doing.

ANENT THE KNOWN QUALITIES OF MATTER

Some recent psychologists, reverting to something like the theory of "visible species," point to the similarity between perspective images in sense and those visible on the retina or on a photographic plate, in order to prove that it is not the mind that transforms things into images, but that the organs of sense and the lines of perspective in outer space supply every detail of the transformation. The confusion, partiality, etc., found in sensible images, they say, are perfectly accounted for by the position and condition of the observer. I heartily agree that the "mind" does not transform nor originate anything, not even itself. Mind is a pure light, not a sieve nor a principle of perspective, selection, or distortion. What the mind sees is an essence evoked by the body: this essence corresponds exactly to the activity of the organ employed —retina, nervous system, brain, psyche. Nothing but a certain impatience with the weakness—which is also the glory—of human discourse, because it *is* discourse and not (what is impossible) intuition of facts, leads us to desire that our living visions should lie in their objects, and be parts of the latter. Of course, the image seen by looking at the retina or at a photographic plate will resemble the image seen by looking at the object which casts that shadow. This is no more singular than that the image seen by looking at a mirror should re-

George Santayana, "Anent the Known Qualities of Matter," Humanities Research Center, University of Texas. © 1969 Daniel Cory. Written probably for *The Realm of Matter*.

semble that seen by looking at the objects reflected there. Meantime, we have not even broached the question whether the essence seen in such cases is like any essence embodied materially in the various objects concerned. The fact that objects substantially so various as landscape, mirror, photographic plate, and retina, yield the same essence to inspection, suggests that this essence is original in each instance—a similar response to a formal similarity in the various stimulations—and not the essence of any of those objects. Various poets may sing very similarly about the Spring, yet the song, however trite poetically, is always a new fact, utterly different ontologically from the object that provokes it. It is as with the gramophone which causes the dog to hear his master's voice: that worthy man and this wretched disc of metal present the same essence to intuition; but that essence, as the dog hears it, never existed materially in either agent; its magic never was and never will be audible save to the canine ear.

PSYCHOLOGISM

At the opposite pole of criticism from the dialectician, the empirical critics of knowledge may be found bearing unwilling witness to the fact that essence is the only native theme of mind: for in reducing all reality to phenomena they unwittingly reduce all known objects to essences. The honest effort of this school is to stick to the obvious and to discard all dogmatism and fiction: it is the stout spirit of Protestantism applied to logic. The obvious, they think at first, is the facts— events and things in the world of practice: but on closer inspection these things and events retreat into ideas of the mind: and later, if the edge of criticism is not blunted by use, the mind and its ideas retreat

George Santayana, "Essence and Attention," Humanities Research Center, University of Texas. © 1969 Daniel Cory. Although Santayana penciled, "Psychologism" at the top of the first page, this does not adequately represent the subject of the essay. The current title was contributed by the editors. The context indicates that this little essay was probably intended for *The Realm of Essence* (New York: Scribner's, 1928).

into the given phenomena. Phenomena are still supposed to fly in flocks and to be easily recorded and predicted: the empiricist is not a sceptic in spirit: but his unquestioning faith calls for plain, homely dogmas, and prayers in the mother-tongue: and he finds that the only words in the true vernacular are groundless, variegated, fugitive data: what I call essences. Essences are the stuff into which an incredulous logic and a sensuous physics collapse when they endeavor to be absolutely accurate. Essences are what phenomena become in a phenomenalism that is radical and consistent. Only, whilst the universe of phenomena contains nothing but essences, it is supposed to create, shuffle, and destroy them as if they were things.

Such phenomenalism, in spite of its conventional credulity, is a violently artificial system and reckons without its host, who is human nature [sic]. Experience and knowledge are clarifications of animal faith; a vital attitude, full of mute implications, subtends all its overt data, and frames them in. Experience and knowledge are by no means composed of a multitude of clear intuitions associated or conjoined; they are developed by dint of large habitual discriminations in a total object of intent at first utterly vague, and always remaining obscure and questionable in its minute texture, no matter what distinctions of place, quality, or form I may learn to make in it. I first believe in the world, and as I pick my way about in it, I gradually distinguish its most notable contrasts, such as good and bad, far or near, light and dark, myself and things: and these contrasts enable me to distinguish object from object in practice, without giving me the least power to say what each object is intrinsically. For this reason essence is not readily discerned in ordinary living and thinking. Attention is a symptom of alarm, or at least of stimulation; it is initially fixed on objects of intent, asking what they are or what they will do: and when this practical question is settled, or ceases to interest, attention lapses altogether, and the essences which served as signals or as discriminating marks seldom become objects of attention on their own account.

Substance must be in flux and contingent, otherwise it could not exist. Its permanence, when it is permanent (for being contingent it may at any time be created or destroyed) is an external relation of its essence to its locus in time and space. Substance may be conceived as the continuity and heritage, quantitative and qualitative, proper to many moments: substance only means things in the gross, in their natural contiguity. The permanence of substance is itself a perpetual accident, observable only *ex post facto*. Substance is the very frame or body of contingency.

A thing, then, is nothing essentially identical with itself at various times, but only a series of transformations of substance, not so radical at any one moment that, for some practical purpose, the thing may not be *called* the same. In other words, things and persons remain the same so long as the same description, in any special regard, remain[s] applicable to them for some purpose; as a man always remains his father's son, and identical in that particular. It is only by virtue of some such essence describing a fact in some respect, that any reasoning is applicable to a fact at all; if a man is and must remain his father's son, lawyers may reason about his rights to an inheritance. If the word son remained a proper name (as it might be in his father's lips when speaking to him or of him) no reasoning could be based on it; only instinct or experience could suggest what the word meant, that is, what the natural object called son might be in itself, where it was, or what it might do or become. In a word, the relations of things are natural and those of essences are logical. In order to perceive a logical relation it is not enough to have an essence present in intuition. The internal relations which in most cases constitute the chief part of the given object are not logical in their sensible or pictured pattern; they are aesthetic for intuition, and in themselves they are essential. The essences of those parts of course have essential relations in that whole; but their juxtaposition is not dialectical: it forms a fresh essence, which again has dialectical relations only as a whole. The Andes and the Amazon have separate essences; a magician might transfer one of them bodily to Asia without the other; but they are parts of the essence of South America, which would no longer be embodied in nature if either the Andes or the Amazon were removed. So each word in a sentence is transferable to other sentences; but essential to that sentence in particular. A particular juxtaposition of elements defines a particular essence; but the elements, taken separately, need not have been so juxtaposed. In the case where the elements are taken only as elements, like the letters of a spoken word, they are intuitively not distinguished as units; only the word is heard; the letters are only physically separable, in so far as they involve different motions of the tongue or the air. So colour is not intuitively sep[ar]able from visible extension in human apprehension; either term alone would be really an abstraction, because it had never appeared except as an interfused and unspecified element in a single actual object. The elements were never noticed or defined; only the whole was noticed or defined which, as we say afterwards, contained them. But this way of being contained does not imply either existing first or being found first, so that the whole should be literally composed or put together out of them. The whole was one which when analysed, and thereby turned for intuition into a wholly new set of essences, will disappear: and in its place the parts which were implicit in that whole realm will appear as new units. Substitution is itself possible only in the realm of nature, impossible in that of essence; you may substitute black for white in a particular place, or in your experience, but black and white will remain what they were and cannot exchange their natures. So the lights and shadows of a picture are not ordinar[il]y seen individually; only the painter's eye notes their shapes or intensities. A tree is seen to have a certain bulk and relief: and a psychologist may discover that such an object would never have been apprehended if just such lights and shadows, in their substantial physical basis, had not conspired to qualify the impression which, expressed in intuition, yields the essence of plastic form to the eye when I say: A knotted oak.

Here we see that the so-called elements may not be true elements: *no* lights, *no* shadows appear to me when I see the round: the round alone is given; but by a shift of attention the same stimulus may be made to yield the essence of chiaroscuro. A shift of attention can work wonders. It can transform a sound into a thought: it can recover a meaning in what was meaningless, or lose the familiar meaning and find only the strange sound. That I may eventually say to myself that a word was nothing but a sound, nothing but so many syllables, so many noises in succession, does not clip the wings of the original word, as it came to me in use. The winged word was the original datum; it was a[n] object of imagination and intent, a goal of the spirit. The subsequent analysis is not of that essence, but of the physical basis of it, the material act of pronouncing the word and receiving the consequent auricular stimulus.

There are cases at the other extreme in which relations are constitutive of the essence intuited: as when I am actually analysing and saying 2 + 2 are four.

Between these two cases lies the typical case of dialectical implication, where a word or other sign intervenes to make one essence signify another, quite as if essences were things.

PSYCHOLOGISM

A doubt may here occur to the critical reader. If matter is merely a name for the convertibility of objects, would not its nature be more clearly and honestly expressed by calling it convertibility in objects rather than by calling it matter? The word matter suggests that our understanding has gone deeper, whereas in fact it has stood still.

I reply that such a phrase as "convertibility of objects," or as "possibility of sensation," is indeed honest transcendentally, because it describes the subjective approach to belief in matter: my belief in a concretion of expectations. But such a phrase is not clear, nor honest scientifically, because any mere potentiality is a lame object: it can stand at all, even in myth or language, only by leaning on the actual facts which suggest it. The potential is either something actual but unknown, some existing seed, or else nothing in itself; and merely an expression of groundless presumptions in us, who in the presence of the actual expect developments *which there is no reason should ensue.* Is there no reason why the sensation of water is convertible into that of ice or steam, and is my expectation of such a change under given circumstances a pathological expectation? If not, the potentiality I poetically attribute to appearance is only my subjective approach to the discovery of something actual, namely, of a substance actually contained in both objects and passing from one to the other by transitions too fine to be traced by my summary sensations. Clear thought and honest science must develop animal faith and not retract it. I must either renounce my expectations, as an honest sceptic would, or else believe them to be justified by facts independent of the empire of expectation over my own mind. These facts will not be mere potentialities. If objects are convertible, it must be by being actually continuous, so that they inherit from each other their time, place, quantity, and quality, even if in all these respects the variation may be incessant. The convertibility of objects is accordingly an indication of the persistence

George Santayana, "Psychologism," Humanities Research Center, University of Texas. © 1969 Daniel Cory. Intended probably for *The Realm of Matter.*

of matter, and matter is not a name for that convertibility but for the substance undergoing conversion.

A further indication of the properties of matter is found in the distribution of objects. The obvious essence of a thing does not involve the choice of any particular place or time in which it should appear. As Spinoza puts it, if there were twenty men in the world, the essence of man, while it described the constitution of each, would not involve the fact that there were twenty of them. That fact, from the point of view of man's essence, would be a material accident. There had happened to be twenty seeds predisposed to take on the nature of man, on twenty propitious occasions. The prior distribution of seeds and occasions, not the helpless present phenomena they have produced, determines the place, time, number, duration, and intensity of these phenomena. A plum pudding is a describable dish, and a recipe for it might be given: an epicurean poem might even describe the taste of it. The cook-book and the ode are insufficient to produce it. The requisite and properly predisposed substance must be found elsewhere, wherever they happen to be. Nor can the ode and the cook-book inform me how many occasions in what particular households will give them the proof: the multiplication of puddings is an accident to their nature.

The only attachment which an essence (say the Pythagorean proposition) can have to existence is that matter somewhere (say in Pythagoras) should be so predisposed by the previous embodiment of other essences that when circumstances are favourable it can proceed to the embodiment or to the intuition of that particular essence. Discourse, though immaterial in itself, gives a sort of embodiment to intuitions, as matter does to forms. But the distribution of these particular intuitions, and the existence of the discourse in which they occur, would be an absolute accident if it were not attached to the distribution of matter in the body of the discoursing animal and in his environment. Were there no material conditions of existence, no essence could ever appear or be exemplified; or if the being proper to essences is called existence, they would all necessarily exist once only and for ever. Repetition, production, change, and dissolution would all be radically impossible. Each of these facts, whenever noted or believed in, accordingly affords evidence of corresponding mutations and diversities in the substance they modify. In other words, matter is the principle of individuation, of concretion; it renders possible the existence of cases or instances of anything. That any essences should lodge locally or temporally at any point in an existing world or in a discoursing mind, compels me to invoke a non-ideal principle, involved in their being here both more and less than the single and eternal essences they are: and this non-ideal principle is matter.

Finally, in close confirmation of this concrete character of matter, is the knowledge of it conveyed by moral experience. Death, separation, and error divorce the spirit from the essences to which it was wedded, or which at least it wooed; it is matter without or the flesh within that is responsible for this treason. Matter, which is the principle of existence in things, and of mutation, is also the principle of imperfection in them. I know that in their ultimate philosophy many people deny that there is anything imperfect: they say everything is a necessary element of perfection. The motive for this contention is clearer and nobler than the meaning of it. Since things ought not to be imperfect, we wish to believe that they are not so. Yet if we really believed them to be perfect, we should rescind the category of the better and the worse which we are constrained in practice to apply to them: and by our optimism all the deliverances of conscience would be nullified in order to feign that conscience is omipotent. In reality the nucleus of values is always some particular nature; and experience proves, what the conditions of animal life imply, that particular natures do not often reach full satisfaction. Even if every dog had his day, here or hereafter, there would remain the other three hundred and sixty four days of the calendar which cannot be expunged from the book fate. All forms of life are strangled more or less, and many are strangled altogether, not to speak of the infinity of life that never comes to birth at all. The world is accordingly infected with imperfection. This imperfection is constitutional, because the material conditions of life and of moral aspiration presuppose it; and it is a real imperfection, which it would be better not to have found, not a false sense of imperfection in a world really perfect, which would have been spoiled without this false sense of imperfection which it contains. But if imperfection exists, which the world would not be spoiled by correcting, whence this ideal, and whence the imperfection which falls short of it? The ideal, let us assume, comes from the aspiration of a spirit conscious of its goals, ultimate or immediate; the imperfection must therefore come from some contrary predisposition in things, some inertia in respect to these demands of the spirit, imposing on the spirit all this difficulty and defeat. This principle of inertia is matter: for although matter is the most dynamic thing in the world, and the seat of all energies, most of its energies are chaotic in respect to the particular tendencies of any given animal, or tribe, or idea. Thus matter, whilst secretly and *in parvo* the source of all spirit, in the gross and publicly seems its inveterate enemy. Why have we no better senses, and no better command over the senses which we possess? Why does explicit thought lag behind the mind's prophecy and intention, and why will not the right words come to express it? Why is the spirit unwilling in some, and willing in others to so little purpose? Because the flesh is weak, or torpid, or rebellious. The principle of this double helplessness of spirit, within and without, deserves a name, and the proper name for it is matter. It is the name given to it spontaneously by spiritual men; but a scientific conception of matter will confirm this intuition, and show how the same principle that determines existence, in-dividuates cases, and distributes events, also imposes imperfection on the world, disappointing more or less every spirit that lodges in it. By its scantiness or superfluity or previous infection matter spoils the ex-pression of those tendencies which take root spontaneously in its particular parts.

Substance, posited in the first instance by animal faith, as the object of pursuit and of eventual knowledge, thus gradually reveals its more specific functions. It is a matter unequally distributed, lending a point of reference in the existing world for the essences appearing to in-tuition, individuating their instances, individuating the minds that behold them, and the occasions on which they do so, and explaining the moral predicaments of the spirit in a world irresponsibly fertile and innocently treacherous.

NO PSYCHOLOGICAL SUBSTANCE

Another obscure notion which the discovery of essence removes is that of a psychological substance, such as feeling, experience, or exist-

George Santayana, "No Psychological Substance," Humanities Research Center, University of Texas. © 1969 Daniel Cory. Intended for *The Realm of Matter* or for *Scepticism and Animal Faith*.

ing ideas. Reflection, guided by the conventions of discourse, assures us that we exist as minds, having passed through a series of experiences and retaining some sense of them and of their order. Relying on this conventional assurance and leaving it unanalysed, some philosophers have thought they could dispense with all other beliefs, so that experience—a succession of mental events with the memory of them—should be the only substance in the universe. The suggestion is vain: experience actually has external conditions and is chiefly a cognisance of external objects, without which the distribution and continuity of experience itself would be inconceivable: for the projections of memory would be mere fancy and would exhaust their objects, if there was no natural locus to which these objects might be severally assigned; a locus that should fix their true order, and render separate series of them possible. Without nature there could be no experience; the very notion of experience forbids: there could be only transcendental thought. Apart, however, from the incoherence of psychological idealism, the discovery of essence shows at once that experience is nothing substantial. Experience is intuition, or the fact that some essence appears; but the fact that an essence appears does not prove that an object exists constituted as that essence suggests. When the essence appearing is that of experience—a succession of mental events with the memory of them—it by no means follows that such experience has existed: all that need exist (although at that moment it cannot be given) is the actual intuition of that essence. But the existence of this intuition is discovered only in a reflection which credits its own images to be true knowledge; and this belief in a bit of past experience repeats the essence intuited before, adding to it a faith in its character as a revelation of facts, which although they may contain the intuition of experience once more, can never be given to any intuition. It is impossible therefore to reach any fact, such as the fact of successive experiences, by any intuition; facts can be reached only by animal faith, or belief in the existence of things or events such as intuition describes. Experience must be posited by faith in experience.

Now the moment I perceive that my own mental life is not a fact given to me immediately but an object of intellectual belief—of a theory vouched for only by the fact that I find myself entertaining it—I have no further reason for believing in this theory rather than in any other. Knowledge being not demonstrable but only indicative, its own existence is, for knowledge, only the hypostasised object of another indication; and if there is a substance at all that substance is not presumably experience. In other words, if knowledge has any object or any validity, that object need not[1] be other cases of knowledge, *ad infinitum*. Either there is nothing but essences without existence, or what exists may be describable by any other essence as easily as by the essence of experience.

So far, I have seen that experience is not evidently nor *a priori* the substance of all knowable things, but I have not excluded the possibility that it should be by chance actually substantial. What excludes this possibility is the deliverance of the experience which I happen to have, and the character of the world which I cannot help conceiving. When I trust my notion of events deployed in time, I see that they long preceded and greatly overflow experience on every side; they subtend, connect, support, and explain it; besides giving validity to its fundamental beliefs. Experience itself then appears in its natural place, as the mental notice taken by animals of their earthly surroundings and vicissitudes.

But this is waking experience, synthetic and somewhat rational; there is a deeper, more wayward, more vapid experience usually going on within me. Might not this dream-life, when reduced to its elements, be actually substantial? Might it not be the intrinsic reality of all that appears to me in a material guise? Might it not be the true matter?

Experience or mental life is the subject-matter of literary psychology. It is a series of intuitions. The immediate objects presented in it are essences; and the literary psychologist, who attempts to record or discover or imagine experience as it comes, should evoke these same essences again; but not simply. Like the author of a novel he occupies a point of vantage with respect to the thoughts of his characters: all their thoughts are his, but not all his thoughts are their. He can compare the sentiments of each with those of the others, and with the circumstances in which he has placed them. This supplement to a flux of imagined experience, such as those personages go through, is not optional; it *must* be present to the literary psychologist. Without it he could not project the various intuitions he develops into fixed points in space and time, nor into personal lives. It is by "introjection" into separate bodies that imagined lives are distributed in retrospect. It is also commonly by imagining the actions and aspects of these bodies that their experience is conceived; but even where it is evoked only by

1. The original, later corrected, had "cannot."—Editors.

words, or by some musical or sympathetic suggestion, it cannot be attached to the natural world nor to any historic person, even oneself, except by conceiving it as the experience of certain recognisable bodies in the presence of certain recognisable things, at certain assignable times. It is evident that the life of these bodies in their environment is the substance of the experience assigned to those persons; the experience itself being a partial and biassed perception of those material facts, or an emotional or reflective expression of them.

It may be said, however, that experience or mental life is one thing, and psychological substance quite another. The latter need not be a series of intuitions of essence; it may rather be defined as unconscious or unintelligent feeling; an object of introspection rather than of memory: for whereas memory (with the literary psychology which remodels or extends memory) repeats intuitions which it assumes to have existed elsewhere, introspection points to an object which was not an intuition, but a blind feeling. Now, it seems paradoxical and confusing to give the title of feeling to anything which is not the intuition of an essence. The difference between a feeling, such as pain, and a perception, such as sound, lies entirely in the characters of the two essences intuited. Some essences are those of things intensive only, others of things extended as well; others (given in thought rather than in sensation) of things extended only, or merely relational. A deafening thunderclap is given, at least initially, only as intensive; so is pain, when violent, until it is perhaps localised and distinguished in quality from other pains, and taken as a sign of some particular bodily hurt. The intensive presence, however, must surprise me, I must have the intuition of that shock, before anything mental, anything experienced, anything capable of figuring in literary psychology, or deserving the name of a feeling, has arisen at all. The thunderclap and the pain are alike physical only, until some essence of each is intuited, or some note of them taken. Certainly I may, by homonymy, *call* the electric discharge in the clouds thunder (although it is also lightning) before any sound has been heard; and I may *call* the nervous shock or the muscular contraction pain, before anything has been felt; but this is to pass more or less frankly to the realm of matter and to psychologise in behaviourist terms. It is proper and necessary to do so if psychology is to be scientific: and I think it on the whole advisable (following the pre-Socratics and the Stoics, who made the psyche material) to use the terms psyche and psychical for the obscure inward *ground* of experience, leaving the terms mental and psychological to describe the experience itself, and that literary account of it which is the only account of it that is possible. I may then *call* that state of the psyche, which immediately preceded the intuition of pain, a pain also; as I may call that event in the atmosphere which immediately preceded the intuition of thunder, the thunder itself: but I must remember that this is thunder, as the other is pain, only by courtesy, as we may indicate a man by his office when we do not know his proper name. The proper names of those objects will be assigned to them by natural science; for as to pain and thunder, they are the proper names of essences given to me in vulgar intuition.

The distinction of essence thus clears the notion of the psychical of all false obscurity, leaving it legitimately and provisionally obscure on account of our avowed ignorance, as embryology, biology, and chemistry are still obscure. But this obscurity need no longer be confusing, since it expressly designates the substantial processes, whatever they may be, which culminate in the intuition of the essence in question. These intuitions alone are experience, compose mental life, are recoverable in memory, and describable in literary psychology. They form in their totality—and there is no knowing how deep down in the realm of matter, nor how far afield, they may not occur—the realm of spirit: whereas the psychical, as I propose to use the word, in contrast with the psychological is a part of the realm of matter itself. The psychical may be, and is, substantial in respect to the mental, being a mode of substance and a habit of matter by which the mental is generated; but for that very reason it is not mental, and is not to be discovered by any sceptical analysis of experience.

PURE FEELING—PAIN

Since everything in physical life, which is the basis of spirit, suffers continually from friction, buffets, and partial failures, we need not be

George Santayana, "Pure Feeling—Pain," *Columbia Manuscript Collection.*
© 1969 Daniel Cory. In the upper right corner of the first page Santayana penned, "Distraction": the essay was written probably in preparation for *The Realm of Spirit* (New York: Scribner's, 1940).

surprised to find spirit also perturbed; so perturbed, that a hasty and passionate sentiment may be tempted to identify spirit with pain, regarding all happy feeling as mere relief. That the happiest and most spontaneous feeling is preceded by *physical tension* of some sort may be granted. That is only another way of saying that potentiality precedes exercise in every natural function, since an organ, preformed for such exercise, must exist if any action having a moral colour and a spiritual actuality is to result. But this physical preparation and readiness, rising under proper stimulation to conscious tension or expectancy or excitement, was never initially a pain. The sense of excitement, the conscious impulse, and in fortunate cases the joyful action, normally visit spirit before any sense of contrariety, or any moral distraction, and it is only by arresting and contradicting innocent will that sorrow, anger, or terror enter the young spirit.

That birth is painful, that there are pain-nerves especially prepared, as it were, to alarm or torment us, does not contradict this contention. Pain may very well be the first and only distinct sensation in some particular life; but the child must have been alive to feel that pain, and in his vegetative growth and pre-natal torpor, there must have been many a process which, if accident had raised it to consciousness, would have yielded pleasure or complacency rather than pain. This is what I mean by saying that *normally* pain is not primary in experience, but belongs to the sphere of distraction, interruption, or defeat: things which cannot arise unless some forward impulse is afoot in a medium fundamentally favourable (since otherwise that organism would not exist) but crossed by manifold currents that may prove hostile or fatal.

The notion of pain-nerves, which might conceivably twitch alone and evoke an absolute feeling of pain, without moral grounds or concomitants, suggests a distinction that has some speculative importance. Why should a spirit, without any previous allegiances or purposes, on feeling this twitch, feel it as evil? Is evil included in the definition of pain, and intrinsic to that feeling? Or must we distinguish the direct sensation proper to the pain-nerve from the general revolt or tremor of the whole nervous system that ensues? I suppose the function of pain-nerves is precisely to provoke such a revolt or alarm; and that it is this function, rather than the specific sensation which the nerve might theoretically yield if stimulated alone, that renders pain evil. Conceive that the effects of stimulating the pain-nerve have been arrested or reversed: would not the absolute sensation conveyed by that nerve become at once morally neutral, or positively welcome? So the taste of

tobacco, in abstraction, may be said to be neither pleasant nor unpleasant; but in the first instance, if violent, it will provoke disgust or
even nausea; whilst later in proper doses of the right quality on the
right occasions it may merge delightfully into a general slightly nar-
cotic, slightly luxurious saturation of the whole inner man. We may
say truly, from the autobiographical point of view, and reporting the
moral experience of a spirit, that the taste of tobacco has become wholly
different, that from nasty it has turned to pleasant, friendly, and even
indispensable; but this variation is evidently due to the total reaction
of the system on a specific stimulus, now become habitual, and not to
the sheer and absolute contribution of gustatory nerves.

In pain it might be well to distinguish the passive or aesthetic quality
of the absolute datum from the vital or moral burden of the feeling in
the context of life. Why should a certain sharp or unwonted sensation
be evil? In itself, what harm does it do? In itself, how should it be hateful, or hateful to whom? The essence of hatefulness or evil seems specific and detachable from any object describable in other terms. No
other ground of hatefulness or evil can be found in things except the
very essence of evil or hatefulness sometimes attached to them. And
we can conceive why this moral essence should be sometimes attached,
and why it should be detachable. When we feel pain, there has been
a general insurrection or revulsion in the psyche at some inner accident
or at some intrusion. Various stimulations differing entirely in aesthetic
effect, as heat differs from cold, when intense and sudden, may equally
interrupt the even course of vegetative life, creating shocks and distress, and even becoming intolerable. A desperate, blind impatience
then fills the psyche, and when conveyed to the spirit provokes a pro-
nouncement, an anathema, against the intruder. The sensation is hardly
distinguished at first from the posited agent that produces it; both are
called evil; or when the distinction between agent and effect is introduced, as it soon will be, the sensation is called pain, for being evil, and
the agent, for bringing trouble, is called bad, wrong, wicked, an abom-
ination, or a devil.

If this analysis be accepted, we may conclude that in itself no sensation is evil; that the aesthetic quality in a pain, if acceptable to some
other psyche, might be an indifferent datum or a pleasure; and that the
moral essence or evil in the pain, the intolerableness of it, is a symptom
of *distraction*. A previously current life has been deranged, something
poisonous introduced, a stoppage or an agony created; and these are
evil to the spirit.

A moral complication arises when the agent is discovered to be one's own psyche. In disease, although the evil lies in oneself, it is usually perceived to be an infection or contagion coming from outside; and even weakness and old age invade us like foreign forces, and a passion or a nightmare seems an incubus, a hideous fury sent by some god to torment us. Yet sometimes these mythical projections collapse, and the vice is too central, or too closely entangled with our remembered actions to seem an external force. We beat our own breasts, and see that our enemy is a part of ourselves. The drama of conscience thus set in motion is often very crudely composed; the man identifies himself with some part, perhaps the frailest and most superficial part of himself, or even with pure reason or spirit, not really parts of himself at all. In such cases he may become his own theoretical enemy and most cruel tyrant, accusing himself of pervasive corruption and depravity. These are thin mental aberrations, akin to madness, and kept within harmless or nearly harmless limits only by the fact that they move on a merely theoretic or hypocritical level.

But the psyche is in reality a most imperfect mechanism. False starts are frequent; passions are suppressed, or inopportunely developed, or excessive; so that apart from all the troubles due to fortune and to an intractable world, there is always more or less civil war, more or less fever, confusion, and failure of nerve, in the action of [the] psyche herself. She is right in crying *peccavi*: but though the spirit suffers from these vital errors it is deceived if it hopes to renounce an animal psyche altogether, and dwell in nobody. The infinite is not an organ of life.

If in a simple primitive feeling like pain the distress is due to latent distraction, an important principle emerges; namely, that unimpeded action in the psyche is the basis not only of the existence of spirit but of its joy, freedom, and dominion. Pain would cease to be pain, in the sense of being an evil, if it did not come from an arrest of function, or rending of an organ. Evil is psychic impediment or conflict. And if we ask, Impediment to what? Conflict between what? we may reply boldly: Impediment to intuition; conflict between physical movements one of which, at least, would culminate in clear intuition, if it had free play. Vital organisation is a great dumb art, mechanically creating and re-creating structures and processes; an art which when eminently successful ceases to be dumb and breaks out into spirit.

Inorganic harmonies, like those found in the stellar universe, are inevitable. Such equilibrium may be changed, is always changing, but can never be broken; and there is no occasion for spirit to arise, since there are no potential harmonies already prefigured and selected in the parts, so that their development or destruction may be felt as the moral fortune of individuals. When harmonies are organic they are precarious. They are precarious only because, in their organic potentiality, they are persistent; there is a psyche, an elastic self-propagating trope, pulsating in that body, maintaining itself alive under difficulties, and ready to recover its normal dominion on the first opportunity. Therefore, until that vital focus is altogether quenched, there is occasion and meaning in a spirit watching the fortunes of the individual, celebrating or lamenting them, and stretching its intellectual vision over past and future, and over the surrounding world, in so far as the inmost bent and potentiality of that psyche may be responsive to them.

Intuition, then, with all its transcendental superhuman privileges, marks the goal and possible triumph of our animal life. We cannot feel the blindest pain or the meanest pinprick without opening up a vista for the spirit towards its ultimate vocation; because the distraction, agonising or trivial, from which we then suffer, implies the possible absence of distraction: and this would mean perfect spiritual clearness, perfect spiritual peace on a large or small scale.

On the other hand, this omnipresent vocation to live in the spirit, far from separating the spirit from our animal lives, rests on the fact that the spirit is incarnate in us, and is the spirit of our own heart, seated there, looking out from there, and seeing all other things only in the light of our personal tragedies. In other words, the spirit is not a bodiless divine intellect or universal ego, but an intellectual expression of private moral predicaments and human passions, existing only because they exist, and present only where they are present.

The profound saying of Aristotle, that spirit comes into us from beyond the gates need by no means be rejected; it need only be interpreted as the mythical expression of a moral truth. The *deliverance* of the spirit is here turned, in the Greek manner, into a fable concerning its *origin*. The spirit does not materially come from outside: if not born within a living animal a spirit would have no excuse for being, no moral direction, no place in the world; but it is bred there precisely in the act of looking abroad, of stretching the sensitive scope of that psyche beyond the limits of the animal organism and its vegetative life, in order to trace the movement and picture the form of external things, travelling far into the past and the future in the act of doing so. Thus adventurous thought, having found a bride at a distance, and starting now from those foreign regions as from primal facts, sees its mother-psyche as an object amongst other natural objects and itself, the intellectual spirit of truth, as something infused into the psyche by the divine authority of the truth itself. And in reality the psyche, in lending herself to intellectual interests, has transcended her private life in idea, and become to that extent foreign and contemptible in her own eyes; so that she may well say, in her motherly rhetoric, that this spirit rebelling within her against herself is a changeling and a stranger, a haunting devil or a visiting god, or at best a vagrant and ungrateful child. Yet all this is but a fabulous drama enacted in her self-consciousness, when in her own interests she discovers the conditions of her existence, the greatness of the world, the infinity of possible Being, and the petty fatality of her home passions. Her despair, her conversion, her self-abasement and her self-transcendence, which she attributes mythically to daemonic influences, are but variations of direction in her own life, adjustments of her impulses to fact and to truth, until she seems to have been born anew and to have escaped defeat and death by humbly accepting them.

IV

The Relations of Spirit to Time

CONSCIOUSNESS AND TIME

The present, if reduced to an instant, seems to have no temporal scope, yet experience has such scope. On the other hand, there are logical impossibilities in the notion that the present is extended in time. If the present underwent change during its lapse, there would be several presents. A sustained present is indeed not impossible, but it would be sustained by continuing to have the same quality, so that any part of it would do for a present as well as the whole.

There is accordingly no advantage in supposing the *actual* present to be lasting but changeless. The fact that the *specious* present contains duration aesthetically is irrelevant; because it would be no aid towards perceiving an extended object that the seat or source of perception in the observer should itself have extension. On the contrary, as what subtends the various radii of an arc is the point at which they meet, so the point of origin of the sense of duration should be single and should occupy no part of the specious time it subtends. If it has a duration of its own, that duration can be no part of the time it perceives. For, though in relation to its object it is out of time, nothing prevents it from being what it pleases on its own plane: either instantaneous or sustained in physical time. Being sustained, while not helping it to perceive duration, might be more congruous with the nature of its organ, if it should turn out that this organ was a temporal as well as a spatial complex; for then the active phase of the organ being sustained, and covering many instants and movements, its hypostatic function—the consciousness of duration—should be sustained also.

At this point we are thrown back upon the nature of physical con-

George Santayana, "Consciousness and Time," *Columbia Manuscript Collection.* © 1969 Daniel Cory. The text indicates that this essay was written before 1920. In the upper right of the first page Santayana penned, "Realm of Consciousness"; the piece was clearly intended as a chapter of the book he later published under the title *The Realm of Spirit.*

tinuity. If the efficacious phase of the organ (the state of it which involves sensation) is prolonged, the question arises whether the first efficacious moment of it has duration or not. The answer would seem to be that the first *moment* has duration, being an infinite collection of instants, because the mathematicians tell us there can be no *instant* next to, or immediately after, any other; immediate transitions cannot then be between instants. An infinite number of instants of rest, for instance, must precede any beginning of motion; and an infinite number of instants of motion must precede any instant at which motion is going on.

rest	motion
r, r, r,	m, m, m,

There is no last instant *r* next to any first instant *m* ; an infinite number of *r*'s and *m*'s always intervene. The transition in quality from rest to motion must accordingly take place from a continuous rest to a continuous motion. This would hold even if we decided that motion and rest can be properties inherent in instants (a hypothesis of doubtful intelligibility) or are based on such inherent properties of instants. Infinite collections of instants having these properties would always have to elapse, before instants lacking those properties could begin. Changes must occur in blocks, every point of which is deep within the frontiers of its own country. Qualities reside in continua. Whether continua are not composed of infinite discrete points is not prejudged, and need not, for this purpose, be determined. For this infinity would itself compel every quality to stretch over an infinite number of points before it yielded to a different quality, since one point can never touch or yield to another.

The only means I can conceive of avoiding this conclusion would be to deny that instants have spatial or temporal relations at all, and to raise them to metaphysical monads. This expedient, however, opens so wide a gulf between instants or points and the natural objects they are supposed to constitute, that it becomes hard to see how they can constitute them. I suspect that by this path we should soon arrive at the conclusion that the points or instants are not substantially but only transcendentally related to things; i.e., they are not elements intrinsic to the things, but foci in which the things are conceived or imagined. And that the focus or seat of perception is punctiform and tangential in respect to the specious field deployed before it, was the view I was just now urging, which I think will be shared by all who understand what is meant by a transcendental principle.

The first plausible solution would seem to be this: that the actual present (not envisaged) is instantaneous, whereas the specious present (envisaged but not actual) displays duration and might even embrace the whole landscape of history. Whether the apperception of this duration lasts or is instantaneous is indiscoverable by studying its deliverance. The question is irrelevant both to the actuality of the apperception and to the length of aesthetic time it surveys. Actual mental existence has no intrinsic date. It is dated subjectively by the events it views; as we all say popularly that we are living in the past or future, or are plunged in this, or absorbed in that; or as philosophers say they live in the eternal. Objectively, and by the scientific observer, actual mental existence is dated by the material processes that underlie it, which are its organ and, when observable, are called its expression. These material processes are certainly extended in time; a single instant of nature would have no *sense*, in any sense of this word. Just as a painter's composition, considered aesthetically, has no place within or without the material picture, nor within or without his own brain, but dwells only in the realm of essence, so perhaps the act of conceiving or viewing the composition has no place in the world of evolution (except through the physical existence of the painter and the picture) but belongs to the realm of consciousness alone, which constitutes a different dimension of being, not intrinsically temporal.

It would follow that all experiences, whatever their conventional date, are in themselves coeval. As they are equal in actuality, so they are indefeasible in existence, and to call them past or future is an impertinence, hypostasising a perspective. The order of these experiences, in the realm of truth, is indeed irreversible, because it is true that they take perspective views of one another which are respectively past or future: it is true that for the ages before Christ the ages after Christ are future, and that for us the ages before Christ are past. And these fixed perspectives in the realm of consciousness express the order of material evolution which (as we have seen) is reversible only in description, not in process; for each stage of material evolution continues the elements given in the previous stage—both the substantial and the methodological elements—simply redistributing and reapplying them.

But no such continuity or derivation obtains in the realm of consciousness, where each moment (like each individual animal in the realm of matter) is a new birth. In consciousness the relation to matter is out of sight, and the moments have internal relations only—dialectical, moral, eternal relations, such as unanimity or mutual relevance—and the temporal order attributed to them is either a false assimilation of them to their ground or material objects, or else a transcript of their mutual perspectives. For some moments, in respect to a part or the whole of the essence they envisage, may repeat or 'remember' others. Those remembered—i.e., placed in reproduction towards the beginning of specious time—are called past; others are imagined—i.e., given without a clear place in specious duration—and are called merely possible or alien to oneself: others are placed, perhaps intermittently, towards the end of the temporal sequence surveyed, and in their characters are called possible, while in their station they are called future. All these conceived experiences are past, alien, possible, or future only by imputation. In other words, time is an intrinsic and measurable medium only in the realm of matter; in the realm of consciousness time is only a principle of perspective. The Kantian philosophy on this point, and in respect to consciousness, deserves to be taken to heart, consciousness being its chosen field; though it should be banished from our minds in considering those other and deeper realms which it ignored.

That material events are precipitated in an irreversible direction, so that one is before the other, is true, and must be somehow interpreted materially by the natural philosopher: such a movement belongs to the essence of matter. But it is not true that any event is in itself present more than any other is. This point of view—as the double meaning of the word present indicates—is that of consciousness. Present is what goes on now, for me here; and in themselves all events are present in their day, and are at the centre of time. Not that we can call them simultaneous, for the diversity in their dates is infinite, discrete, and continuous in one dimension. Since an infinite number of instants intervenes between any now and any then, what shamelessness to assert that some of these intervening instants were more nearly present than others, when the stress of presentness, so to speak, is passing through them with an impartial and infinite rapidity! They are indeed nearer or farther from the one we call present arbitrarily—because we are egotists—but they are all equally possessed and equally dispossessed of presentness. Existence, the more closely we view it, grows more and more unseizable and unstable; the opposite being the case with essence and with truth.

Yet this fleeting presence of events is their due, and it is in passing that they have their being; they are no more ghostly than childhood, which indeed is the present become human. The ghostliness of existence is imputed to it, because most of it, in perspective, fades behind the mists of the past and the future; but the opposite and reversible character of these two ghostly screens proves how subjective they both are. Every future becomes past without changing its inherent quality; and if we were not animals, with minds hanging on the flux of matter, we should be incapable of conceiving that any experience called past or future had ceased or had not yet begun to be. Either, we should say, these events never occur at all,—they are merely essences imagined now,—or they occur in their time and are integrating parts of the context of existence. In this latter case their material or psychic actuality is intrinsic; external imputations, such as fall upon them through expectation or retrospect lodged in other quarters, cannot affect them. The events of 1920 are future to the writer, to the reader past; evidently in themselves they are neither, and relatively to you and to me, they are always both. For I can only expect, and you can only recall them; and we should both be dreaming, and there would never be any such events to recall or expect, unless they always held their allotted place in the realm of truth, and in themselves were actually passing and present.

There is accordingly no march of events out of limbo into a momentary existence and back again into the shades. The whole world of fact, with all its pulsing moments and their relations, pants in the rush of existence, infinite against the doubly infinite background of essence, like the stellar universe against the abyss of space. No part of existence lapses into non-existence or rises out of it. Only the superficial and reversible perspectives of consciousness (fantastic in their deliverance, though in their own plane existing facts) introduce this double twilight of pastness and futurity, and these impossible degrees of semi-existence, egotistically calling crepuscular what they see dimly, and noonday reality what lies under their nose.

As to the summation or retention of the past in the present, we may distinguish a retrospective fallacy from a physical fact. The fallacy lies in supposing that because we feel that we are living the past over again, we are actually repeating integrally a past experience. The fact that we know we *revert* to anything proves that this second experience, conning the old theme, is not the original experience of the same, even in our opinion; and the identity of the theme itself is probably largely illusory; for how do we know what it was, save by hypostasising the memory that remains to us, which external evidence often shows to be strangely transformed? Belief in the exact recovery of an essence present long ago gratuitously identifies a present appearance with an absent one; or perhaps it tries to do even more, palming off the two experiences for a single fact, in order to dazzle and afford people that strange exhilaration which they sometimes find in talking nonsense.

The physical fact concerned in retention is that many a moment continues the movement of the preceding moments, either by sustaining or by repeating it after an interval. Hence, for a time, reverberations of previous events may be constant or occasional. These reverberations assume, under various circumstances, the character of generation, habit, or memory. But nothing is sustained or reproduced integrally. Things are merely absorbed and enter structurally into the thing that absorbs them, until the crossing of various structures confuses them all, and makes exact reproduction impossible.

This may be seen going on in the light of day in the case of language. Words, phrases, literary effects are repeated *ad nauseam* and yet, after revolutions or migrations, no people can keep its diction or pronunciation unaltered; and the turn of language in the end is so transformed as to be unintelligible to anyone who remains faithful to antique usage. And if we take a longer time we find even the various species of expression passing into one another. Gesture and inarticulate sounds yield to song, song to poetry, poetry to economical speech; mythology becomes physics and physics mathematics; while the imitative or telepathic communication of the lower animals, or of future generations of men, may hardly deserve to be called language, and certainly not literature. Nevertheless each of these phases of expression continues the physical processes that underlay its predecessors: everything is continuous but elusive, repeating the past only generically and containing the future only materially; as a mother repeats the nature of her parents and contains the body of her child.

The difficulty in describing specious change is a literary difficulty. We feel time and events lapsing before us, and we have but to find phrases that will fix and revive this feeling. It is hard to rein in our words and thoughts to such an introspective purpose; for their natural function is to disregard immediate data, and to awaken in us conceptions of objects quite different from the essences given. In defining physical change, however, the difficulty is of another order. We are then bound to propose consistent notions, and such as do not evade or contradict the facts they are meant to explain, such as the fact, for instance, that changes occur. Aesthetic essences—which poetry and music may be needed to suggest, and which words can seldom define —may quite innocently be wholly incomparable with the occasions that call them up, as pain is incomparable with wounds, or heat with friction, or sensible extension with an infinity of points. And though of course no essence can contradict itself, it may easily be vague or misleading when its logical implications or dreamful variants are taken to express the nature of any concomitant fact. Self-contradiction itself is one of our data; and the attempt to identify contraries tempts even some logicians. Such is the landscape of dreams. But in the realms of existence we are concerned with spheres from which contradiction is excluded; not that we can impose our logic upon nature, but that however nature is constituted our ambition is to describe its constitution faithfully. So long as our description remains ambiguous, therefore, it has not quite hugged the facts, whatever they may be. Physical change must according[ly] be consistently defined, and the definition must not abandon the subject matter to which it was to apply: it must be relevant to the aesthetic change which we are trying to understand and to translate into physical terms. If this were impossible, we should have to agree with those philosophers who maintain that aesthetic change is all the change there is, so that all existence—even this perception of aesthetic change—is changeless. Motion would then be an aesthetic but not a physical category, as beauty is. What physical change is, if such a thing actually occurs, must be determined by natural science and mathematics.

Nevertheless the literary difficulty in describing aesthetic change, and the scientific difficulty in defining change in existence, are not disconnected, because the terms used in science to symbolise material facts are themselves given essences, and although we may prudently take these symbols lightly and drop half their quality (including their uncertain degree of definition) in predicating them of things, yet we have no other substantive terms in which to conceive things, in contrast to data; only a certain system, not belonging to the data, and intended to veto everything in the data which contradicts it. It may well happen, therefore, that the true theory of physical change or physical time should remain, as it were, in the air, physical change and time not having, any more than matter, a literal aesthetic representation in the human mind.

There is accordingly no paradox in the circumstance that the physical relation of before and after should not at all resemble the intuited essence of motion or change. In consciousness there are many degrees and varieties of persistence and of change, and the two elements seem unintelligibly mingled. There is blank duration; there is a persistent presence of some further essence during this duration; there is felt motion; there is the intuition of some essence (other than motion itself) which is the term of this motion—something new or gone; there is finally the sense that what is present has succeeded to something which is absent—a curious contradiction if we understand it to imply the givenness of what we believe is not given now, but was given at some other time. Perhaps what we believe is only that the *object* is not now by us in the existent world; the essence of the absent, however slightly defined, being certainly present when we feel the absence of that thing. But confusion breaks out in appearances the moment we use them in their concreteness as predicates of things, or even as terms of thought. If we consented to admit the complexity of being, such confusion would be avoided, since there is no contradiction in the presence of appearances conceived as such, nor in their different perspectives and shufflings. The specious world is tangential to the material world, and its magic dimensions are superadded to the three dimensions and to the temporal measure of nature.

The sense for elapsing events may be analysed as follows: to endure, and to endure without change, is proper to every datum initially; we may hold it, or revert to it in primary memory; and in holding or reverting we carry ourselves consciously along. This enduring felt self is a second essence concomitantly given. The force of the psychic processes that yield these essences of the lasting need not be constant; but any consequent retrocession or paling in the datum, when not reflected upon, does not constitute any change in the essence mentally identified or sustained—the theme of consciousness for the time being remains the same. But on this background, which is pervaded by specious duration, some special factor may appear at any point, and join the procession, in our picture, from there on; and then (still having

the whole specious duration before us) we see the difference between
the first part of that duration, unaccompanied by the additional feature,
and the second part, where this feature appears.

This is the character of what we actually intuit in perceiving change:
but in our naturalistic language we interpret this synthetic essence as
a sign of successive detached events, and say that we are seeing the
additional feature arise; it is something new. This assertion is not good
introspection, but it is a beginning of good science. It is truer than
the appearance, and begins to make sense of it. Introspectively we are
surveying a stretch of specious time in the first part of which the
event called new is absent, in the second part present; the shock or
surprise which an explosion may cause is itself such an interlarded
event; for unless we are rendered unconscious by it, we continue to
feel the previous silence, and the previous calm attitude of our soul,
in the background of our consternation; this enables us to feel that the
explosion has occurred and is not a fact without a known beginning,
like our own existence. So that we are unfair to our data when we say
we have lost our former serenity and are all surprise: the truth is only
that, like a thunder cloud covering half the sky, our surprise is gaining
on our serenity. Each shock is like a little awakening, that leaves us
still half lost in our dream. We do not, then, feel change by changing,
but by not changing—which is not to say that, in some respect irrelevant to this perception of change, our own condition is not varying:
but our sense of the sudden shock, or the rush of events, is like (and
perhaps contains) our apprehension of impending blows; as they have
not yet fallen it is impossible that we should draw our consciousness
or their futurity from their operation; we draw it from the life of our
body now; not by travelling with the flux we intuit (which outruns
the present) but by looking at it—a mere essence of succession—
through the window of our present apprehension.

Certainly we travel too, and change psychically—though far less
precipitously and intricately than the simplest material thing: even
our deepest layers of dream are thin and sketchy. But we change insensibly, and it is only those features that appear in one part and not
in another part of the same specious duration that we see to change.
Psychic change in ourselves, and any *total* exchange of data we can
perceive or believe in only *ex post facto*, on indirect scientific evidence.
Our psychic birth or extinction evidently cannot be changes observed
by us: no more can any intervening mutation in our psychic condition.

As when born we do not remember that we were once unborn, nor when dead that we were once alive, so any other break in our actual existence will prevent rather than introduce a sense of interruption, and will tend to cut us up into fragments serenely ignorant of one another.

The complication that lends retrospective intent to memory is obscure. Exact repetition of an experience would exclude this perspective, since the original experience did not take its object in the past: yet to do so is the intellectual nerve of memory. When we are most confident that we recall the past exactly we are also aware that it is far away; we float into remote spaces, knowing that the event now going on went on then; a contradiction which common sense solves by saying that it is going on here now only ideally.[1] But this is not enough; for whence the notions of then and there, with the conviction that the present image occurred also in that other setting, or (more simply) that it is an object lying in that setting exclusively?

I conceive that the answer to this question needs to be rather bold; all else would be mere fumbling and avoidance of the issue. We must admit that intentionally the specious present covers all time. As the eye, looking in any direction, plunges indefinitely into space, to see what it may find there to arrest it, so the sense for time sweeps along to infinity, ready to survey the whole chain of events, and to note the place of each in the series. This place is given to each event, not by a roving eye, or an intrinsic feeling, focussed there for a moment, but by the eternal relations of that event to its neighbours. We may accordingly literally re-view events we have viewed before, since all of them are always virtual objects of our attention; for intelligence initially, in its cognitive attitude, is not addressed to what may chance to be already given, but to anything there may chance to be, and therefore to everything. But this native scope of cognition is miserably arrested by the accidents of place, organs, interests, and sloth; the spirit is willing to be omniscient but the flesh is near-sighted. As we can, therefore, we confine our attention to what is near in space or in influence to the organs of our thought; and as these distances or influences are modified or reversed by new instruments, turned on things from fresh points of view, various vistas cross and recross the same field, or extend it in sundry directions.

1. Santayana's marginal note: "Distinguish this contradiction from the innocent recurrence of essences."—Editors.

The sense of pastness attached to objects in memory is accordingly not fundamentally a sense that they are not now before us, but rather that they are before other objects present to us also, raised to practical actuality by the fact that we are disposed instantly to react upon them, whereas direct reaction on past or future objects—though they may be just as vividly present to us mentally—is inhibited by our lower and saner nervous organisation.

A misunderstanding to be avoided here is any suggestion that we somehow *perceive* all events in time, or all objects of ulterior experience. This is impossible; the future cannot affect us at all because true perception involves the dynamic presence of the object, and dynamic relations flow by definition in the direction of genesis only. Moreover, most of the past is cut off from perception at any point, either of time or space; most of the details would block and blur one another in transit, and no living being has tentacles that reach to the whole breadth of the present, so that even in perspective it cannot bear on him in its entirety. There is no physical or dynamic universality in sense; what is comprehensive is the intent of the spirit; as when an orator, without seeing or conceiving the individual members of his audience, addresses them all, or even all the world, and all future generations: indeed, fundamentally, according to his spontaneous poetic instinct, he may address the dead also, though they cannot applaud him. This universal scope of attention belongs to the essential framework of apperception; in catching one wild colt we make the lasso ready for the whole herd.

Into this framework the data fall and take their places according to the accidents and mechanism of perception. We accept at first sight and install in office whoever presents himself as a candidate, in the order either of genesis or implication, until perhaps some rival claimant appears. Nor are the offices to be filled numbered or defined beforehand: the occupant largely determines his post: but it has a certain initial topographical position; we know what sort of a post it is, however its functions may ultimately be developed. This initial scheme or grammar of apperception expresses the responsive machinery which instinct or experience have so far endowed us with, yet at every stage it is like a language which, however special and limited is a mother tongue, [moves] forward to undertake the expression of everything.

CONSCIOUSNESS AND TIME

Attention can obviously be sustained. The sense of duration is elementary; in pain for instance the most vivid part of the sensation is often that of dragging through a still persisting past into a future constantly arriving. This is the deliverance of consciousness at such times; it might conceivably be an illusion and we might have before us nothing but the static essence of duration, the changeless idea of change. In fact, however, we can hardly be wrong in predicting duration and continuity of the outer world (though not on the scale nor in the units of our ideas). The world is in process, and in much more rapid and complex process, than the drifting and summary data of our senses. Yet the sense of change and continuity is true; there is real change and real continuity in the world and in the psyche which it signifies to us. It is indeed the persistently varying assaults of matter that calls away our attention from whatever we might be inclined to fix and to contemplate: and as this change of objects is not complete, but the two overlap, one waning and the other waxing, we not only change but feel that we change, and that it is the changing world that is carrying us along, often regretfully.

Consciousness, since it follows and traces a sustained flux, would seem to share it.. We might be tempted to assert that it, too, lapses continually, essentially, and irretrievably. But there is another side to the matter: for in noting any change consciousness bridges it, and if, like substance, it was essentially in flux, it would be as incapable to [sic] passing from a term both really and ostensibly past to one both really and ostensibly future as anything that changes is incapable of retaining the qualities it has surrendered. It would seem that what reviews a sequence must be tangential to it, must stand still, as it were, at a certain distance, to watch the march past, and take the salute.

Such an image or analogy, however, is misleading. The relation of consciousness to its objects is not geometrical, and any graphic symbol tends to materialise it, whereas consciousness is not a point nor a peep-

George Santayana, "Consciousness and Time," *Columbia Manuscript Collection.* © 1969 Daniel Cory. Another early attempt to deal with some of the problems discussed in the previous essay.

hole, but a cognitive energy. There is doubtless a reviewing post, some relatively central and relatively steady organ: but that organ, which I call the psyche, is material, and by no means consciousness itself. Consciousness is only the winged observation which the process in that organ sends forth under appropriate stimulation: it is as mobile as the reaction of this organ, altogether insubstantial, and quite incapable of standing aside to receive shocks, collect, or compound them. Consciousness is no material receiver, or material distributor, as the psyche is; consciousness is the fact that, while all this is going on, the psyche becomes aware of sundry essences or objects, and that something is given or known to it. If therefore some relatively permanent ego is required to retain and bring together the moments of a flux, if the flow of it is to be observed, this ego must be some nucleus in the psyche, or the psyche as a whole, or the man; it cannot be consciousness. Consciousness is volatile, and itself on the wing.

Externally considered, consciousness is certainly in time. It begins and ends. Like any other continuum, it has no first instant of being, but there is an instant at the beginning, after which, at any moment, it already exists; and another instant at the end, at any moment prior to which it was still existing. Consciousness like every other existent fills time; it lasts between assignable instants each time it arises, and beyond those instants ceases to exist.

The strangeness of such absolute limits troubles our reflection; we say nature makes no leaps, because we hate to make them. But the shock of absolute beginnings and endings is unknown to nature, which is full of them; and our own experience, which illustrates them, cannot feel them. No one is surprised to be born, or horror-struck at having been annihilated. It is only reflection that suffers in contemplating such miracles, and wastes its sympathy on the impossible. In the routine of life, too, nothing established seems to need justification, unless something else, equally established, is impatient of it; and nothing absent is missed, except when the present is pregnant with it and labouring to give it birth. That consciousness should have arisen, though but a moment ago, is nothing startling: so soon as it exists it takes itself and its random objects for granted. It has no alternative in its empty mind: the infinitely improbable fact is the simplest thing in the world to it: because it is the whole world it knows. Wonder begins when knowledge extends, and imagination contrasts its own impulses with the habits of things: and it is only when the absolutely infinite realm of essence is discerned, every part of it equally likely, *a priori*, to have existed, that the vanity of all surprise begins to dawn upon our reason.

Whether the continuity of consciousness between these limits of time, or the continuity of anything, might not be composed of an infinity of instants, may be left to mathematicians, as well as the corresponding question about the continuity of space, motion, and matter. I understand that a continuum composed of discrete points, if these are infinite in number, offers no logical difficulty, but rather solves the difficulties that had been supposed to exist, before the mathematical infinite had been studied with the docility and sympathy which, like every reality, it demands of the mind that would understand it: for to approach a fact or an essence with egotistical demands or postulates is to shut the door in its face. The same spirit, however, requires that when we have satisfactorily elucidated such an essence as continuity, we should not assume that, because such a structure is intrinsically possible and has become easy for us to conceive, therefore it "must be" the structure of the world before us. Substance, not being obliged to exist at all, was not obliged to exhibit any particular kind of existence. It is merely a matter of fact, to be decided for us, as far as we can decide it, by the evidence. Any argument seeking to coerce consciousness *a priori* to dwell in indivisible instants, infinite in number, or matter to dwell in points, is futile. All you can show mathematically is that such *might* be their distribution: to show that it actually is such would require conclusive evidence drawn from observation. Even in the case of matter such evidence can hardly be secured, because while our observation of matter is direct, it is not distinct enough, nor near enough to the scale of the object, to reveal its intimate structure. When it comes to observing consciousnss, however, the case is altogether hopeless, for consciousness cannot be observed: it is observation of other things, and even in memory, what we remember is what we thought or observed, and in what order; and this includes, and involves the fact that our attention fell on those objects successively; but even then we cannot observe or determine how attention itself arose or sustained itself. It seems that we shall never be able to decide, therefore, whether it occupied the infinite number of indivisible instants between two points of time, or the undivided duration between the latter.

What we can observe in consciousness is its deliverance; this is complex and changeful, yet integral; because the unity of apperception (which involves neither simultaneity nor indivisibility nor homogeneity nor distinct boundaries in the data synthesised) is the condition of awareness having an object or datum at all. The datum may be as small and the awareness as brief as you choose: but if it is a datum and there is awareness of it, there is a definite fact of apperception, and the unity of apperception individuates it. It could not be what it is, had its parts appeared separately.

Now, we have said that consciousness considered in its external locus (as every existence may be considered) has a beginning and an end, and lasts between those limits.. This duration is not incompatible with its integral deliverance; to suspect that it may be, and that synthesis must be confined in an indivisible instant, is not to have a firm hold on the qualitative difference between matter and spirit. It is like the barbarous argument of some psychologist that because the deliverance of consciousness has unity the *organ* of consciousness must be punctiform, and that therefore the brain with its diffused and perhaps dispersed processes cannot be this organ. A punctiform organ could have no structure, and could therefore never have any relation to the complex, changing, diverse deliverances that consciousness. affords. Besides, the brain *is* the organ of consciousness; and why should philosophers protest that it is impossible, after God has proved the contrary? In the same way, the unity of consciousness in respect to any deliverance it may make, does not prevent consciousness from lasting, and its deliverance being often sustained. You may still say that consciousness resides in instants, if they are contiguous and if an infinite number of them are passed through whenever we are conscious of anything; for then it will not matter to this cognitive integrity whether consciousness occupies these instants severally, or the interval they fill as a whole. It will always be a group of instants, not a single one, that subtends a thought; for it happens, it grows, it gropes, and what it is observing or saying comes gradually to a head; the approach is felt together with the issue. The deliverance of an instant, if not repeated in a varying context by its successors, would hardly represent a recognisable attitude of the psyche, nor any adaptation on its part to anything comparatively stable in nature, or determinate in the ideal world, be it form, truth, or habit.

I say that the deliverance of consciousness is, as a matter of fact, integral. It is certain that the eye has scope, that thought takes cognisance of complex matters, and that knowledge is cumulative. Doubtless a part of this accumulation is an accumulation not in consciousness—inhibitions and potential sequels which keep the datum from being practically misunderstood, without visibly enriching it. In other words, education remodels instinct as much as it enlarges thought. Yet it certainly enlarges thought too: a sailor *imagines* this circumnavigable planet, and the varieties of the human race, as the untravelled townsman does not. In other words, there is a transcendental unity in apperception, and whatever is at any time in mind, is in mind together. This obvious fact may be obscured and the assertion of it embarrassed, if we make too much of it, usurping the rights of other complementary truths in our zeal to publish it. We might, for instance, tend to ignore the stealthy ghost[s] that flit through the mental scene, even in the broadest daylight of attention. Apperception itself frequently lapses, or contracts its range. Those shadowy forms, however, though rightly or wrongly we may credit them with a more definite being in their own realm, are for consciousness just shadowy forms, and fall within the unity of apperception in that capacity. Otherwise, they were absent altogether, and we later invent or falsely project them, and say they were "virtually" present, because we know that they were ready to be perceived at any moment. We impute them to the past only because they have come out clearly since, and belong to the same context as the former objects. Such latencies, far from outrunning or disrupting the unity of apperception, show stress of the psyche, which has responded, and is ripening for further responses, to external things by a change in its own habit. The basis of concrete consciousness can never be simple; to look for its seat in an atom is a pure aberration. An atom, to justify all the vision and labour of the mind, would need to be affected by the relations it stood in to the rest of psyche, and through the psyche to the rest of the material world. But an atom, by definition, cannot be diversified inwardly: it can therefore, taken alone, be the basis of nothing complex or changing. Only a system of atoms can form the psyche, because only a manifold can be diversified, or could furnish consciousness with such objects, many and shifting, as we know our consciousness regards. Perhaps, if ultimate atoms are indivisible, one of them, when encircled by a vortex of other atoms, might be the centre, in some sense, of the system which was conscious; its absolute necessity and ubiquitousness for consciousness. A thousand things might have been attended to if apperception had been differently focussed; but they were omitted and did not come to consciousness at all, because the constitutive synthesis of attention neglected to incorporate them in the present datum. All the latency and potentiality are in the realms of essence and of matter: in the characters which might have appeared but did not, and in the readiness of the psyche to present such objects, when the proper stimulus is applied to it. What seeds are in the ground, and what flowers might or will grow from them, is nothing to the point; what is under ground is under ground, not in the light of consciousness.

The integrity of consciousness is elastic in scope; it covers on occasion everything that any one recalls or, as we say, has in mind at any time. Of course the features in this field are not due to any fecundity in consciousness itself; they express the fruitfulness and plastic . . .[1] but the consciousness would still arise from the entire system, and its unity would express the substantial modes—the collocations and movements —of that system, not by any possibility the central atom alone. This unnecessary central atom is not more unnecessary than an indivisible soul or ego, which some philosophers think it profound to postulate. A punctiform soul would be as incapable of synthesis as a punctiform atom. Synthesis is an ideal, a modal, unity in a manifold; the substance of it must be plural and changing; the unity of apperception which supervenes expresses hypostatically, in actual thought, the modal unity of its organ, with the multiplicity which this organ contains. A bare unity in the substance would preclude, far from facilitating, this unity of experience. It is like a picture, the aesthetic unity of which would not be enhanced by reducing the picture to a dot; on the contrary, that dot could only be apperceived by becoming a dot on a background also visible. In fine, the organ of consciousness is certainly a life, the operation of a complex psyche, and not any sort of simple unit.

The analogy of this extends to time. Consciousness does not express a momentary or sustained collocation of parts in this psyche, but rather a movement there, or an attitude, that is, a mechanism held ready for movement. Its least restless occasion is an equable flight, or a determinate straining for flight of a determinate sort. It is then that consciousness is what we call clear, steady, and sustained. A certain swing, a certain equilibrium and declared circuit in operation is requisite before any particular object or feeling can be fixed or aroused; and consciousness can never exist without some object or feeling: you cannot be conscious and conscious of nothing. Just as there must be commotion in the spatial organ of consciousness, so there must be progression there towards a definite cycle of life; the process that is to be expressed in consciousness, and to create its expression there, must first have a particular character and scope of its own: how else could it determine

1. This is the end of a page; the sense indicates that a portion of the manuscript is missing here.—Editors.

what sort of essence should be its messenger in the conscious world?

Now a process (the minimum required to subtend consciousness) contains many moments. Shall we say that, when consciousness exists, some of these moments are past, others future, and only one actual? That is, in one sense, the fact when in a material process we select an instant (empty of movement) which divides that process like a watershed; yet only in one sense, because the actual instant does not contain any part of time or existence, which occupy it only in passing.[2] The flow of consciousness, viewed from the outside, is subject to just such partition by a moving instant, or mathematical present; but consciousness itself is the sense, more or less persistent, of objects or feelings and their movement; it cannot in its outlook be either confined to one instant, nor hedged between two instants, so as to stop short at them. The time it knows is not its own date but the felt duration of its objects; and the apperception that spans that specious duration, while it grasps nothing but a moving and sustained present, is not subject to the same compulsion as a material flux of being in all its parts either past or future. Consciousness has the privilege of *actuality*, in a sense not applicable to the other realms of being. It is not passed through, it is a point of origin, a centre of radiation, a carriage window from which the passing landscape and the distance are surveyed. It may regard and know nothing but changes, or even change in itself—which is a particular essence and may be felt intensely when no term can be fixed which it starts from or in which the change issues. But this specious change will die away in a vague recession without horizons, suggested but not explored. Pictorially, indeed, this vagueness is a clear datum like the haze in the landscape. The act of apperception, however, lies neither in any of the moments surveyed, nor extends to the unassignable limits of the changes intuited. Consciousness does not share the temporal structure of the specious flux which it spans nor of the material flux which underlies that experience and in which the organ of consciousness, the psyche, participates.

Should we say, then, that consciousness is out of time? Is it supernatural? If it were out of time it would not be an existence; we should

2. This is true even if time and matter are discrete (which I do not venture to form an opinion about) because even then a group, containing an infinite number of points, would be the effective minimum of time or of matter. [Though originally part of the body of the essay, Santayana indicated in the margin that he wished to introduce the preceding sentence as a note.—Editors.]

not be able to say of it (what is true of it preeminently) " 'tis here, 'tis here, 'tis gone." If it were supernatural it would not dog the steps of an animal; it would not require a psyche to produce it; nor would it be likely to be so dreadfully interested in the life and death, the adventures and passions of an individual body, or a tribe of men. Consciousness is so truly in time that of all existences it is the most ephemeral; renewed only to lapse again, and mocking all its deliverances by never repeating them. It vanishes without a trace, for it contains no substance; and it is merely on the rhythms of an alien substance that it hangs its intermittent being, like the sounds of a bell on its swinging. As for being supernatural, it is the very fruition of nature; without it, all this prodigious engine would have slumbered on in a sort of half-being. It may be a human prejudice, but it seems to us, at least, that nothing is more natural than to care which way things go, and to weight the mechanism of life with preference. Without it existence would seem to us ghostly, and necessity trivial. Yet without consciousness the world would be a mathematical limbo; no pang felt, no light seen, no place far or near: and all the industry of nature in producing so many plants and animals would be wasted: for nobody would care to live or to be beautiful. Let me say something rash, and which in a materialist may sound strange, although in truth it is a corollary to materialism: all nature lives, cares, and is conscious, in as much as it is all concerned in the process which culminates at times in life, consciousness, and preference. If a man is a genius, though his bowels have no genius of their own, his bowels unwittingly minister to it, as much as his brain: and I do not mean providentially or magically, for in truth his bowels may be a hindrance to him also; but organically; because he could not, but for what they are, have been just the sort of genius he is. The moral life of the world is late, local, ephemeral; but it is a natural expression of the world, and at a greater or less remove, an expression of the whole world; for the whole world has made just this sort of moral life possible and inevitable.

Natural, surely, consciousness is; but it is immaterial. It is not amenable to the same laws of dynamics, nor to the same anatomy in space and time, as substance is. But nature is more than substance; it is a system of movements, forms, and transformations, which have their specific being in the realm of truth. This realm is non-natural in one respect; it is eternal.[3]

3. The manuscript ends with the note, "Nothing more yet written."—Editors.

THE RELATIONS OF SPIRIT TO TIME

The mind is an emanation of nature, something rooted in animal life: but it is no mere complication in the movement of bodies, observable externally; it develops in a new invisible dimension, adding an immaterial moral intensity, called feeling or passion, to the vicissitudes of material life. Thus mind extends in two directions, longitudinally, through physical time, keeping pace with the changes in the body whose mind it is, and with the world surrounding that body; and at the same time it extends also vertically, in a direction from which, as from a watch-tower, the flux of existence, forward and back, may be surveyed synthetically. It is the essential privilege of mind to enrich the moment in which it exists with perspectives toward other moments. Mind is therefore proper only to organisms, arising when the tension of their organisation towards ulterior things becomes conscious of those things and of itself. For organisms are charged with instincts (or unconditioned reflexes) set to go off only in specific circumstances; so that an organism has to wait for the occasions on which it may do the trick which it is primed to do. Until then it is sullen or restive: when the occasions come, or seem to be coming, it grows keen; when they have come and gone, it is pacified. Now these organic predispositions and impulses, working themselves out more or less smoothly in the press of events, would be simply *tropes*, that is, rhythms or patterns in the flux of existence, if nature, at such points, did not generate spirit, synthesising those tensions into feelings, and those patterns into perspectives swept by an intuitive glance. Out of tension in the longitudinal physical dimension, arises uneasiness or terror or lust, out of tension along the mental tangent arise emotions, images and ideas. These feelings being spiritual, transcend their position in the flux of nature by their intent, and survey that flux, or some part of it, by their summary intuitions. For they pack within one moment of time a conscious refer-

George Santayana, "The Relations of Spirit to Time," *Columbia Manuscript Collection.* © 1969 Daniel Cory. Santayana wrote this essay in a small notebook. The use of the word "spirit" in the place of "consciousness" suggests that it is a later work than the two preceding pieces.

ence to other moments, and a sense of transition from one moment to another.

Now primary instincts, or pre-formed reflexes, form the very structure of the animal psyche, and so long as life lasts they are persistent. Fatigue or satiety only half suspends them in sleep: your sleep is always vaguely nibbling, your cat is always ready to jump, your urchin is always looking for mischief. So on the mental side, though the intensity of attention varies, the field open to attention remains continuous and comprehensive. Though I may blink, I continue looking, and the prospect endures; things come into it and drop out of it without breaking its general sameness.

And the sensuous prospect, be it observed, is initially infinite. In looking forward, I look for all that may ever come; in looking about, I look for everything that may be there, at any distance. Yet this infinite prospect is empty and vague, like a dark night: it is but the projection of my indecision and ignorance. I am simply waiting, sullenly or eagerly, for what may happen to come.

In a plastic organism, however, not all the instincts are performed and invariable. Conditioned reflexes may be established: the animal may be trained. The great trainer is experience: there are so many things I am impelled to do which are impossible, and so many that would be possible, if only I could change my conduct a little. The occasions on which an instinct is checked or diverted, if that instinct is plastic, remain grafted into its structure: when the instinct reawakes, those twists are re-enacted. The mind then rehearses that experience.

Is this rehearsal memory? Yes: memory has intervened, bringing not existentially the same images which the open senses produced in the presence of the original objects, but other images, such as the dreaming psyche is able to produce now; images less brutally imposed, less suddenly withdrawn, and grown ductile and transformable in the uncertain limbo which they people. They are called forth not, like the images of sense, by the impact of external events, but by the obscure currents of life within the psyche. Their roots are spread and intertwined in the same sub-soil in which the instincts are planted.

In an organism not able to learn by experience, instincts may be supposed to excite in the mind simple vacant expectancy. Uneasiness will not be accompanied by any notion of what might come, nor by any foretaste of what is desired. Concrete events will almost falsify even

this vague anticipation; because, on the scale of human affairs, occasions are never exactly repeated; and the movement of the world will
hardly have taken the same direction as the movement of vegetative
life in a particular psyche.[1] Things will never be as they were, nor as I
might wish them to be. Nevertheless, in some respects, the future may
be forecast correctly, as in astronomy and the mechanical arts, where
human ideas and human action have been abstracted as far as possible
from instinct and psychic weather, and adjusted accurately to the
measurable aspects of things.

Even in moral matters, experience is not entirely wasted. Sometimes
the burnt child dreads the fire; perhaps when badly burned, he may
want to put out all fires, even the sun. The wisdom a man may gather
from experience alone is likely to be full of crochets, superstitions, and
manias; and though these will be checked and sifted by contact with
those of other men, we see in the morality of savages what sad stuff
the result will probably be. Not the most rational part of an old man's
wisdom is transmitted or admired, but the most congenial and contagious part. Experience dies with each generation; the psyche in every
child begins again at the beginning; and if the lessons of experience
are to accumulate, they can do so only by imposition from outside, by
example, custom, and institutions. But these traditions imposed, often
superstitiously, by the howling multitude, are apt to oppress the individual in the sober balance of his faculties. They can easily become
absurd, cruel, and detestable: and this in two directions and for two
reasons. On the one hand the original maxims embodied in a tradition
were themselves empirical and incidental. They were but wild shots at
the good, probably far from being prompted by deep self-knowledge
or a wide acquaintance with the world. On the other hand, even supposing the original maxims to have been just, a new generation, under
different conditions, may find them inapplicable and, if insisted upon,
odious. Human nature is not exactly the same in youth and age, in man
and woman, in all climates and epochs—and what living judge of values
can there ever be save the heart of each individual, no matter how
singular or unprecedented?

Apart, however, from personal idiosyncrasies, the mere establish-
ment of a morality or civilisation will abolish the sort of experience
out of which it grew. Tradition, by the time it is sacred, has become

1. This happens occasionally in some odd circumstance, when a prophecy is
fulfilled.

obsolete. The trained and indoctrinated child, if ever he dares to call his soul his own, will wonder why these imposing fictions were ever adopted, and he may rashly disown them. He may then easily perish under their ruins, before, perhaps, he rediscovers their utility.

Thus from the casual and headstrong character of moral conventions, and from the radical variability of human nature, it follows that a system of morals, to be just, must take into consideration all the living interests which it touches; and that in order to remain just, it must be no less plastic than the souls and the societies over which it presides.

This is not easy, and many a conscience suffers violence in the process. Conscience moves along the spiritual tangent, in the vertical direction; manners, customs, and each man's sins, move along the horizontal level, with the other events of this world.

The synthetic nature of mind renders its relations with time very perplexing. Is feeling or intuition a spiritual act resident in one moment? A prick or flash might seem to be instantaneous, yet feeling existed before, for that surprise to impinge upon and interrupt; and feeling persists after, with the continued, actual, fading sense of that very interruption, as well as of a whole universe in the background. Does this intuition, then, reside above or beside the flux of events, so that different points of physical time can be observed by it at once, together with the transition between them? Is intuition a sort of super-temporal bracket, embracing some part of the flux of existence, and virtually, perhaps, embracing the whole world? That is doubtless what pure spirit would be, and what mind actually is, in so far as it is synthetic and stretches in the vertical direction, thinking the world, transposing it into an idea, conceiving it in its truth and under the form of eternity. Yet this is only the ideal self-forgetful dimension of thought, in its cognitive ambition. Surely in its existential capacity this ambitious thought is an event in natural time, has a beginning and an end, and even while existing moves from an initial phase to a widening view, to a clearer logic, and to a final summing up, which dismisses most of the lumber to keep only the relevant issue. But no matter what temporal vistas may be patent within the field of intuition, we are compelled to date this intuition, taken as a mental event, at the time of its organic cause. I see when I open my eyes; and the date of my seeing, though not seen, is the date of my looking.

This temporal or historical position of mind, in the midst of the existential process of nature, will have to be described by the natural philosopher according to his analysis of physical processes in general. Something, in any case, must be continuous, or the moments would not be successive; something must break in, since the continuity exhibits changes. There are also in nature certain recurring types or patterns of change, which I call tropes; and it is to certain tropes in the life of the organism, not to particular instants there, that I conceive mind to correspond. Now a trope is saturated with change, since it is a form of it: yet a form of change is not itself an event, but an essence which an event, and only an event, might exemplify: so that tropes belong intrinsically to the realm of essence, and when nature exemplifies them, also to the realm of truth. If a trope be the basis of a feeling, we can perhaps understand how, in the vertical direction, this feeling has an open field and an enduring vista, since the trope is super-temporal; while at the same time, in the longitudinal direction, the trope proceeds from a first instant, when it begins to be repeated, through expanding phases, to a summary and perhaps memorable result, when the trope has been completed. For instance, when we open our mouths to speak, the trope which our words will constitute is already initiated—though accident may cause it to lapse half-executed, or to acquire a fresh complexity; and our feeling exactly betrays this truth about things, since we know vaguely that we have something to say, and we may clarify our meaning in the act of expressing it, or may stop short altogether when we feel suddenly what a wind egg it was. In adult speech, when the grammar of the language and a stock of current phrases have been acquired, we have some intuition, when we begin to speak, of the whole sentence we are about to utter: often words at the beginning are governed, as to gender and number, by those which are to succeed. Intuition in such cases is prophetic; and the general meaning of the whole suffuses all the parts as they arise successively, and continues to suffuse the whole, when this has been finished and remains, as a whole, available to recollection. The trope, at its first stirrings, has awakened the spirit, and in executing itself has filled the spirit with the sense of that trope. There is no thoroughfare in the organism for tropes that cut across the rooted habits, as evinced by the difficulty of pronouncing a foreign language correctly: and no synthesis arises in intuition when the essences suggested distract attention from the theme in hand; although, just as the foreign language might ultimately be learned, so the most irrelevant essences, which would make nonsense in a given context, might be actually synthesised in a single intuition if viewed in

a different perspective; as for instance under the category of mere being
or of irrelevance itself or of contradiction. Speculation too has many
languages, and those we do not happen to be using are not necessarily
gibberish.

In any case, the deliverance of an intuition is just what it seems to be;
and it is in reference to that deliverance, or in the vertical direction,
that spirit is transcendental, synthetic, and poetically originally. In
glancing toward the past, present intuition re-evokes many ghostly
images, in glancing towards the future, it finds no definite resting-place,
but only projects the general medium, the mere type of opportunities,
demanded by its present equipment for life: for the psyche can expect
or prefigure only what it is ready to perform. The domestic landscape
will be expected to remain much as it is, and people the same people;
but sharply scrutinised I do not think that the idea of the future ever
copies that of the past, or merely projects memory forward, while re-
arranging some of its elements. There is an uncriticised notion that
ideas must copy sensations; and Hume thought he was rather bold in
suggesting that perhaps a shade of blue, intermediate between two
shades seen in the past, might actually be summoned up in imagination.
But can imagination *ever* reproduce exactly an image produced earlier,
under different conditions? The prejudice, once challenged, seems to
dissolve. Suppose in a dream, or in a brown study, I have a vision of
the walls of Avila, which in the past have surely impressed my eyes
many thousands of times? Which of those thousands of images comes
back to me now? Surely not any one of them, in its precision and detail;
some fresh, perhaps curiously distorted picture, doubtless determined
by the mixed propensities of nervous reflexes to revive, modified by all
the cross-currents and new dispositions of my present life. I am sure
that if I could arrest and paint this dream-picture, it would prove gro-
tesquely original; and the problem would not be so much where I got
those elements as why I so unhesitatingly identified them with the walls
of Avila, of which at best it was a futuristic emblem. For how do we
recognise of what original a mental image is a copy? Certainly not by
comparing the aspects of one with that of the other, since the image
given now is, by hypothesis, the only one present. Recognition cannot
depend on comparison, but on an emotional or motor suggestion, which
makes this image *mean* the same thing as the other to my total mind.
And this recognition can occur without any graphic image whatever,
by virtue of a name, or a sort of psychic scent carrying attention in the

requisite direction. So our attention is continually carried towards the future, not by picturing any expected events in particular, but by hunger for action and for experience, or by vague apprehension and the hope of better things.

THE NATURE OF CONSCIOUSNESS

Consciousness is an act of attention, moving from object to object, a changing feeling, having duration, and variety. Its data are always fading in one direction, and growing clear in another; it has an insecure but extended range over space and time.

Consciousness is not a datum. The datum is some essence, which may be a group or movement of essence [*sic*]; the intended object is some substance or some substantial mode. Consciousness may of course itself be thought of eventually; but only by a later or outlying exercise of consciousness.

Consciousness, since its existence begins and ends, must begin and end at some absolute instant of time. But these relations of consciousness to time are not given in consciousness. What is given is a temporal and spatial field of indefinable extent, in which the lapsing duration and simultaneous variety of objects is immediately given too. This field is without a definable centre from which consciousness could be said to survey it. Attention moves without losing its hold immediately or absolutely on what it has surveyed; its continuity is, for its own observation, only the continuance or continuity of its objects. It cannot be localised or dated intrinsically; intrinsically the whole apparition which it surveys is a transcendental centre which it always occupies and which moves with it. Extrinsically, and conventionally, its date is that of the organic process which immediately supports it; and since its roots are there, it may be assigned, by courtesy, to that place also;

George Santayana, "The Nature of Consciousness," Humanities Research Center, University of Texas. © 1969 Daniel Cory. Reflections occasioned probably by Santayana's reading of E. B. Holt, *The Concept of Consciousness* (New York: Macmillan, 1914). The title was supplied by the editors.

but in truth it occupies no place. The participation of consciousness in time is more genuine and internal than its participation in space. An omniscient observer would see that it arose, declined, and expired with the process that supports it; but never would he be able to see that it grew out of its roots or hovered above them. It is only from without, by virtue of the place of the organs it changes with and the objects it considers, that its roots in space could be found. For itself it is always in a sustained present time, and in the centre of the universe. Both specious multiplicity and specious change are given in its immediate object: it is equally synthetic and transcendental in respect to both.

But if we consider consciousness from without, and as it really exists and flows, we see that its phases succeed one another, in time, and are discrete; at any instant consciousness may cease, without any change in what preceded: and the survival or revival, of certain strains in memory is an added contingent fact to their original appearance, which the actual extinction or distortion of memory can never modify. But there is no such discreteness in the spatial status of consciousness. The specious extension given is an organised and synthesised extension; its parts are, in their size and position, *intrinsically* relative to one another; and the total has no definable centre or limits. Only when the *organs instrumental* are instrumental in producing this consciousness, or the *objects intended by it* identified in the physical world, does the consciousness assume a relation to real space at all; and it is imputed only.

The *date* of consciousness, as distinct from its temporal flow, is also extrinsic and imputed, like its position: it has no date, but is conventionally assigned to that of its organs or expression. An attempt may sometimes be made to impute to it the date of its object—as when people suppose that in vivid memory they *go back* to the past, or in prophecy pass into the future; but this is sheer confusion. The date of what we perceive or think of is relative to its surroundings, which we do not perceive; and the same is true of the date of our perception.

The data of consciousness need not be either psychic or existent. They can be essences of any sort. The existent object—the one the body is reacting upon directly or indirectly—is only believed in. The sense of its independent existence is conveyed by this conscious adjustment to it, and involves expectation, fear, affection, or command; all forms of faith, not of intuition. In other words, perception expresses attitude rather than observation. It is a judgement having phases and practical implications rather than contemplation of a distinct present object. We look before we know what we shall see; and we recognise the object without consciously describing it.

Consciousness is based on a mode of substance—on a physical process—and gives to this diffuse existence a synthetic expression. This expression is a fact in itself: it is hypostatic.

What is, or was, called a state of consciousness is rather an instance of consciousness; consciousness falling for a certain time on a certain complex of objects. It corresponds to a state or sustained process of the organ. It is not strictly a *state* of consciousness, because consciousness is not a substance that can change its form; but an awareness that can change its objects. Perceptions, feelings, emotions are not states of consciousness; they are states of the psyche involving consciousness of certain essences or things.

This is quite obvious in the cases where the essence is well articulated. A triangle is anything but a "state of consciousness." This essence is not, like consciousness, an actual existence; it exists only speciously, in that it appears; what exists actually is the consciousness of it, the hypostatic expression of the substantial process in the organ, which leads the man to think of a triangle at all.

Consciousness arises and vanishes; it is a fact, an event that actually takes place; but it is no tight little datum like the perceptions or ideas of the English psychologists; it has to be exercised, it has to be lived through. The tight little datum is never more than an essence.

The perfectly inarticulate consciousness which the child has of his mother is not, strictly speaking, *in* the child. It is certainly no part of his head, nor of his soul, nor is it properly a *part* of his consciousness, but the whole of his consciousness while it exists. It reveals a group of "neutral" qualities; but as this intuition varies with the state of the child, and in particular of his brain, it may loosely be said to be *in* either. The English idiom puts the matter fairly enough when it speaks of what we have or keep "in mind," without saying "in the mind"— good language not having yet reduced mind from an activity to a receptacle. Speech also keeps clear of paradox and confusion when it says that the child *has* these feelings, without saying that they are he or a part of him. But to say they are a part of the mother is to deny that they ever were born; and what cross-section of the good woman, I wonder, would they be found in?

SUBSTANCE

I venture to think that the essential principle of error in philosophy has always been the same; namely the metaphysical abuse of notions which in some special field might be legitimate or necessary. The Pythagoreans made metaphysics of mathematics, the Socratics of grammar and ethics; the English made metaphysics of analytic psychology, and the Germans of the criticism of knowledge. People perceived long ago that the Platonic ideas were falsely hypostasised when turned into celestial intelligences or natural powers. So people should now perceive that the "sensations" or "ideas" of the English psychologists were falsely abstracted, since they excluded both the objects that move and evolve in nature and the spiritual activities of the mind. Those sensible images are found, when we forget what we know of ourselves and of nature, and contract our gaze upon the immediate, to fix its character without interpreting the fact of its presence. This labour of analysis and scrupulous inspection is not calculated to disclose the structure or extent of the universe. To suppose that all reality is experience, and all experience such as you have had, is to make metaphysics out of humility, sceptical parsimony decreeing a little universe, while denying the great one, and decreeing that little one by an inconsistency: for the immediate really supplies only some homeless and isolated essence, and no psychic facts, much less a series of them.

As everyone knows, this very inadequacy of the English school provoked an unexampled consciousness of the machinery of intelligence. But here again the principle of error—metaphysical projection—intervened. The categories of interpretation by which human minds, here and there, may have read their experience were turned into principles generating the universe, *a priori* rules by which the visions of an absolute Dreamer must pass from phase to phase of their expansion until having absorbed European history and Protestant . . .[1]

George Santayana, "Substance," Humanities Research Center, University of Texas. © 1969 Daniel Cory. This essay is a rejected portion of Santayana's review of E. B. Holt, *The Concept of Consciousness*. The review itself is reprinted in *The Idler and His Works and Other Essays* (New York: George Braziller, 1957).

1. This is the end of page VII of Santayana's manuscript. At the top of page VIII "the infinitesimal." concludes what is presumably the same paragraph. The discontinuity of sense indicates that a portion of the manuscript is missing.—Editors.

Psychology in its turn has not escaped the ruinous honor of being turned into metaphysics and has been commissioned to support the whole universe on its slender resources. Indeed, it has begotten three differently impossible systems, one based on the hypostasis of consciousness itself, another on the hypostasis of ideas supposed to be definite, and a third on the hypostasis of feelings and dumb stresses acknowledged to be vague.

We all know the immense difference between feeling and not feeling, noticing and not noticing anything; and this is what we call being conscious of it. Why we are conscious of some things and not of others would be a hard enough question for a scientific psychology to answer: but unfortunately it is not allowed to investigate that question in peace. For it appears presently that not all we are conscious of is something substantial and sufficient unto itself, whether we notice it or not. A great deal of what engages our attention dissolves irreparably when we turn from it, and is evidently unsubstantial. Such are images in mirrors, dreams, perspectives, emotions, beauties, iridescent colours: such, in a strange and deep sense, is the whole past.

Indeed, a hasty and impassioned reflection may jump to the conclusion that no permanent object or principle inhabits the world at all, but that everything equally is an illusion, and has no being apart from the fact that we are momentarily conscious of it. This would be genuine idealism; but no philosopher of the West has held it with conviction, and most of our idealists are incapable even of conceiving it. A subject thinking, or a method of evolution in feelings, or a set of Platonic Ideas forces itself on their substantiating intellect. They cannot sink into mere consciousness and live.

If we eschew the metaphysics of consciousness, we still have the metaphysics of sensations and ideas to lead us astray. What shall we do with those discovered elements which do not seem to form a part of the substance of nature? Some of them seem quite homeless there, like the two beautiful worlds of religion and music; others are attached to things only when these are in specific relations to our persons or organs, like perspectives and foreshortenings, values, and colours. Since nature seems to disown these foundlings, might they not be laid at the door of consciousness? Might they not be made to fill consciousness up, and be its substance? Now this, which Avenarius called introjection, because it drives the objects of experience into the mind, and the mind into the brain, is a great confusion. Consciousness is no receptacle, it is no breeding-place: its objects are its objects, not its contents, as a barbarous phrase has it; which is as if the visible world were called the contents of light, or Rome the contents of the roads that lead there. Consciousness is a spiritual act, a cognitive energy falling like a light on certain things, not because it contains these things (could it perceive them if it did?) nor has any fecundity or principle of evolution in itself capable of producing them, but because in the course of nature the spark of consciousness is kindled by the contacts of things, making them incandescent, and giving to some of them an inkling of some of the others. All these appearances, even the most unsubstantial and fugitive, have an essence altogether different from the consciousness that perceives them. True, many of them do not exist except while consciousness surveys them—like pain, for instance, or dreams. Yet by applying the inapt category of substance and attribute people take these homeless essences for qualities of consciousness, as if consciousness were a canvass on which they were painted or a *camera obscura* in which they shine; forgetting that in that case a second consciousness would be needed to see them there. This aberration has become so habitual that people sometimes carry consistency and absurdity so far as to speak, under pressure, of green feelings, extended perceptions, and joyful landscapes.

The worst of it is that by this procedure external things can no longer be distinguished from consciousness; for if colour and extension are qualities of consciousness in dreams, why not in waking life also? Thus consciousness threatens again to become the only seat and bearer of existence, and all nature evaporates into an idea, or system of ideas, with which consciousness sometimes amuses itself. In our metaphysical haste, in our impatience of complexity, we have fallen into absurdity. Awareness has been turned into a locus or a power or a system of evolving images; at first of those images only which did not seem to slip easily into the context of nature, but ultimately of all images and of all objects, including nature itself. God too, I need hardly say, becomes either a notion that consciousness entertains at a certain stage in its progress, or else a popular symbol for the creative activity of consciousness itself.

Recent philosophy has made a discovery which shows a way out of many of these confusions. The immediate objects of consciousness are not ideas in the mind, nor are they necessarily material objects. They are just what they are, having logical or aesthetic being without materiality or even existence. The variety of them is endless, and they have not as we find them and in their several given fields, any natural spatial or temporal relations to one another; they are not, therefore, constituent parts of nature nor ideas or perceptions in any animal and developing mind. They are the lines, movements, relations, equations, propositions, colours, pains, beauties which changeful animal minds come upon from time to time, and may return to and repeatedly refer to, whether they be qualities of natural existences or not; in fine, they are every conceivable sensible or intelligible essence.[2]

Here again, however, where light might seem to be bursting on us, we are wrapped once more in a metaphysical cloud. Professor Holt tells us that these qualities are the "substance" of minds and of bodies; that they are "active," especially when they are propostions: that they "generate" their consequences; that a law of nature, expressed in an equation, is a "purpose"; and that the universe is a set of "purposes in conflict" with one another. Thus the new Platonic Ideas, in spite of the democratic advantage of their number and variety (for they include all possible themes of experience) thus suffer the fate that befell the old Platonic Ideas in their moral and logical dignity: they become metaphysical existences and powers. The generative equations of Professor Holt, which are purposes, bear a striking resemblance to the Intelligences of the Celestial Spheres, the angelic purposes that propelled them in perfect circles, obedient to the duty that "keeps the stars from wrong." To fix a law of nature is to fix an essence like a Platonic Idea, save that instead of being plastic and presenting the end or result of some creative operation, as the Greeks naturally did with their moral and artistic genius, we fix forms of change instead, which an impartial study of nature shows to be in truth more deeply rooted there than any types of structure or excellence. For the animal world is rich in fossils and the moral world in revolutions, but gravity and electricity seem to hold their own. If they too should some day yield to other laws, we should suppose that some law might obtain in this very mutation of laws in nature; at least that would be the last refuge of form in a world that if too closely scanned threatens to disown form altogether. The Platonic Ideas were a noble and by no means inappropriate harness for

2. Santayana clearly intended to add a further discussion of related issues here. His note to himself reads as follows: "Go on in criticism of Berkeley's ideas. The walks in a park. How long are the two converging lines? Are they equal? Where do they end? Are they straight, or do they curve round you, to meet again at the other end, behind your back?"—Editors.

reality: daily life, religion, even zoology and medicine could get on
after a fashion with those moral and rhetorical categories: but what
we call the laws of nature are far more exactly and constantly exemplified in existence than the Platonic Ideas of man or of the state. In
this lies the real advantage of modern philosophy, if we only would
make use of it: that besides that poetic and empirical morphology of
nature which divides it into things, persons, and detached events, we
possess a second, in mathematical terms, covering the continuous
change and evolution running through those plastic types that come
successively to the surface; so that what Socratic philosophy did for
morals and politics we might do for the dynamic mechanism of nature
and life—that is, observe and define what is intelligible in them. But
to suppose that equations or laws or aesthetic essences, such as colours
or sounds, provide for their own embodiment and dance down the
avenues of time in troops and choruses, is more fantastic than Platonic
metaphysics without being truer. Forms, truths, and essences are timeless, even if they refer to time, as history does: and so are all propositions and their terms. They are also without place or extension even if,
like $x^2+y^2=t^2$, they are formulas for extension and for the relative
position of parts. They could never become the origin of their manifestation at one place or time rather than at another. This in the new
realism, as in Platonism, would have to be left to the "predisposition
of matter"; yet if matter had been deprived of all inequality in character
and distribution, and turned into a metaphysical omnipresent blank, it
too could offer no foothold for the actual and local evolution of things,
nor for the individuality of what fills particular times and places. The
abstract elements of things, raised to neutral timeless and placeless
essences, can never compose things; they are forms and the elements
of forms only, not existences nor parts of existents. They are not things,
but qualify and define them. What composes things is their natural
substance, i.e., what ever indecomposable things are inside of them;
this substance is simply the things themselves, in their previous forms
(for language will speak indifferently of bread being flour, or being
composed of flour). It is the material world in its particularity and contingency that determines which qualities shall be exemplified in it, and
when, or which shall be manifested to consciousness—these not being
all of those, nor always some of them. The physical world, not a metaphysical principle or set of principles, is the basis of everything. The
neutral logical and aesthetic terms, and the types of relation, are deeper

no doubt in the realm of being than any existence, just because not being existences they are indefeasible. Yet like the Platonic forms they are impotent; they are the grammar of experience but not the voice that speaks nor the heart that hears. It is an old lesson, but hard for speculative zeal to learn, that the concrete can never be absorbed in the abstract, nor the actual in the ideal, nor the contingent in the necessary, nor the temporal in the eternal, nor the local in the universal, nor the natural in the logical, nor consciousness in things, nor things in consciousness. We must continue to expect, so long as there are metaphysicians, identifications of this sort, that miss the point and after a thunder-shower of revolution leave everything as it was before.

Professor Holt's book contains a second instance of this love of simplification at the cost of fidelity to the several natures of things. Having decreed the universe to be a complex of neutral terms and energising propositions, he tells us that consciousness is "nothing but" a cross-section of this manifold, selected by the responses of the nervous system. I cannot understand how a particular nervous system, one existing here and now, can flow from the terms and formulas that would describe equally well one that did not exist; but leaving that point I find it very plausible and luminous that the nervous system, by its responses, should determine the *range* of consciousness, that is, what objects consciousness shall regard, and under what form.

This is much the way in [which] we actually travel through nature, catching a traveller's glimpse of those aspects of it which we have the interest, intelligence, time, and education to perceive. These aspects are precisely those which our system is enabled to react upon by natural sensibility or by training. Furthermore, what we gather is not a mere abstract of the facts: we colour them by our passions and private associations. As an indication of the field from which the objects of consciousness are drawn, Mr. Holt's simile is excellent: but he has chosen it, naturally enough, to favour unduly a little equivocation he has at heart; namely, to identify this field of objects with consciousness itself. A flash-light is not merely a point of vantage, an outlook; it is a set of rays that actually fall upon the surfaces exposed to it, marking them with patches of light, so that an observer at a different station would see the same precise lines dividing the light from the shadow. A flash-light playing on the dome of Saint Peter's will leave a line of demarcation at a particular great circle of the hemisphere; so that from the side this line will appear as a concave curve, like the inside of [a] crescent.

If for the flash-light, however, we substitute an eye, which is a real organ of consciousness, the parts of the dome visible to it and lighted up, so to speak, by its movement, are not deliminated [*sic*] in any such way upon the object; they are not perceptible at all from another point of view. They are determined by a merely ideal system of lines defining the perspectives that appear from one out of an infinite number of possible stations. The fact that I occupy a particular centre determines the limits of what I see, but it does not divide the object, as the flash-light does, into a dark and a bright portion. For this reason, if I had amassed no experience, I should believe the object to have the shape of its visible part, as the young moon is thought to be materially a crescent by the ignorant: and I should suppose things to change and grow as my knowledge of them did, like an idealist. The part of the object I see is therefore deliminated [*sic*] subjectively but not objectively; and this part is erroneously supposed (until the illusion is corrected by reason) to be the whole. That is why, in current language, we speak of our ideas of objects, as if what we saw was something private and subjective, and the real objects were beyond our ken: and on this foundation we know, alas! what idealisms ensue and what denials of knowledge, out of scruple to keep to what we actually know. No: the object is not private, only the view of it is: the real substance is not beyond our ken, but is seen through a glass darkly, inadequately and redundantly: so inadequately and sometimes so redundantly that but for the impact and relation to our body, which always can identify afresh the object of intent, we might doubt whether what we see and what excites our vision had anything to do with each other. The crescent is still evidently a glimpse of the moon; even the Man in the Moon might pass for an equivalent; but is Diana merely the moon in a highly figurative presentation, or is she a merely ideal essence, or some ghost of a human huntress, associated with the moon by imaginative accident?

I know the advocates of the immediate are now fervid: the conviction that nothing occult can exist seems to kindle in some minds a sort of religious fire. Yet I cannot share that zeal, because it seems to me extremely probable and not at all distressing that nature should contain a thousand things and a thousand dimensions (as Spinoza believed) which we have no faculty of perceiving, so that much must always remain occult for us, though familiar and obvious, no doubt, to other creatures, or at least perfectly definite and clear in itself. When we are born into this life, however, we are and feel ourselves to be, in the bosom of nature as a whole; all that affects us (and its range is vague to our apprehension) all we react on, or might react on, is our initial object and concern: what controls our destiny is what we address ourselves to, from the very first, in struggle or prayer. It is therefore wholly false and inhuman to say that we know our ideas only, or are shut up in our own experience. Our experience is a manifestation of what is not experience, and our ideas are the conceptions we have managed to form of other things, material or ideal. Everywhere, from the first alarmed awakening of consciousness to the last philosophy, we envisage other creatures, or God, or matter, or truth, or what you will, but not ourselves nor our experience itself. Mere sincerity would vouch for this, if we were reduced to expressing our actual belief, and the deliverance of our intelligence; but we see this inevitable faith justified by the fact that consciousness is the spiritual expression of an animal reaction, and as the reaction responds to a pressing environment, so consciousness rightly salutes objects independent in their existence, vaguely apprehended in their nature, and formidable in their approach. What consciousness learns of this object, however, is by no means its entire constitution. A child at the breast feels its mother to exist, and it is truly she that he is aware of; but his idea is inadequate, not merely because incomplete but because mixed with other things and nebulous. So is our idea of nature, in our science and philosophy, and I fear always will be. I am not sure whether this opinion condemns me to the dishonourable but merry company of dualists: let Minos and Rhadamanthus assign me to the place where I belong, I am resigned. Our ideas, I say, are not our objects, but our description of those objects; as various theologies are not various Gods, but various descriptions of one God, which is why they disagree. True, the degree of error and irrelevance in these descriptions may be so great that the original intent to describe a felt and ominous reality may be buried under the poetic flowers of the description; as if out of the moist and querulous impressions of the young child we tried to frame an account of motherhood and of the mother. It is by no means the case that our ideas are constituent parts of our objects, nor even that the qualities they predicate of the object are necessarily to be found there. Not constituent parts; because the ideas are opinions, judgements, spiritual acts, and the objects are substances—incongruous things: not necessarily true in predicating what they do of the object, because the essences that consciousness predicates form together a complex essence, or description of the object, which is a symbol, but no part, of it: for it usually reports the movement and place of that object in relation to the observer, but adds something and, for the rest, leaves out almost everything. These symbols or ideas neither are nor are thought to be objects in themselves— except for reflection, when a science of symbols arises, if ever it does. The object symbolised is accordingly known directly and immediately, not by inference from another object known first; for the ideas are not known first, but only, if at all, long afterwards; and even if they were known, they could not be taken for symbols until a direct knowledge of the object had been attained, and the two could be compared; as is done when we learn to read.

Mr. Holt is tired of temperamental and personal systems of philosophy: it is a scientific, universal, dogmatic philosophy that he wants. Indeed, the neat literary unity of a system may well seem cheap and impertinent when substituted for the tumultuous variety of the real world. We should try to accept this indocility of things, and be docile to it. In that way we might reach the system which is in them, instead of one which we create for it out of our personal resources; we should discover "the demonstrable, coherent structure of all being, running through everything that is." This is a fine and natural ambition and if we had no memories we might all entertain it. But the immensity and heterogeneity of things, which makes them overflow any personal system, makes a total scientific survey of them impossible as well. And even if it were possible, such a total survey would be useless; for infinite wildernesses of fact would be opened up in it which neither affected our life appreciably from without nor enhanced it inwardly in contemplation. A personal system, on the other hand, being a work of studious imagination, done by a man presumably interested in right culture and in the good, throws the universe into a human perspective, and is a better thing to possess, if it is morally adequate, than infinite passive knowledge would be. It contains less and is not so bewildering, unwieldy, and portentously dull; yet in another way it contains more, since it focuses what it needs to notice of the world upon human destiny, renders it picturesque, and lights it up with a thousand rays of terror and humour. That such systems of philosophy differ from one another is no scandal; they ought to do so, like languages and works of art, provided the facts they report are genuine. The trouble with systems of philosophy is precisely that they pretend to be systems of the universe, not recognising their selective and judicial nature: if they would only abandon that grotesque pretension, and give out that they are works of meditative art and helps to wisdom, they might still show their faces in public; and it would not be hard for an honest historian to discriminate their genius from their errors. To be a philosopher in this private and ancient sense requires, of course, a certain wholeness of temperament and intellect, a certain geniality, even if it be of the cynical sort; it is not enough to have studied the sciences, not even the new logic. The sciences, no doubt, inform us about the universe, while the philosophers inform us chiefly about themselves; but that is nothing against them, for are not we philosophers the most interesting thing in the world? What the sciences tell us is fragmentary as well as miscellaneous; I am afraid neither the substance nor the limits nor the fertility of the universe will ever be exhausted by those researches. For that very reason they can go on indefinitely, from wonder to wonder in discovery; and it is well for the philosophers who live in an age of science to inspire themselves by it, if only they do not give it a false finality. As for me, I welcome this new sense for the dignity and reality of abstract being. This generous infusion of "neutral entities" into a *Weltanschauung* that had become so limp, psychological, and sentimental, this fresh recognition of a universal mechanism, and of the mathematical form of all "causes" and "forces." But I hesitate to believe that "the substance of both body and mind" is thereby discovered once for all.

COSMIC ANIMISM

A different consideration, of a speculative kind, may throw light on this whole subject. Spirit, in its actuality, is a form of life, an awareness that life comes to have vividly when it reaches a certain degree of concentration and a certain scope in responsiveness. Complete concentration with infinite responsiveness would yield the perfection of spirit. In imagination there would be a perspective of the universe in time and space, without admixture of error, yet a perspective taken from one

George Santayana, "Cosmic Animism," *Columbia Manuscript Collection.* © 1969 Daniel Cory. Rejected version of Chapter II of *The Realm of Spirit.*

point, variable, and not at all the same as the complete truth. In will and emotion there would be a unified sense of destiny and power, moving in harmony with life at that point, but by no means dominating all conditioning movements and all ulterior events. Many of these would be contrary to the life expressed at that point by spirit, or irrelevant to that life; the perfection of spirit not lying in attaining omnipotence—a mad ambition—but in attaining conformity and harmony, in spirit, with the order of nature, which though ultimately fatal to each form of spirit, existentially, is friendly to them all morally, and allows them as much room and perfection as is materially possible.

This finitude and definiteness of the life expressed in spirit are essential both to spirit and to life. Without them life could not have a body or a career amid obdurate circumstances that must be surmounted, modified, or accepted; and spirit would not have its intellectual curiosity and discipline, its loyalty to truth, its moral freshness, its dramatic experience, its saintly renunications, or its heroic allegiances.

If we attempt to conceive the whole universe as the organ of a single spirit, all these vital and spiritual characters become impossible. The world could not "exist," much less "live" if it did not change and by changing create a physical time, determining thereby a removed truth about the past and the future. To retain or foresee this truth is a primary function of spirit; yet if the organ of spirit were the whole universe at each moment, the truth could not appear to that spirit at all without appearing altogether and all at once, as it belongs to the essence of truth to subsist and to the essence of spirit to conceive it subsisting. But that would preclude change in the knowledge of truth; and since omniscience would remove or compound all the vistas of time, it would thereby kill the natural life of spirit and congeal (or exalt) it into a *nunc stans*, an all-embracing moment of knowledge incapable of movement or variation. But would such a moment be a moment of life? Involving no antecedent and no consequent, no process of anticipation and discovery, of pregnancy and expression, would it be an act of thinking? No: and the legitimacy of that conception (which I have no wish to deny) lies in another quarter. It is a poetic, dramatic, mythological conception. In it the truth, and the other goals of spiritual aspiration, are hypostasised and personified, as if already attained, and as if the attainment could constitute the whole life of a spirit, living in that moment of consummation. These anticipations, if physical, are fallacious. The goals of spirit, when momentarily attained, can be "ends" only morally; they cannot be material stopping-places, or forms of a possibly sustained life. Having touched that consummation, spirit would either perish, yielding up its breath in homage to its object, or else would pass on to other interests and other ideas, such as the natural psyche always has in store. This relaxation would not imply forgetfulness or treason towards the revelation of that supreme moment; it would rather supply fresh materials and new occasions for a return to that insight, as music in its pauses and gush of invention may be only preparing to revert with a greater volume to a fundamental theme. As music can exist only by being executed, and the themes, taken as essences, are not music but only the forms that music may take, so spirit can exist only in the process of feeling and thinking, in the passage from one term to another; the morphology of its objects, for instance of truth, not being by any possibility the morphology of spirit itself.

Thus it is absolutely essential to spirit to live in an environment other and deeper than itself; an environment which it may discover, which it may celebrate and love, with which it may attain harmony in repeated but distinct moments, each an act of apprehension, of expression, and of prophecy.

Might not the cosmos, taken in its temporal process, be the organ of a universal spirit, not omniscient, not dominating the whole past and the whole future, but retaining a vast memory, where the structure of things still kept plastic the organs used in the past, and animated by vivid prophecy, in so far as that same structure already contained, in germ, the organs destined to mould the future? The world would then be a solitary giant, living a natural life, impulsive and pensive, artful and wise, but ignorant of his origin and ultimate fate, or of any reason or necessity in his existence, his preferences, or his powers. A Polyphemus, a Pfafner, if you will; but hardly the sort of animal in which spirit would be likely to be much clarified, if we may trust the analogy of our own bodies. It is not in their internal operations, or even in their generative impulse, taken as a physical promise and power, that our bodies bring spirit to light, but rather in the outer organs [of] sense, and in the vicissitudes of fortune amid recognisable external objects and kindred persons. Solitude is sought by hermits, but only because they know society and prefer to converse with the few great ultimate companions of the soul, rather than with a multitude of distracted men and women. A god having nothing but his own body to observe or to care for would breed, if anything, a busy vegetative consciousness; and his solitude would not be a disillusioned choice of company, but a beastly immersion in his own flesh.

Pantheism, in so far as it is a religious conception and posits true spirit in the universe, does not therefore arise at all by virtue of inspection and analogy, as if the cosmos were too like a human body not to have a corresponding soul. On the contrary, the more such inspection is practised, the slighter that analogy appears, and the more remote from spirit grows the principle seeming to be at work in the world. The source of pantheism is the same as that of popular belief in deities, and popular dramatisation of natural powers and events. Pantheism is a universalised myth, the sympathy of man with nature overflowing into an intuition of infinite life, knowledge, and bliss, seeming to flow from that unfathomable power which excites these feelings in us. It is a common delusion that nothing specific could arise unless a great quantity of the same thing existed previously, ready to be drawn upon. In genuine observers pantheism tends to become nothing but a religious or conceptual mask for naturalism. Where on the contrary the spiritual nature of the universal deity remains dominant, as in India, observation becomes unnecessary and fancy can take its place, the world in any case being reduced to an unsubstantial and self-dissolving apparition, and the spirit—the divine spirit in us—feigning, denying and outlasting a thousand worlds.

Spirit, in such an absolute idealism, seems to have it all its own way, and whilst not literally distributed over those various universes (which never truly exist) yet pervades the whole reality, in the sense of being the seat of all illusions. But this absoluteness of spirit conceals a horrid secret by a mere trick of inattention and eloquence. Spirit, that makes possible all this fugitive experience, ought to be in itself perfectly collected, lucid, and calm; something not itself, then, engages it in these vain dreams, catches its light on contingent objects, and stains it with alien colours, so that after all we virtually reinstate the naturalism of common sense. Everything in the spirit, if not spirit itself, is the work of matter; and if we insist that the spirit retains its exclusive actuality, yet all that fills and diversifies the life of spirit assaults it by an alien fate. We are left with the cheap satisfaction of calling the vision a passing delusion and unreal, though like the ghost of Banquo it will not down. Is not the crime that pursues us more deeply our own than the intellectual exorcism by which our philosophy would disown it? We may flower into spirit sometimes by divine grace, but our substance and soil are earthly.

Monism has a nullifying result. In making all things one, it washes out the essence of each of them, even of that one to which they are all reduced. Thus it seems a grand conclusion to declare that all is spirit; but if all is spirit, spirit must possess all the attributes and perform all the functions of matter. In what respect, then, would it still be distinctively spirit?

If, on the contrary, we retained a spontaneous dualism, we might perhaps hope to trace spirit by some special operation proper to it in nature, seeing that we have experience of many events that matter, without spirit, would never produce. Which are these events? Those actions and works which we forecast in idea, and perform intentionally. A circumspect philosopher might at once observe that our intentional works and actions, such as writing books, are never performed by spirit alone: they are performed by our bodies, guided, as we suppose, by our thoughts. But these thoughts, which seem to bloom in our bodies, are rooted and were planted there by physical agencies not impossible to trace: by contagion through the actions and words of our elders, by impressions coming from things and arousing impulses that spirit in us was very far from inspiring or having any notion of, such as the impulse to fight, to eat, or to make love. Therefore, although we do not normally write books or even letters without conscious intent and some prophetic anticipation of what we mean to do, the existence of this intent and this anticipation in us is materially conditional. They could not otherwise, in their purely spiritual capacity, have any connection with the rest of our lives, arise at a particular date, be relevant to a particular occasion, or know what lever to turn so as to secure the performance of the intended act. Even as it is, they know nothing of those levers, and commonly have but an indicative vague notion, clarified as the action proceeds, even of the result they mean to obtain. Frankly, it is not the anticipation or the intent that do the work; they merely summon it, half in the dark, into existence; and behold, into existence it comes, though often not quite as expected. Yet in the absence of any notion of the hidden mechanism by which both the action and the anticipation of that action are produced, we are reduced to living by guess-work and implicit faith, attributing our actions to rhetorical motives that perhaps were never really ours, but that describe

our action and secret passion in the conventional dramatic language of
our society. Very little actual intelligence or purpose, often none whatever, accompanies our lives. But there is abundant language at hand,
to describe behaviour and disposition in moral terms; and whenever
a man is manifestly selfish or gluttonous or drunk or sneaking or in
love, we are quick to supply him with an imaginary consciousness, and
if we are clever, with just the thoughts and words suitable to his observed character. These thoughts and words were probably never ours,
nor those of our audience, that declares them true to life or inspired
by the insight of genius. They are life-like not because they ever were
experienced by anybody, but because they put graphically before us
the gesture, the temper, the consequences of human life as observed.
Poetry and wit are behaviouristic without knowing it: and psychology
is a science of observation. It is only indirectly allied to spirit, in that
the visible performances and predicaments so set forth may put before
the psychologist a vivid picture of life in its moral upshot and emotional
ups and downs; suggesting the unobservable experience of others, and
clarifying his own.

In strictness, then, there are no events that nature might not produce
without spirit, except the inner life of spirit itself. Since this inner life
is essentially invisible, imponderable, and impossible to place in the
context of natural objects, there is no means of discovering where it
exists and where it does not. We are reduced to specifying the occasions
on which, by spontaneous sympathy, nature excites in us the sense of
an ambient or a planning spirit. Religion and poetry thus have a free
field, but superstition may also invade it; and in philosophy there is
need of caution, if we wish not to mistake dramatic convention for
spiritual insight.

The chief witness conventionally invoked for the presence of spirit
in nature is the otherwise unaccountable character of certain events.
When are events unaccountable? When they are unfamiliar, or seen
suddenly in an unfamiliar light? Not much profundity is required to
convince us that the commonest and simplest events are unaccountable
logically. They are contingent, and therefore unaccountable in existing
at all; and nothing can account for the form or law of their connections.
Gravity, motion, time, change are names for brute facts. If spirit must
be invoked to account for all these unaccountable facts, spirit is evidently at the root of everything. But alas, if spirit be conceived as one
more fact, its existence too is perfectly unaccountable; and its connec-

tion with other events or power to produce them is not only unaccountable but incapable of being represented in any image, spirit and nature not having any dimension in common. We can see things grow or change, though we do not understand how this happens; but we cannot see spirit intervening to make them change or grow. The appeal to spirit therefore only multiplies the insoluble problems presented by events, if we aspire in any intellectual sense to account for them.

But the advantage of appealing to spirit lies in another quarter. Spirit, unaccountably existing amid unaccountable events, is conceived to *wish* to exist, and to *wish* that events should take one course rather than another; whereas matter is conceived to exist and to change willy-nilly. Add, then, to unaccountable events an unaccountable wish that they should occur, and morally you have accounted for them; while the wish itself does not need to be accounted for, because morally, when we wish to do what we do, the whole event is explained perfectly. The insertion of an imaginary spirit into events does not help in the least to explain them causally; it overloads the facts to be explained; but it assimilates them to facts which, for dumb emotion, do not need explaining. We reduce ourselves, and we reduce the universe in idea, to the condition of the innocent bride finding herself at last in the bridegroom's arms, forgetting all past difficulties, unconscious of future troubles, not pretending to understand herself or her love or her lover, but simply crying: I am so happy! A wave of conscious bliss may thus quench all cavils about existence; and a wave of resolution, a firm prophetic resolve, master of its instruments, may mystically suffice to assure us that the planned events will occur, and that they will occur because we willed them.

Spirit, in its prosperous moments, thus becomes in its own eyes a magician; its life suffuses all life, its light suffuses all nature, and nothing need be taken into account, save the victorious crescendo of its inner music. In this sense, and in this sense only, events are accounted for when they are attributed to the intervention of spirit.

The problem for the historian or the psychologist is not to distinguish those events that require spirit to produce them, but to distinguish those that suffice to produce spirit. For as the bride's happiness is not the ground of her youth, her prettiness, or her good fortune, but these the cause of her happiness, so the source of all will and ideas, and of spirit itself, lies in the existence and energies of men's bodies, not the source of their bodies in their ideas or their will. This is so obvious

that we might wonder at the contrary impression that seems to prevail
in people's minds, or at least in their language. Yet the illusion is not
unnatural, and not so great an illusion in effect as it would become if
taken literally and logically analysed. The intended objects of ordinary
perception are physical, and common sense never conceives them to be
other than physical; yet the vehicle of this perception is imagery, and
the vehicle for reflection and utterance concerning those physical objects is words. Now both words and images are creatures of the psyche,
existing speciously only as they traverse the spirit. Terms of spirit
therefore necessarily fill the foreground of experience, although the
source and object of this experience is avowedly the world. In other
words, apprehension is naturally poetical; it is emotional, dramatic,
and animistic; so that the world that comes before us when we open
our eyes is saturated, for our apprehension, by the quality of our own
animal life.

This quality, among other things, is prophetic. In a psyche organised
to meet future contingencies there must needs be much restless preparation for action, and many a budding rehearsal of the great things to be
done. These rehearsals often carry conscious foretastes or images of
those actions, as well as the will and propensity to do them. Otherwise,
this immense psychic preparation would remain unknown to the spirit:
and such indications as come to light eventually are still terribly inadequate to convey the historical springs and physical machinery of
life. Yet in time conventional tropes and proverbial notions about
human motives and purposes establish themselves in the mind, sufficient to indicate in dramatic terms and on the human scale the origin
and issue of ordinary actions. Not of human actions only, but of all
nature, which comes to be conceived on the same dramatic model.
Hence much animism and mythology, which may range from close
observation and semi-humorous attribution of spiritual intentions to
things, as in fables about animals, up to the wildest cosmological
dreams and multiplied theogonies. Such fabulation is taken by sane
people with a grain of salt, and great uncertainty remains as to the
degree of literalness of conscious metaphor intended. People often talk
in parables with a keen sense of their own wit and invention, leaving
the facts thus satirically sketched to work themselves out as they may
in the shadow; and even in the most critical science figures of speech
have to bridge the gaps in experimental knowledge, if not to supply
axioms for the whole construction.

The great difficulty, the rooted illusion hardest to extirpate, does not regard fabulous physics but fabulous psychology. It is in ourselves that we are fundamentally deceived. Spirit awakes in us like an infant king born to the purple but helpless; yet soon childish ignorance and royal pride unite to produce in it a sense of absolute power. Painful is the education of young omnipotence, and apt to issue in disaster. The spirit, convinced of its authority, may obstinately defy circumstances and prefer ruin to compromise; or else, in order to maintain the illusion of freedom to do as it will, it may turn into the path of least resistance, adopt fashionable vices and dominant opinions, and profess to lead in whatever direction it is carried. The ruin in this case is moral, as in the other case physical; spirit perceives in time the nature of moral dominion. Zeal wastes itself in commanding, fuming, and criticising, unless the will represents physical powers capable of giving shape to physical events; and in some measure such potentialities always exist, since otherwise indignation and zeal would have no fuel in the psyche to burn, and no reason for taking their actual direction. With this vital root in the organism, and the easy contagion of moods and gestures in an animal society, what seems a purely spiritual passion may start great currents in the world. An opportune word may precipitate a coalescence of forces in an unexpected direction, and perhaps bring about the triumph of an idea long nursed and proclaimed in vain. The secret of power is intelligence, but not as callow intelligence might suppose. You may command only by obeying; and the dignity of ruler, be [it] in the world or in the heart, hangs on obeying the hidden, constant, irresistible physical currents of order and of change, while defying the ignorance and delusions of the hour. Your victory will not always be a victory over your enemies; it may be a victory through them. The collapse that would follow their nominal triumph, the shame that would bury it, would vindicate your insight. Spirit, like any other living natural thing, has its internal troubles and victories; but in respect to the rest of nature the office and possible success of spirit is a success not in control but in expression. If then it has expressed the deepest currents of life in the world, and forecast their possible culmination, it has done for the world all that spirit can do: to enjoy, to understand, and to judge it.

The darkness cannot be expected to comprehend the pure light of spirit that shines in it, but will confuse that light with the drift of psychic powers which it renders half visible. When a man feels his rising wishes or courage or intentions he may say it is his "spirit" inspiring him; but this "spirit" is then only a name for his passions, for the impulsive and prophetic powers of his psyche, of his animal life. These may be on the point of working a revolution in the world; but he may fancy that the half-phrased thoughts or hopes that actually cross his mind, and are perhaps true omens, are the source and cause of themselves and of the actions and effects ensuing. This "rationalised" view of his conduct is conventional, and if taken seriously superstitious; yet it serves as a model for "rationalising" events occurring in human society or even in nature at large. The error here is double: anthropomorphism on the surface, easily detected and discounted; and, below that, a profound ignorance and misconception regarding that human life of the mind which is taken as an exemplar and thought to be self-explaining.

The notion—expressed on a grand scale in religion and mythology, but seldom examined psychologically—seems to be this: that wishes and projects occur of themselves for no reason and that, when they have occurred, they cause actions and objects to conform to them. This notion is drawn from the more sophisticated levels of language and conduct, where planning takes place. In planning a house or a conspiracy we express our ideas as eloquently and precisely as possible, putting them down, perhaps, on paper; and we check the plan too zealously by our guiding motives to ask ourselves why we have embraced these motives or entered at all upon such a work. Then, with our heads heated and our wills sharpened, we cannot help seeing friends and enemies everywhere; and we vividly imagine prophetic schemes and explicit ideas to have inspired every event that occurs in the world. If by chance we ever ask ourselves whence came such various wills, especially when sharply contrary to our own, or suddenly favourable, we have only one answer ready: From sheer wickedness or from sheer kindness.

Now this moralism is no less absurd in psychology than it is in physics. Was it kindness or wickedness that caused fish to breed in the water and human beings to drown in it? Is water, like Neptune, wicked and kind by turns, and is that its whole substance? Can the need for water or for air arise in animals before they have been born in that element? Could they be prepared, without a prolonged evolution, to exist in a form that can consciously demand that medium, or suffer agonies in its absence? Will is therefore neither wicked nor kind, but constitutional. An animal exists as it can exist; and its will is the report to consciousness in him, when he is conscious, of the direction his nature has acquired. This direction may be opportune; then he will be a normal, good, and healthy creature, with a sane will; or the direction of development acquired may be unfortunate or fatal, and then he will be sickly, vicious, or insane, and the whole world in his eyes a chaos of injustice.

But the case is not so simple. Were conscious will merely a sense of effort or precipitation, a blind impulse, it might perhaps be still thought to be absolute and substantial, as some philosophers actually interpret matter to be essentially a felt energy or strain; yet this semi-animation in matter would be too evidently the sport of material relations and material laws to be confused with spirit. Spirit eludes place and date and mathematical calculation, being essentially a moral and intellectual commentary on events. What lifts will into this region is the fact that far from being a mere strain or impulse or effort, it is a preference or choice between ideas. This gives it its conscious freedom: the occasion and the alternatives may be material, but the preference and the choice —in intent, if not in performance—are spiritual pronouncements, moral events.

Hence the very common persuasion that mind and will, in the form of a choice between ideas, inserts itself into the course of events, and determines their direction. Free will selects the idea preferred, and nature then executes that decree, and realises that idea in the material sphere. This is often a true description of experience as it flows; it is autobiographically accurate. But the level of autobiographical accuracy is the immediate, the most superficial of levels; and only the solipsist could even aspire to regard it as the sum total of the facts concerned. I have already noted the astonishing silence of subjective idealism on the most important of questions, namely, how initial phenomena are produced, and in what order they may be expected to appear. Their real cause and origin, as everybody knows, is the body and the physical world around it; but this basis having been removed in theory, all expectation and all collateral assurances about what exists, ought to lapse, and an abyss of nothingness ought to be felt to open beneath, around and beyond the present moment of consciousness. No such abyss arrests the imagination, because scepticism is only an academic pose, or a mystic defiance of convention which lasts, in a sincere form, only for a moment, and yields at once to the return wave of conventional sanity. The world, masked perhaps under a new nomenclature, re-asserts its existence; especially the social world, which allows the sceptic to conceive it in psychological terms, as a tangle of biographies; and he may forget to ask what evidence, on his principles, he can have of its reality. Everything continues to be talked about, for instance by Comte and by John Stuart Mill, on the assumptions of common sense, that is to say, of materialism; and this framework remains standing under the name of an intellectual fiction, to support and interrelate the scattered sparks of human consciousness which, according to them, constitute the sole reality.

There is therefore, for the psychological idealist, just as much and just as little spirit in the universe as for the materialist; only that in-stead of being spread out over the material world, and concentrated in animal psyches, it is spread out, *as if there were a material world,* over absolute vacancy.

IMAGINATION

There is one element in imagination, as in all mental things, which is immaterial, namely, consciousness. But consciousness, a cognitive and synthetic function of pure spirit, is similar in all instances of it, and contains no ground for its own existence, much less for the various qualities and movements of its objects. The qualities and movements of material things, however, (as we shall see in the Fourth Book) do supply a natural ground for the existence of consciousness, and for its varying intensity and scope. They also contain the only possible ex-planation of their own variations, which, as exploration proceeds, ap-pear more and more minute, complex, calculable, and continuous. The existence and flow of imagination are controlled by matter.

Imagination, in its beginnings, is continuous with perception. As the waves, says Hobbes, after the wind dies down, give not over rolling,

George Santayana, "Imagination," *Columbia Manuscript Collection.* © 1969 Daniel Cory. A notebook entry, with "Chapter IV" written over the title. The reference to the future "Fourth Book" suggests that this was not meant for *The Realm of Spirit,* even though it might naturally have fit there.

so sense, after the object is removed, retains its motion: and fancy is decaying sense. Yet this connection of imagination with the external world, obvious in the beginning is soon lost and obscured, owing to the hidden cerebral labyrinth in which the currents which carry imagination with them meet. It therefore seems, after a little, that the course of imagination has nothing any longer to do with what is happening in the world of matter; and its liveliness and fecundity are attributed to the will, or to genius, or to chance—or to some other pompous synonym for ignorance. Youth, love, and wine, however, are well known to quicken the imagination; and opiates to swell it and make it monstrous; while hard labour and a sound digestion quiet it, and fatigue and an-aesthetics may arrest it altogether. These indications are telling; and ingenious observers can succeed in tracing almost all the figments and vicissitudes of the fancy to some prototype or impulse in the material world.

Dreams, they say, are guided by profound and tortuous passions, which during waking life are relegated to the background or suppressed altogether; and it looks as if in each man there were several levels of ideation, and several types of character, which may be suspended or renewed alternately, with comparatively little intermingling of their currents. It is to these submerged lives within that a life wedding eloquence, intention, conversion, and madness may be traced, as well as voluptuous reveries, fictions, revelations, and dreams. The wealth of the imagination is thus seen to be greater even in plain men than hasty convention supposes; but no advance is made in understanding the mechanism of the objects that appear in these various fields of ideation. To attribute them to the passions or interests which they entertain is idle: for what, then, institutes these passions, or directs them in the choice of their objects? It is pure verbiage to attribute ideas to a tendency to form those ideas: either the ideas have no ground, or the "tendency" that produces them must be the operation of some object or organ otherwise discoverable. These objects or organs can, up to a certain point, be found in early surroundings, startling accidents, sex, etc.; but the thread of objective causes is soon lost, and words or vague physiological analogies have to supply the place of precise knowledge. How, for instance does "sex" operate on the imagination? The conventional account of this mystery (and psychology here is little more than convention) would be that nature has attached pleasure to certain contacts and to certain images; that what is pleasant is retained if possible in consciousness; and that erotic reveries and dreams obey this interest in keeping pleasant images and sensations before us. But errors and inversions of fact simply saturate this account. Nature has *not* attached pleasure to any contacts or images taken in themselves; whether these objects are pleasant is due entirely to other circumstances, such as the ripeness and momentary activity of sexual impulses: the very same image and contact being annoying or indifferent or repulsive, according to the residual underlying mood of the man. Even the acme of sexual experience itself may be almost pleasureless, when it is not craved or is crossed by alien preoccupations. And as to images, the light of pleasure plays upon them most inconstantly and only in occasional moments; like the spell of beauty, actually felt, the power to stimulate lust is a most adventitious property coming to them from without, and like reputation according to Iago, got without merit and lost without deserving. Nature has attached no pleasure to any specific object but pleasures involved in profound and untraced reactions of the body, when they happen to be set in motion when some image is before the mind, suffuse it for a moment; and the poor idolater may afterwards fancy these images have pleasure to give, while it was the warmth of his own blood that, by chance, lent them all their charm; and when the blood has thoroughly cooled whole cohorts of houris will not warm it, so as to make themselves seem beautiful again. We must remember, too, how arbitrary the qualities are that arouse desire. The charm of youth and bloom, for instance, is sometimes overwhelming, and it is far more closely related to probable fertility than to sensual pleasure; so that, if these qualities please, it is because they stimulate passionate desire, and if they stimulate it is because, by their physical operation, they are already found [to] excite sexual reaction. The whole conventional introspective view of such a matter is accordingly foolish and merely rhetorical. The hold which any image ha[s] on the soul is, in its basis and substance, a hold which one material object has on another. If my hand is caught in the wheels of a machine, the fact that my attention is chained to these objects is not referred even by the silliest of idealists to a genius on my part spontaneously interested in imagining such a situation. Yet that would be the only consistent view for the rhetorical psychologist, since when my brain is electrified by erotic effluence of some passing body, because the material meshes in which I am caught are less visible, he tells me that my sinful attention spontaneously selects that image and that my secret pleasure tempts me to keep it in mind—no matter how cruel and distracting I may actually find that obsession.

Nevertheless the movement of fancy is so vigorous and incalculable, and it seems often so irrelevant to the surrounding facts of nature (for perception and imagination run on side by side) that mankind has always supposed that the mind had a life of its own: people have supposed that the soul is a separable substance, or that mental life moved on an independent plane of existence, parallel to the plane of matter. How natural this illusion is appears in the superstitions of savages, who all believe that souls of their enemies and of their relations survive their bodies, at least for a time, and continue feebly to exercise their malign and sneaking influence. For while the world of imagination is reputed to be a separate stream of being, it is not (except in the theory of a few philosophers) cut off from influence on the material world; on the contrary, just as it takes from nature themes for mental elaboration, so it is thought to impose on nature its designs when formed; and the material and the mental flux (people think) influence one another, but hardly in the same sense; since mind draws its materials from nature, only by a kind of reproduction, or of sensuous photography, while it bestows on nature new forms at will, by a kind of magic. This barbarous commerce is still admitted in popular psychology; and on the same level the belief in surviving ghosts, in groundless ideation, and in creative will, flourish congenially together.

Now the objects given in animal perception are not ideas. Sensible qualities are predicable of the objects, and not of the consciousness of them; what is hot is the fire not the mind that perceives the heat. How then should the very same qualities, present in imagination or in dreams, become qualities of the mind? The object that wears these qualities (if there is one) must be of the same sphere as the material objects in which these qualities were originally found. Let such a material object seem not to exist behind the images of the fancy which, though both inadequate and redundant, is unmistakable, and sufficient for significant reference of the visionary appearance to the mechanical reality. The problem is thus raised to a much higher generality, when we consider that even in perception the immediate *ground* of our perception is in the brain, not in the perceived object; and that the quality attributed to the object by sense is not always present in it bodily, but is often a fanciful translation of some relation or some dynamic process subsisting between the object and our bodies. Now in fancy too the brain is undoubtedly active, and therefore the same *ground* for ideation exists as in the case of external impressions; while the non-existence of an object such as is imagined is only an exaggerated instance of the non-existence of an object exactly such as is perceived. In both cases there is a real object, inadequately and redundantly presented; but in fancy and particularly in dreams, this inadequacy and redundancy are extreme, so that we may say there is little relevance left between the natural causes of the dream and the aesthetic essences it discloses; while in the case of perception this relevance is considerable, though far from entire.

Accordingly, reveries, thoughts, plans, dreams can have none but a material basis. Although we are ignorant of what this basis is in its middle course, so to speak, we see its extremities, in the determining influence of blood, sex, age, and environment, on the one hand, and on the other in the motor tendency, in the artistic expression, in which imagination invariably issues. I watch the landscape, and it is admitted that here the images visible to me, as the clouds gather, or the trees sway, vary with the changes in the material object, and because of them. It is further known that I should not perceive these external changes, go on as they might, if I had cataracts in my eyes, or a lesion in my brain; the immediate ground is therefore not the mere existence of the object, but its operation upon the inner parts of my body. Later, by my fireside, I see those clouds and swaying branches again, or rather a half-formed, ill-focussed, fugitive ghost of them; but my sense of their identity, my recognition of their presence, is far surer than my memory of their exact aspect. What does this mean? That the immediate ground of my former perceptions, the effect the objects produced in my brain, has been partly reformed within me (nervous processes being very mobile, and quick to acquire habits) and especially that the motor attitudes and general reverberation of those impressions is almost exactly renewed. Nay, sometimes, it is not until the images are recalled in reverie that the full sentiment and magic of them is felt; that is, in the haste of actual perception, other stimulations interfere with a full digestion of what the eyes drink in; but at a moment when impressions are less crowded and loud, the whole system settles, as it were around the revived movement, and the imagination grows poetical, moral, total, warm. But what now? I find myself, pencil in hand, reproducing with a motion the curves of these trees and clouds, bringing them (though in a qualified form, with the unconscious bias of my temperament, and with my sign upon them) in material shape again before me, and before all men drawn upon a sheet of paper. This drawing, let me observe, is no copy of the image actually flickering in my mind's eye; it is a tentative, surprising creation of the hand, far more complex and true than that unseizable image. All I can do is, as I draw, to say (like any bystander) yes, yes, or no, no, to my gradual miraculous reproduction of what I had once seen; but see no longer. That is, I recognise the object more easily than I imagine it, and I reproduce it more fully and accurately than I recall it. What is the meaning of this? Evidently that the trees and clouds soaked my body in their subtle but manifold emanations, and bent and predisposed it to random imitative reactions: and that to this bodily *enacting* of the objects before me, this mimicry of my environment by my whole organism, original perception, later imagination, poetic emotion and artistic impulse were all incidental. How this profound and pervasive, though almost insensible, imitation of all things by the sensitive body occurs, I am at a loss to conceive; I beg the physicists and physiologists to make some effort to tell us. But I am aware of it in myself; I observe it in others, especially as time subdues [?][1] them to the element in which they live; and the very existence of imitative arts proves it, I think, beyond cavil. The imagination, while we labour, is an accompanying observation of images that come unbidden, that change, vanish, and reappear, as the artist's work proceeds, according to the dryness or exuberance of his momentary condition, his freshness, fatigue, or incidental excitement —for any stimulus stimulates the whole brain. Nothing could be more false and superficial than to suppose that the given images govern the work, and are themselves groundless or voluntary. To choose my images I should need to possess them already so as to know what I wanted. But why do I possess those I do, and not other and better ones? And why do I wish to summon or focus any of those I have? All that can be said is that the *body* presents these images, and no others, and that the *body* knits itself together to enact this impulse and not that. A man's body is his genius.

---

1. It is difficult to get an accurate reading of this word.—Editors.

V

The Relativity of Morals

THE UNIT IN ETHICS IS THE PERSON

Man is born dependent. He did not create himself, as he may like to imagine afterwards in his insulated self-consciousness. He had to be begotten by a blind accident; he had to be fostered, carried, suckled, and protected for nine months before his birth and at least for nine years after. His utter helplessness on coming into the world condemns him and all mankind to live more or less in society.

Nevertheless both in the womb and in the world each human creature germinates darkly but spontaneously after his own fashion; and if cast up when not too young on some tepid South Sea island, he might grow up alone into a Caliban or an Ariel. Poets, hermits, and ancient philosophers, not to mention madmen, have dreamt of that sort of life, and sometimes attempted to practise it; and there are periods in adolescence and also in old age when the intrusion of other people becomes rather a nuisance, and when rapture as well as comfort can be found only in solitude.

This latent impulse to isolation, this dream of independence, this possibility of living alone with God, with nature, or with thought has the deepest biological roots; and it supplies the moralist with his ultimate criterion in two directions: politically, for judging the justice and rationality of institutions, and spiritually, for opening the gates to freedom in art, in love, and in religion.

The dominance of social impulses in man, imposed by his mode of breeding and by his tribal life, cannot destroy the organic unity and singleness of his person. The biological unit is the individual body, the spiritual unit is the individual soul. Society, with the religions and philosophies that may prevail in society, has no other footing: if the individual were not social there would be no society. Persons may be

George Santayana, "The Unit in Ethics Is the Person," *Columbia Manuscript Collection.* © 1969 Daniel Cory. Probably an early draft for *Dominations and Powers.*

very much alike by nature: they may have grown out of one stem like grapes in a bunch; there may be little or nothing exceptional in any of them. Yet the common hereditary essence repeated in each can exist only in these repetitions; it can figure in the world only because one or more persons exemplify that essence and are moved by those passions.

Now the nature present in individuals of one race is not identical in all, nor at all times in any person: it involves a cycle of human seasons and a contrast of sexes. The picture of society therefore exhibits many a trope, many a pattern of complementary figures and responsive changes, which envelope the individuals: and in this formal sense society has a unity and character of its own, quite other than that of its members. It is not an animal but an institution.

There is also a psychological sense in which an individual may transcend himself. His thoughts will embrace all his familiar surroundings; and his habits being necessarily social, his passions will be social too. The scope of his affections may eventually extend over the whole world, or even to an imagined infinity: yet this love and imagination are lodged just as snugly in his private animal heart as is the most sordid instinct. Somebody must feel everything that is felt; somebody must say or do everything that is said or done. It is only by a conspiracy of individuals that society can act, and only by the voice of individuals that it can be judged.

This fact is so obvious that it might seem hardly worth mentioning; and the contrary ways of speaking are so clearly metaphorical that we may let them pass with a smile. Yet the truism that only animals are animate, and that only individuals can speak or think has important implications. One is that in the most docile and gregarious creature there is a possibility of independence, and a point at which rebellion will occur. The most irresistible social influences sweep down upon a living organism already endowed with a life of its own, which it cannot rescind without perishing altogether and ceasing to be a slave of society or an enthusiast for it. The most tempestuous propaganda and the most cruel persecution must reckon with their host. Man was not made for the Sabbath, and the Sabbath must find some accomplice in human nature, some tender spot in the imagination, before it can hope to be honoured or even conceived.

If anyone, therefore, ever recognises a duty or amiably considers another's pleasure, he does so *necessarily* on his own authority and by obeying some impulse within himself. And if he is ever tempted away from his highest good, as his radical nature and capacities define it, this happens because his moral condition is largely chaotic, with intermittent passions differently sensitive at different times, and fanned by variable breezes: so that trivial but tempting occasions may entice him from the deeper allegiance of which he is but vaguely conscious. The best is distant, and the steady repressions it would impose have never been deciphered. He will never upbraid himself for his inconsistencies and treasons, unless he can find those neglected loyalties alive in his heart. If he can, he will have retained or awakened reason and conscience within himself, and will be capable of shame and repentance. But if the temptations have ceased to tempt, or the unity of will and character to assert itself, he will regret neither commissions nor omissions; and everything not demanded by his present temper will drop out of his moral world. The public may call him a villain; but he will despise that judgement, and think the public a gang of tyrants or of hypocrites, or positively possessed by the devil and enemies of light.

The principle of right choices in morals—call it reason or conscience —is accordingly a power of synthesis in the will, by which all impulses rooted there are collated, and a resultant course is discerned to be the best possible. This acceptance of the best will be sacrificial but rational: and any failure to act accordingly will be due to weakness or distraction, not to moral doubt. Such a synthesis is possible only in an individual mind capable of integrity; so that social bonds have moral authority only if they can justify themselves to the inner man, and subserve a spiritual life.

PSYCHE OR TROPES

The most remarkable and solid unit in the moral world is the individual person: nor are any beginning or endings in nature more unmistakable than birth and death. Neither, indeed, is absolute: a life is a trope; a

George Santayana, "Psyche or Tropes," *Columbia Manuscript Collection.* © 1969 Daniel Cory. The provisional title of this interesting fragment was meant by Santayana as a note to himself for its future placement in *The Realm of Matter.*

substance runs through it which pre-existed and which survives: while the recognisable trope itself does not disappear with the disappearance of each of its instances, but defines them one after the other. Yet by falling into this recognisable human form, modified in each case by circumstances, that flowing substance generates a man. How? A seed, a fostering environment, food, and time are required for birth. The elements absorbed would be impotent of themselves to compose such a being; the seed must contain a material nucleus of order—I will call it a psyche—by which the requisite elements are selected, arranged, and kept for a time (which we call a life) in organic circulation; else they form sediments, or are exuded, until the organising force of the psyche proves too weak for its many commitments, so that the circulation ceases, and death ensues. There is no psyche in the residuum: yet the human trope does not become in consequence suddenly obsolete; it continues to develop out of the seed which the dead man, or his contemporaries, had shed in their prime, and is reproduced with slight variations in their offspring and descendants for indefinite ages.

Such, in the rough, is the most notable instance of genesis which a philosopher can observe; and he can observe it from within as well as from without, a fact which may compensate in a measure for the rough view, all out of scale with the presumable texture of nature, which the outside presents to his senses, or even to his biological science. Generation is a miracle to his mind, but to his instincts it is a destiny, even more irresistibly insidious when not understood than when foreseen and desired. The inner human cycle of hunger, playfulness, hunting, love, and paternity proves to experience that genesis and the ordering of human life are perfectly spontaneous and blind inwardly, however familiar or mechanical they may come to seem when surveyed from a distance.

A philosopher whose reflection remains on the level of humanism might be content to say that there exists a miraculous supermaterial power, the idea of man in God, perpetually renewing its operation in nature. This expresses the broad facts, though without accounting for the occasions on which they arise, or the variations which they show. If a divine idea operates, it operates only under conditions, the chief of which are that the psyche be transmitted by sexual fertilisation, and that its growth be fostered by a suitable environment. Moreover, the most rapid glance at the world will show that the human psyche is only one among many; all animals and plants are generated and preserved in a similar fashion; they all go through the cycle of birth, propagation and death. Indeed, the analogy runs deeper. The seasons, the weather, the rise and fall of human institutions, even celestial and chemical motions obey some such vital rhythm, yet with this notable difference, that in inanimate processes genesis is from the end of one trope to the beginning of the next, whereas in living beings the propagation is from the middle of each trope. After its fertile prime, individual life has a waste end, a decline in which it is addressed to death, not to reproduction. Some animals, however, go through metamorphoses; they seem to change their species without surrendering their individuality; the whole grub passes into the butterfly, wholly unlike itself and yet not another. The psyche here has several forms of life in store, to be developed alternatively or in succession, producing bodies of different aspect and scale, which nevertheless are bodies of the same soul, or the thoughts and the acts dictated by the same passion may carry out a single impulse in entirely different transcripts and expressions. This is presumably the native method of nature, the sequel being a precipitate, not a copy, of the previous fact, and transformation rather than persistence of form being the very condition of existence and life. And it is not insects only that pass through dissimilar phases of growth, in which a superficial observer would not recognise the same animal: all seeds are strangely dissimilar from the full grown plant or animal from which they come and into which they develop; and even in man there is much transformation from birth to old age, both in aspect and powers, with a succession of different instincts, long latent and perhaps never actually exhibited. The notion that like comes from like, and that it would be miraculous if any thing arose that had not preexisted, is a shallow empirical impression: never justified strictly, since things are never just as they were, and justified roughly only by projecting generic images, words, and other convenient essences upon the substance of things, and supposing that they exhaust the reality; when in fact they serve merely to name or to transcribe it. Sensibility itself, the latest begotten and most original child of nature, this empiricism thinks, must also be like its parent, or else inexplicable and spurious; whereas, even on its material side, it is a wholly new trope, involving subtle suspended reactions and cross-associations in the nervous system; the mental transcript of which, when by a lyrical impulse the psyche transcribes it mentally, must be doubly and trebly original. As intuition is the most living form of life, the keenest edge of existence, so it is naturally the most novel and variable, playing like light reflected from summit to summit in the waves of animal effort and readjustment which from that keenness and agitation sink again, normally into a calm, to sleep the pregnant sleep of universal matter. If there were an eye that could trace this matter in all its shifts and collocations, it might perceive the individual necessity of every new form and sudden insecure embodiment of essence, and of every repetition, itself conditioned and unstable; the fairest things being on the whole rare, yet occasionally and in certain fields frequent like wild flowers; and the large issue of events always unprecedented, an unintended continual culmination continually breaking down, and yielding to some fresh posture of affairs. In this flux the tropes which such an eye would recognise and name would be multitudinous and of all sorts and lengths; their appearance would be always a result, never a cause, and their monotony, when they were monotonous, would itself be local and temporary.

The human eye, however, cannot trace the flux of matter in its true texture and complexity: it can note only here one trope and there another, within the range of its own vision and on its own scale. And when these tropes cross and are superposed, as in human experience occurs inevitably (some perceptible tropes being mechanical others moral, some vital and others literary) reflection becomes sadly confused; for all these units are superficial and precarious, none of them belongs to the inmost, efficacious texture of substance, and yet the human mind is tempted to make them the measure of things, as if the meter of nature created the words and was all their burden. But nature is not such a bad poet; the numbers bubble unbidden up from her heart, and she does not know the style in which she babbles. Hence a comic predicament for the acrobatic philosopher of nature—serious human philosophy being that of spirit: that none of the phenomena or laws or measures which he may note are true parts of the object which he wishes to study. They are tropes, and the flux of nature is not a collection of tropes, but a pervasive flux of substance in which the tropes are only resulting figures, as the tropes of rhetoric are in living speech. Science is therefore but a mask for nature, as the senses and their perspectives are other masks; and I must be content to play wih her in these assumed characters, in so far as her part and mine are rôles which I can study and learn, and a visible pageant; although meantime both she and I are living our true lives, even in acting that comedy and wearing those masks, as actors and actresses are silently and sadly toiling in their private persons, and growing old in the real world, even when still bravely playing their same young parts upon the stage.

RELATIVITY OF MORALS

The root of self-transcendence, both in idea and by actual transformation, lies in the very essence of existence, far beneath the level of religious aspiration. Existence is intrinsically a flux: that is, it consists in a passage of recognisable characters that arise and lapse by accident, in an accidental field. By "accident" and "accidental" I mean without relevance or justification found in the nature of that which arises to its arising there and then, or to its lapsing. The field does not logically require that particular occupant, and the occupants do not logically require that particular field: in a word, existence is being in inessential relations. Ready proof comes for this fact in that the occupants continually vary. Such a flux and such a jumble are harmless and merry enough so long as nothing cares whether it exists or not, or in what surroundings it finds itself; but when there begin to be elastic and self-recovering organisms the ground is laid for moral experience, for care and for self-knowledge. The instinct of self-preservation, struggling to maintain certain characters in being, causes those characters to be noticed and esteemed by the awakened mind. Good and evil enter the world. Desire, suffering, love of life, fear of death sharply divide the self from the world that feeds it and starves it, has formed it, cruelly tempts and deceives it, and soon destroys it altogether.

What labours, what migrations, does not primitive man undertake in order to find a better lodgement in nature? What deadly feuds and vendettas does he not hand down from generation to generation in

George Santayana, "Relativity of Morals," Humanities Research Center, University of Texas. © 1969 Daniel Cory. Santayana's notes identify this as intended for a section on "Militant Ethics" in *Dominations and Powers*. No such section was included in that book as published.

order to get rid of troublesome rivals? And in despair at his own help-lessness, what offerings and vows does he not make to invisible powers, that they may smoothe his path for him, or rescue him by miracle from his predicaments? Vitally, industry, war, and religions serve the same needs, and are sweetened by hope of the same happiness.

Different types of men, in different circumstances, appeal more to one or to another of these arts; and as the arts develop they impose special images and maxims upon the expert mind. The good itself assumes a different form when a different art is employed to pursue it. The thrifty mind, the pugnacious mind, and the religious mind cease to exist at once or by turns in the same person. They dominate different classes; until the warrior thinks it beneath him to labour, and the priest thinks it a virtue in himself not to fight.

Conflict with nature or with other creatures sharpens the animal will and integrates it, so that the simple-minded man practises religion with a view to accomplishing his will against his enemies and helps his friends without a thought of reforming his own will or surrendering it. Only when two wills begin to struggle in the same breast can religion begin to become spiritual. It is essential, however, that the two wills should be both spontaneous; and the first inner conflicts of a child, in-clined to do forbidden things and torn between impulse and fear, issue in the kind of religion and morality that Kant called heteronomous. These form but a grumbling conscience and a grudging virtue, from which the free soul longs to escape; and from this source come the reactions against religious and moral discipline rather than any clari-fication of the purpose that such discipline may serve. There are, how-ever, spontaneous alternatives enough offered to the human psyche, and conflicts of free impulses within it, to lead reflection very quickly to radical intuitions and to sweeping judgements about the worth and the worthlessness of life.

One such radical intuition proclaims that life is a dream, all vanity and illusion; and this is no mere fancy of some disgruntled poet, but the ripe conclusion of many sages. Verbally it is indeed sophistical; because if *all* is illusion, illusion becomes the standard of reality, and the vulgar dogmatist is himself again. Virtually, however, this com-plaint pierces to the deepest of ontological contrasts and of spiritual choices. Why, when existence is a flux, does anybody dream of per-manence? Why is the clearest and most vivid perception called an illusion, if we find it does not last? Whence this anti-natural demand for arrest? Vitality on the contrary demands novelties and creates them; and nothing is more exasperating to a lively body or a lively mind than to be pinned down and prevented from moving.

Yet there is one thing that is equally intolerable, and that is to be forced to move in a direction that arrests and reverses an impulse already afoot. If nothing in particular were afoot in us we should not be alive; we should not even be material factors in the world, with specific properties and effects.

Here we touch the legitimate, the essential character of the demand for permanence, and the root of it in ourselves. Existence involves movement, and conflict of movements; but each movement has a particular direction, and the first law of motion is that all motions continue in the same direction and with the same velocity, unless modified by external forces. All recognisable and reliable movements, spontaneously enact some specific rhythm, trope, or law: did they not take, as far as possible, a particular course, they could not be original, free, or vital movements. The flux of existence is therefore a concourse of movements each of which has a method in it, and as a movement tends to preserve itself, and to continue for ever. But usually, if not always, it does not continue for ever, because it merges and dissolves into other movements. Relatively to any moment, however, there is always a form in the processes going on, often exact repetition of a cycle, sometimes development of a psychic impulse towards an end gradually discovered but unmistakably recognised when attained. Originality in particular instances of a passion may be combined with repetition of it in the life of the world, as happens in the tender passion, and in the formation of the family.

The play of these forms of motion and types of life over the surface of the flux is studied scientifically in physics and biology, and dramatically in poetic historiography; and there is a danger in both fields that we should define the generic forms too strictly and impute a more complete and lasting ascendency to them than they actually possess. For when we come to the human mind a new motive appears for prizing the permanent and rejecting the transitory, as if only the permanent could be real. Not that movement is less characteristic of mind than of matter. Empirically it is more so: for we find what looks like a divine permanence in the stars and the mountains, and even in the inconstant sea; while in our thoughts all is volatile, confused, and irrevocable, except perhaps the words in which we crystalise them. For the inconstancy of actual thinking is like the inconstancy of luck at cards or at dice. The moral issue is incalculable, but the counters are permanent and precise. Our counters mentally are ideas and socially are words; and both, once coined and stamped, are ideally eternal. Not of course that the ideas do not fade and become equivocal, or that the words do not shift their meanings or become obsolete; yet still each, as at any moment the mind actually apprehends it, presents the precise meaning and character that it presents: and with such counters, and no others, we must do all our reckoning. The ideal web of intrinsic relations uniting such terms manifests its independence and unchangeableness in the sphere of logic, mathematics, music, and theology; for here no sanction is asked for from material events, and intuition is never stopped or disconcerted in tracing and retracing the labyrinth of essence. We have discovered a congruous world in which we may lay up and endlessly review our treasures.

It is because life and nature cross that ideal world, and constantly contradict our assumptions and hopes that we complain of change, and that the great philosopher of the flux was called the weeping philosopher. We are shocked to find that neither material things, nor our friends, nor our minds are true to the idea that we had formed of them. The love of poetry, the trust in inspiration and in argument, then begin to seduce us from animal contact with facts: and the great elegiac, fabulous, dogmatic life of religion superposes itself, sometimes genially, sometimes tragically, on life in the world.

Another radical intuition that comes to swell the stream of spiritual rebellion against nature is the sense of wrong. If inconstancy in things perplexes and saddens, injustice provokes wrath. Wrath is an impulse to punish and avenge: and if mutation leads us to a flight from nature into the spiritual world, wrath calls us back to nature, under moral guidance, to correct nature and teach it how it should move. This is the perennial banner of human militancy: but on each occasion inscribed with a different device.

There is a complication in this rebellion and perhaps an illusion. Any voice upbraiding nature figures in nature: it is in that sense a natural force. And wrath is eminently a natural force: the contradicted animal contracts its sinews, rears its head, and prepares to strike a blow. Yet the animal does not perceive its own agitation. It perceives only the wrongness of the event; and probably it attributes its indignation to insight into that wrongness, and to a purely spiritual love of goodness and justice. Religion in animals has no need of appealing to the secular arm, since that is its only instrument; and their undivided soul thinks it will set things right by its own power and auhority. And indeed, neither reason nor religion could ever bend one blade of grass if they were not first, as they are, movements in living beings, passions that reveal themselves to the observer as gestures and actions, but to the subject of them only as categorical imperatives. His own emotions and ideas seem to the natural man perfectly causeless or derived rationally and dialectically from other ideas and emotions; and then this stream of passions, conceived in ideal terms, seem[s] to him to rush upon the physical world, in order to make righteousness victorious there.

Yet before they have time to make righteousness universally victorious, or before they begin to do so, a strange turn is likely to be given to the reforming wrath. It is apt to turn against the man who feels it. For he sees it working havoc in the world, far more than justice; and he feels it working havoc also in himself, multiplying his hatreds, embittering his days, and perhaps causing him to fall into his enemies' hands and to suffer all manner of torments.

Now wrath against oneself is called remorse. It is no less spontaneous and irresistible than wrath against other things or persons, which it probably includes: for why have I been such a fool and such a wretch, except because I was born under an evil star and people have coerced me? The spirit that thus rises in judgement within me against myself and against the universe never asks for its own origin or questions its own authority. It takes itself to be an absolute principle, or an inspiration from God; and when its accusing voice is persistent, it sets up a second life within one's life, based on repentance, conversion, and a determined effort to make oneself a different man.

These inner conflicts have a simple natural occasion which also determines their frequency and violence: the human psyche is complex and imperfectly integrated. Its instincts and impulses interfere with one another. At the same time the range of human perceptions and interests is so great that opportunities are often missed, or reactions provoked inopportunely. For this reason Socrates said, most truly, that virtue is knowledge: not verbal knowledge, of course, but knowledge of oneself, that distinguishes clearly one's powers and possible satisfactions, and knowledge of the world, that can foresee the fruits of one's actions. If a man's will were simple and integrated, and his information adequate there could be no conflict in his will, nor any tempests in his conscience. His *virtue* would then be perfect, as the ancients understood virtue. The people who repent and reform are well inspired, if they had previously been doing violence to their true nature and capacities: but they will only prolong their moral agony if their new allegiance represents only a hectic or artificial turn taken by their fancy.

If such is the natural history of morals, it follows that there is a complete inversion of the order of nature in striving after or preaching any particular type of virtue as if it were divinely imposed upon all men alike, or even upon the cosmos at large; so that, for instance, sexual intercourse or war or diversity of classes in society, however intrinsic to human life, might be absolutely wrong, and the meteors bedevilled for following erratic courses. In other words moralism, that takes moral sense for the foundation of religion and even of cosmology, is a radical error. Good and evil are relative to natures already existing and making specific demands: but as these demands may be imperfectly determined or conflicting among themselves, or as circumstances may prevent the satisfaction of them, defeat and trouble cannot help dogging the unsteady steps of mankind. In so far, however, as man and as society are thoroughly integrated, the good will become clear in their eyes, and their pursuit of it unflagging: and their virtue will bear appropriate fruit, unless it is so unfortunate as to arise in a medium where the exercise of it is impossible.

The relativity of morals is a dissolving principle where men are individually loose and profoundly alien to one another: they then aspire to vacant liberty rather than to vital virtue, because liberty is a reality to them and virtue only an oldfashioned word. Yet it is evident that in so far as human nature is distinguishable, and its innate demands constant, there will be a nucleus of principle and aspiration common to all men. This nucleus will be formed in part by their common dependence on the medium in which they live and to which they all must adjust themselves. That common medium will determine how far the demands and assumption of each party are practicable, how far hopeless. Probably a part of every political programme would be condemned at once by this criterion, and a part given free passage into the lists. There would remain much that was conflicting among not impracticable ideals.

GEOGRAPHY AND MORALS

Tacitus observes that in the north people are drunken and chaste, while in the south they are lascivious and sober; and Paul Valéry thinks that Catholicism can hardly be at home except in countries where bread and wine are the staff of life; and I remember my old teacher, Josiah Royce (who was a native of California), shaking his head at the Middle West, and saying that great plains produce flat and monotonous minds, whereas mountainous coasts, archipelagoes and islands are the soil of genius and liberty. There may be wit in such confrontations; but I suspect that climates and landscapes influence the mind only in so far as they impose different habits upon the body, and kill off persons of a certain temperament and complexion. Your lewd man will be lewd at the north pole, though he may not like to live there, and your drunkard will continue to drink at the equator, so long as his life lasts; and in every land the seeds of all sorts of faiths and affections may take root, if only they are not stifled by rival growths, already in possession of the ground.

It would therefore be a gross and false geography of morals that should paint upon the map bands and tracts of different pure colours, to represent the territory of different religions, arts or moralities. If these things really flourished in blocks, like corn in one field and grass in the next, there would not be that terrible insecurity and those painful moral and religious conflicts which prevail within states and within families, and even within individual minds torn between different influences, and uncertain of their natural allegiance. The grain of virtue is sown mixed; anywhere any sort of young shoot may innocently appear; and it is but a dubious and changeable flora, always shifting its frontiers, that prevails for a time over this or that region.

This close intermixture of contrary aspirations in men or in cities has unfortunate results. A human being is not a bird that can develop his arts and lead his wild life in solitude, or with a single mate; he

George Santayana, "Geography and Morals," *Columbia Manuscript Collection.* © 1969 Daniel Cory. At the top of the first page Santayana noted, "Good beginning." There is no indication of the date of the manuscript or of Santayana's intentions as to its eventual use.

requires a congenial society to foster him; and he finds instead, unless
he is very dead or very fortunate, little but prohibitions, difficulties,
and oppressions. He is continually forbidden to do what he might do,
and commanded to do what he can't. And if he sulks and rebels and
attempts to live his life apart, or with a few other outlaws, he is not
the happier for that, but only more consciously starved and more
openly bitter.

This experience is so ancient and so universal that wise and fatherly
men have always wished to establish traditions that should forestall
it or mitigate it. Legislation should instil into everyone from the beginning certain virtues necessary for the state; nothing contrary to
these virtues should be tolerated, or be so much as mentioned: people
to whom those approved virtues are happiness should be allowed to
prosper, and the rest should be degraded, ostracised and, if possible,
left to die out. In this way a definite and happy society might be established, in which everyone's will would spontaneously conform to
the law, and each fresh genius would come to glorify the established
order, and none to destroy it.

I do not think that any philosopher who understands the natural
basis of morals can harbour any other *ultimate* ideal. Possible types of
perfection are many, and the essential condition for happiness and
beauty in life is that it should realise perfection of some sort. Without
unison and harmony with his neighbours no perfection can be attained
by a gregarious animal like man: yet the physical intermixture of
temperaments renders it difficult and devastating to impose any one
type of virtue on everybody. A question of geography, the distribution
of human types in space, thus becomes a sort of a preliminary question
for all intelligent ethics. How far, and in what manner, need moral
society be attached to place at all? There is at least one relative centre,
the moveable individual, to which all morals must be relative: for here,
in me, in the sensitive platform which I carry with me as I move, in
the conscious focus of all this, passions and circumstances create sentiment and pronounce judgement. Need all moral society be cut up, so
to speak, into vertical blocks, each covering a part of the earth's surface? Or may some, or possibly all, moral societies be geographically
homeless, and spread horizontally, as it were, engaging here one man
and there another, perhaps only in a part of his nature, and linking
him with those of his own kind in all other places? In a word, need all

moral society be local and patriotic, or may it be partly or wholly universal and voluntary?

A merely horizontal society is always irrational and covers only a part of its members' interests. Food, shelter, and family life must be obtained by local compacts. These could fall within the purview of a universal society only if this society was also all-comprehensive, like a theocracy that not only claimed the allegiance of all men, but regulated all their physical actions, such as the quality of food and the methods of trades. But such meddlesome theocracies can never include all mankind: climatic and temperamental differences render such complete uniformity intolerable, even as an ideal.

MECHANICAL SCIENCE AND DESCRIPTIVE ETHICS

When science traces the structure of things beyond the human scale, it carries the mind into a region foreign to common sense, into a difficult unbreathable air amid ghostly objects; as today we all make use merrily of electric[it]y and radiation, without at all understanding what they may be. The mind of the perfect expert may be intellectually a blank: and in living amongst unimaginable forces he may become confused morally as well; for when science gets out of scale with human nature, human nature is apt to relax its own moral scale; at least no obvious monitors, on the human scale, are any longer conceived to stand about us, compelling us to face them either as friends or foes: but life seems rather a web of methods of interaction, not needing to stop anywhere, or even to traverse any particular predetermined phase.

The tendency to abandon the lines of Christian morals, and sally forth into the open, existed in Christendom before modern science or the mechanisation of life: the excess of humanism had the same effect

George Santayana, "Mechanical Science and Descriptive Ethics," *Columbia Manuscript Collection.* © 1969 Daniel Cory. A fragment intended for *The Realm of Spirit* or *Dominations and Powers*; the title was provided by the editors.

during the Renaissance that the submergence of humanism has had in the industrial age. The modern mind, fed on the humanities, dislikes exactitude: it is a literary mind; we gladly relegate exactitude to mathematics, where it will trouble few of us. In our thoughts and lives we wish to be free, eloquent, splendid, and individual. For this purpose it is not inconvenient to be rich: at least, it is indispensable to have the wealth of a prosperous society at our disposal. Prosperity, indeed, became for the modern mind the aim and criterion of both science and morals. This criterion, and not any scientific enlightenment, prompted the withering scorn, expressed by literary men, towards the Middle Ages; no doubt a genuine wind of adventure and discovery flew then in science, as well as in all the seas: but with it was mixed a great impatience of hard thinking and hatred of plain living.

Since the Socratic revolution in philosophy science had been essentially moral science: it had conceived and described the world in terms of the standard nature and possible perfection of each specific part. The human soul, like the sister souls of all created things, had its functions assigned to it by the Creator. But the analogy by which all these superhuman or infrahuman things were conceived was a moral analogy: each thing had its proper nature to fulfil, and its proper perfection. The age of open romanticism had not arrived; God was not yet a mere extension of the field of human experience; it was not yet the essence of the universe to be sensible or useful to man. Nevertheless, although this metaphysics, grounded on analogy, was generous in intention, it was not really very perceptive or elastic; it read human analogies into matter and into God; and the modern critic might perhaps say that, just as our mathematical physics do far greater justice to the body of nature—in astronomy, for instance—than did the moralistic astronomy of Aristotle, so our haphazard romantic sympathy with exotic ways of living does better justice than Platonic or Christian ethics could do to the spirit in things.

I think such would be the verdict of common sense. We must push forward our frontiers in the direction of mechanical science and descriptive ethics; and we must sharply withdraw in the region of moralistic or humanistic or psychological interpretations of the universe.

Does this mean that common sense can discard altogether the wisdom of Socrates? Must we go so far as to deny that nothing existent has any proper nature or possible perfection? We may discard the Socratic philosophy in our private capacity, being convinced that all natures and perfections are fluid and elastic. Yet it is only in the measure of their definiteness that things can posit or exemplify some type of excellence or beauty; all is approximation; and beauty and perfection sit upon natural things only like wingèd riders, ready to fly off at any moment into the empyrean. Yes; when we *imagine* our nature and remotely beckoning perfection, we may imagine it only as one of an infinite multitude [of] diverse natures and disparate perfections; but when we *exert* or *enact* our nature, when that nature in us chooses and wills, loves and fights, we have thereby taken sides: we have joined the human army; or at least we have set up a standard of integrity and moral ambition for our own persons, voluntarily closing our hearts against all temptations to abandon that single aim, and pursue other perfections. Common sense and manly virtue must take this step: they must defend some particular moral frontier. Each man, each nation, each vested or ideal interest, must unflinchingly assert itself; all concessions, co-operations or federations being, in the logic of life, either roundabout ways of serving extant interests, or the inception of some new particular organism, which will substitute its own interests and loyalties for those which the dying organism imposed.

But now arises a delicate question. Can common sense be satisfied with goods admittedly relative? Can it consent to pursue at home, in its church, its parliament, its schools, and its literature aims no better intrinsically than those which might be pursued by the heathen or the foreigner? If you feel in your bones that your home system is not exclusively the right one, is not your insistence on it a pious sham? It might seem, then, that if common sense is to be perfectly honest and to maintain its moral position with a good conscience, it must include within its frontiers a firm claim to a special divine revelation. The honest man cannot live happy without feeling that he is surely on the right side: and he cannot feel sure that he is on the right side unless he asserts that he is privileged above other men, and the pet of the universe. A fishy claim: so that the heartiness of common sense in morals seems to require an excursion beyond common sense in speculative belief.

A FEW REMARKS ON CRIME

In clinging to our vices we often sincerely regret them, or half regret them. A vice is like a stammer or a wart: the lifelong habit may have been grafted upon us by some early accident, and may be a nervous parasite quite peripheral and odious to ourselves; the victim of it is not pleased with himself for biting his nails or getting drunk or running after loose women. He would much rather that the fiend should let him alone and allow him to satisfy himself more gloriously. Not so with a crime. A crime is too much ours to be regretted. It was wrung from us once only, at the moment when we were most deeply ourselves and most intensely alive. Murderous as it may be, and destructive of what is dearest to others or even to ourselves, every crime has its internal virtue; we hide it jealously, with a terror which is half love; or if it is discovered and we are obliged to confess it, we do so with a certain glow of defiant pride. Some god, we feel, required and prompted it at that hour, in contempt of all mortal prudence; and if the world blasphemes against that irresponsible god, it is because the world is dead, and cannot understand life.

The internal morality of crime appears clearly when the criminal is not a single individual, but a band or a sect or a nation. Within that society, the most intrepid criminal is the most virtuous man. And he may really be an estimable person, sweet and mild in his domestic capacity, and heroic in the fray; the frontiers at which the crime begins may be so remote and the victim so foreign, that no self-reproach reverberates from them to the heart. Necessity and the blindness of war then turn ruthlessness into innocence.

In fact, the first and fundamental crime is to exist at all, existence being an inveterate cannibal, or worse, since it always feeds on some part of its own body. Vegetarians excuse themselves by ostentatiously not eating their own children, or other animals, and calling whatever they devour inanimate. But is anything inanimate? At least, nothing can be formless; and in destroying the forms of things in the hope of preserving our own form, we commit an act of which the violence is

George Santayana, "A Few Remarks on Crime," *Columbia Manuscript Collection.* © 1969 Daniel Cory. Intended probably for *Dominations and Powers*; from a typescript in the Columbia University Library.

certain and the success impossible. Yet we cannot abolish aggression: that would be to abolish the flush of youth, and to decree a general suicide in order to prevent an occasional murder. The only solution, since conflict must rage for ever, is to carry it on with as much chivalry as possible, suffering reason to moderate somewhat the love of life: to teach existence, since it must perish, to perish gracefully, and by a timely connivance to bring the will of the dying into harmony with that of their heirs. In saying this, I am far from wishing to emulate that ancient sage who was called the advocate of death, and whose eloquence drove those Greek young men and women, rapt in a divine despair, to cast themselves into the sea. The flux is in no haste to swallow us; it leaves room for many a feast; Nature is full of sustained repetitions, and it is as legitimate and feasible for us to cling to a pleasant custom as to push for some dire reform. But slowly and imperceptibly the Pyramids change their colour; we must die daily; and it is this gentle renovation of our being, no less than its catastrophes, major and minor, that wisdom might learn to greet with a smile: for there is such humour in it. Time laughs at ambition, and Eternity laughs at Time; and if we could relish this double irony, the great crime of existence, self-destruction would cease to seem an outrage, and the violence of it would become like a lover's violence, tragic but welcome.

On Prudence

Why should a youth suppress his budding passions in favour of the sordid interests of his own withered old age? Why is that problematical old man who may bear his name fifty years hence nearer to him now than any other imaginary creature? The soul is not directed upon herself; more important than her temporal continuity is her reproduction, and more important than her material reproduction are her spiritual affinities, by which parity is established between the kindred exploits and the conspiring thoughts of the most remote persons. If it be frivolous to live in the present, is it not vain to live for the future? And how many are concentrated and contemplative enough to live in the eternal?

On Money

Money, as the modern rich man disposes of it, is not wealth of a natural sort. Natural wealth would consist of visible objects in a man's possession, which the curious and admiring eye might catch glimpses of in his hand or in his shop or behind his park gates. The proprietor of these fine things has a natural dignity: not only the dignity which long and familiar use of them may have given to his mind and manners, but at least the dignity of power, because having found, made, inherited, or conquered these choice portions of the material world, he can share or withhold them at will, and thereby establishes a natural domination over other people, in proportion to their need or ambition. but the modern rich man is not the obvious lord of anything. His mysterious wealth is homeless, nominal, immaterial: it consists of the force of words written upon paper. We live in a fog of finance. The capitalist hardly knows what goods or works or rights or projects his bonds and shares represent: his function is merely to sign cheques and to receive other paper, and on distributing this, to be fed and clothed magnificently as if by magic. Very likely he lives in a flat and travels about restlessly in a motor car; he belongs everywhere and nowhere; he knows everybody, and nobody knows who on earth he is. As he buys or sells his title to some fraction of the unknown, he may well wonder what makes him daily so much richer or poorer, and perhaps lays the whole world of buyable things and persons at his feet. The domination of money is a sort of conventional miraculous domination, like the former domination of religion. How can it subsist?

I reply: by imputation to the rich man of control over some natural increase in the world, due to the general fecundity of Nature, or to that part of it which passes through the hands and the brains of men. The fecundity of Nature may be watched, guarded, or coaxed by a knowing mind: its products may be collected, transported, and exchanged, perhaps on a grand scale; and those who manipulate these operations, perhaps by telegraphing from the other end of the earth, possess the power over these things without possessing the things themselves: they possess their value. Being liquidated and merged in the universal mechanism of exchange, this value at the rich man's disposal becomes a mathematical and fantastic quantity: it becomes money. To-morrow this convention may break down and all this nominal wealth may vanish like a dream. The strong, no doubt, will always seize and hold the good things of this world; but it may be again by an actual mastery and possession of them, and not by an artifice of bookkeeping.

On Self-Sacrifice

Self-sacrifice passes for a wonderful virtue, as if human beings were expected to be perfectly integrated and thrifty, with every impulse and

instinct providentially directed to their ultimate profit. Human nature
is much blinder, more casual, and more generous than that. It is necessarily adjusted to the survival of the race rather than to the welfare of
the individual. The few great masters of life, who have really brought
things to a head in their own persons, have never left children: their
empires have passed to their nephews or to their generals, and their
wisdom to their disciples. As to the prolific rabble, Nature does not care
how unhappy or deluded we are, if only we can blunder through and
keep the world going. The most perfect animals are those completely
subject to the routine of the hive or the ant-hill; they are links in a
temporal mechanism which has solved the problem of perpetual motion: perhaps the human race, too, in America, may reach the same
equilibrium. Is it a sacrifice or a joy to pick up those appointed burdens
and to hasten to deposit them in the public granary? Probably the
question never occurs to those worthy creatures: like good nuns they
find their happiness in rising or sleeping, working or singing, mourn-
ing or rejoicing, according to the chime of the bell or the day of the
calendar. Even the profane, who think themselves free and original, are
soon found treading the same mill: every lover, every mother, every
soldier rushes into the glorious trap; and if all in this self-surrender is
not sacrifice, it is not because the commitments into which Nature al-
lures us are not burdensome and fatal, but rather because there seldom
existed in us before that moment anything worth mentioning to be
sacrificed: it was probably at the touch of those sacrifical passions that
the man or the woman first awoke to a vivid life.

Some enthusiasts, like Fichte, would wish all life to be a hard sacrifice
to duty, so that the whole of it might be truly heroic and divine. Materially such an economy might not be impossible; but morally the
whole would then be without justification or excuse—an acrobatic
feat, forced, painful, and ugly, persevered in by a vain obsession. We
might say of it with the philosopher Bradley, that it was the best of
possible worlds, and everything in it was a necessary evil. Nature is not
so devilishly tense; she plays and loiters, she laughs and breaks out into
a scattered consciousness, which, perhaps, a perfect economy would
exclude; she renders much that is instrumental also self-justifying, by
the pleasure of exercising that natural function. This free play, this inner pause and enrichment redeem the whirligig of existence from vanity, and turn its heavy prose into poetry. And it is only because the
parts are good each in itself that a real sacrifice of any of them is possible; for sacrifice would not be sacrifice if the sacrificial impulse was

all in all, and there was nothing else good in a man which he might surrender. Sacrifice first becomes possible, and constantly necessary, in a wayward being imperfectly unified; and in him it may be fruitful, because by restraining each of his impulses on occasion, and discharging them only in a certain measure and in a certain order, a decent harmony can be established among them. Then the subjection of each fond passion is a reasonable precaution, and the orderly release of them all an admirable discipline: for this harmony when once formed is exceedingly sweet and beautiful in itself, and impossible to sacrifice to anything better. It is never out of place to think and to act intelligently, and there is no occasion to give the hysterical names of Duty or Self-Sacrifice to what is simply a happy art and a rational compromise.

This life of reason is like the crystallising principle that turns the common atoms of carbon into a diamond; it lends to our animal impulses a nobility which they never had in themselves and which they lose at once if they are liberated. The passions are our moral atoms, each, no doubt, possessing an organisation and a life of its own: but how ugly and poor! Cupid and Mars, who prompt in a civilised soul the most sublime consecrations, are in their own persons strangely cruel, silly, and dull; and except in that single sanctuary, where their inspiration is qualified and restrained by many a venerable rite, they are rather demons than gods; their irresponsible fury breaks out like an epidemic or a conflagration anywhere and everywhere in this flat world. There is no more hideous centipede than life in general.

DECISION BY DISCUSSION

A good instance of the domination and impotence of words may be seen in the practice, more nominal than real, of reaching decisions by discussion. Each speaker is dominated by his words, but the decision would have already been reached and would obey the prejudices or in-

George Santayana, "Decision by Discussion," *Columbia Manuscript Collection.* © 1969 Daniel Cory. An essay meant for but not included in *Dominations and Powers.*

terest of the stronger party. Words, spoken or written, are indeed indispensable in politics to propose and register the measures to be
adopted, even when these measures are accepted under duress; an
armistice or a peace requires an exchange of messages and documents.
An agreement regarding the future must name the actions expected;
and a sufficient definition of these actions may be reached by discussion. Practical conflicts may be avoided that might arise out of the mul-
tiple senses of words. Legal, like scholastic, phraseology is often derided
by humanists, but not with self-knowledge on their part; since it is the
humanists that are frivolously enamoured of words and will not have
them made clearer than suffices for a lazy eloquence; whereas by
discriminating various possible meanings the real relations of objects
are studied, and language is made more closely significant of things.
Then the contracting parties, by making the terms elaborately precise,
when they put their names to the final document may be really escaping the snare of words and accurately conceiving the proposed actions.

Discussion of this sort, however, is only such as might take place in
formulating a surrender or capitulation, when the substance of the
agreement so secured is secured by force. Conversation would begin
by declaring that resistance to that force was to be abandoned. Such
is not the state of things when it is proposed to reach a decision by
discussion. The assumption then is that, without any reference to the
forces in play, words by their pure eloquence and their appeal to moral
ideas might bring about a change in the will of the two parties. Discussion is to be a means, not of avoiding a misunderstanding, but of ef-
fecting a conversion.

Conversions certainly are not impossible. Eloquence may sometimes
provoke them, but probably it will be the unintended and unreasoned
eloquence of some action or some simple word; for if words or even
facts have power to change the Will, it is by breaking down some
obstacle or clearing some entanglement in the Will itself. To be truly
converted is to recognise and to become that which one is. But discussion and argument have the opposite tendency. They increase the entanglement, they draw the whole psyche into the net, and dedicate the
passions to weaving that net, closer and closer, and making all frank
conversion impossible. Eloquence and controversy are ecclesiastical
arts; they presuppose in the missionary a plighted faith, an indulged
passion; and this they merely elaborate and fortify by abounding in
their own sense.

There is also a different soberer eloquence that may contribute to decisions, the eloquence of knowledge. Here words are mere vehicles, as inconspicuous as possible, and it is the power of facts that impresses the mind. Well-digested pertinent knowledge inspires confidence even in any enemy, because it so marshalls the circumstances and the probable consequences of the proposed measures as to obviate blunders on all sides and to direct the will of each more securely towards its chosen end.

All the vehicles of power are not grossly visible or expressible in statistics; the psyche too is a great centre for the collection and re-direction of energy. By exciting the psyche, purely moral or emotional appeals may lead to intelligent action, if they call forth latent interests that in any case would ultimately have made themselves felt, and per-haps condemned the achievements towards which the overt will was directed. If, for instance, any proposed measures offend religion, when religion is a living passion or has attracted vested interests into its orbit, an offence offered to religion involves a political risk. Yet such con-sideration of the power of religion is not a religious consideration. Not gods or moral laws or romantic ideals are then feared or respected, but only the psychic impulses in mankind that breed those ideas, and that, being already physical potentialities, may well become overt actions on occasion. Words are habitual and telling signs of such hidden impulses, being a first external ebullition of them; and for this reason to listen to the words of an orator may sometimes be important, since the dominion of words over him (which passes for his dominion over words) may in-dicate what real powers and proclivities, in action, belong to the talking unit that he represents. Yet if there's many a slip 'twixt the cup and the lip, there is many a slip more between the lip and the hand.

Lost words that float away in the air, which is their proper element, or enter the ear only to enrich the verbal memory, form there a magic atmosphere, a realm of logic and fable, from which spiritual powers are conceived to descend into the nether world. This is a pleasing dream; in fact spirit is like hot air that only ascends, or like music that only radiates. When the heat or the sound is spent, the spirit has van-ished. But the fountain of it is perennial. Shakespeare, for instance, illustrates magnificently the proper expressive function of words. True or fabulous history alternately or mingled, observation and pure in-vention, inspiration and ribaldry, tenderness and wit flow exultantly together in an irresponsible current, that never takes itself seriously,

that never corrects a syllable or challenges a thought. Here everything
exists for its own sake; all is poetry, even when it is scurrilous prose,
yes, even when it is rant; for what is rant save disordered inspiration,
that has lost hold of the relevance that valid passion must have to possible fact? In rant, as in punning and quibbling, speech takes the bit in
its teeth, and shows that it is essentiall[y] automatic and indicative only
by accident. Yet the virtuous may find in the free automatism of
Shakespeare, as in that of nature, a great fountain of moral lessons.
Something that lies in the reader unexpressed he finds there expressed
aptly, and that verbal aptness, shaping for him something hitherto
vague but energetic, delights him and makes him feel that, intellectually, he has become master over himself. A quotable maxim now
seems to guide his decisions. That it should be the poet that from time
to time leads us to the top of our little Tabors; that he should trans-
figure for us a part of our vulgar life into a part of heaven; or that we
are ourselves such a poet in every free disinterested intuition of sense or
of passion, seldom occurs to us. We feel the momentary exultation, but
we think it trivial, as its occasion may very well be; or we regard it as
an indirect or mistaken promise or echo of some material advantage in
the distance. So we piously propose to build little tabernacles on earth
for our poets and prophets, not as gates or jumping-off places for us into their sphere, but as miracle-working oracular shrines, where we may
detain them and render them useful in our earthly business.

Piety is really useful in politics, as we see in the Romans and again in
the Puritans, because it disciplines the will to esteem the possible and
to despise the impossible. And it has this beneficent effect in proportion
to its good sense, in other words, to the absence of any poetic or
spiritual transfiguration of the conventional world which might arrest
attention on anything for its own sake, and not merely for its uses. Yet
evidently this utilitarian piety has its limits, and must leave something
positive, some natural perceptions and passions, to form the items in
its reckoning; and these natural perceptions and passions, having engaged spirit, become so many airports, as it were, from which spirit
continually rises into its own sphere.

Therefore piety and the pious working psyche can never have everything their own way; they signed away their earthly allegiance when
they became conscious. This spiritual bee in the political bonnet causes
no end of trouble. A whole class of politicians and ideologues arises
that are private Shakespeares to themselves; and their facility in con-

joining observation and invention into eloquent words seems to them a divine guide to action. But if they make bad poets, they make worse statesmen. A true statesman may indeed use their proficiency in words, which is a real proficiency, for his own practicable ends. Their very illusions give them a capacity for contagious enthusiasm that a clear-headed man may not himself possess. And they probably can do other things than talk, and can do them well, if only their talk is not allowed to govern their action. When this occurs, however, the tragi-comedy of sophistical politics begins.

In this tragi-comedy the solemn reiterated proposal to reach decisions by discussion forms an instructive episode. The decisions to be reached are political and concern prospective action; but the discussion will not turn on matters of fact but on matters of preference. The facts are granted, or taken for granted. Discussion of the evidence for these assumed facts is usually avoided in politics and diplomacy. Instead of investigating the facts, all parties rely on whispered reports, or private information, or malicious insinuations as to what the facts might probably be. To inquire into the facts in open court, under the eye of opponents, might weaken the necessary conviction and firmness with which each party must state its case and propagate its sentiment. If some innocent realist should actually present a full account of the circumstances, expecting to bring about a change of front in all quarters, he would be grievously disappointed. His account would be dismissed unread, and dismissed for not representing any of the *policies* or *principles* involved in the debate. The debate does not touch what exists, or what has happened or what is likely to happen: debate on such points might actually lead to agreement. The debate merely expresses what each side wants, and the effort is to succeed in doing as you like, even if you fail in getting what you require. This was the method adopted by the League of Nations in the Abyssinian affair, with the notorious results.

That political discussion should abstract from the facts, which each party will continue to conceive in the fantastic way that most pleases it, renders such discussion futile, since it stubbornly ignores the sphere in which political events actually move, and only regards different Utopias. Each side will victoriously refute the conclusions of the other by reasoning on its own contrary premises; and each view, even if accurate, will contradict the rest, because taken from a different point of reference and covering a different range of events. One will insist on the present legal status as if eternal; another on the legitimate rights of an older order which this status contravenes; a third on the deeper interests and deeper currents of change undermining all conventions. Thus the further discussion proceeds the more each will be confirmed in his opinion; each system of assumptions will be progressively filled out and made consistent by appropriate fictions, and the contentions of all other parties will seem to become more and more baseless and unintelligible.

Let us suppose, however, that apart from enlightenment, some unanimous passion produces agreement about the facts, as when theologians agreed that the Bible was the literal word of God. The field then seems to be open to moral suasion. There is a natural contagion between will and will, and the force of enthusiasm is felt universally. Not, however, always sympathetically: and here the irrepressible variety of nature breaks out again in the very nest of conviction. Enthusiasm and eloquence become repulsive and seem proofs of madness, when overheard by anyone whose imagination is dumb in that direction. The various animals, if they could hear the absolute eloquence of one another's feeings, would think one another mad. The reasonableness of such diverse sentiments becomes intelligible only when they are conceived not as absolute judgements but as omens of action; since various animals would be eloquent about flying or swimming, hunting or singing, according to the depth to which the psyche in each was engaged in these actions. Pure spirit, if it got free, might perceive the eloquence of all possible passions, but it would also perceive that this eloquence was relative in each case to a specific type of life, and not perceptible to a psyche in a disparate phase of action. But perfect freedom is an ideal limit, and the animal psyche always holds the spirit in leash and remains insensible to justice, even while unintentionally creating the sense of justice in the spirit. The physical expression of any impulse contrary to her own always fills her with ire. Of ideas she can be tolerant, because they are nothing to her but what they are physiologically: childish impulses not momentarily relevant; and though they may worry and fatigue her by their idle strain, she cannot do more than rock the cradle and trust they may go to sleep. The deeper then, the more distinctive and original, spontaneous Will becomes in any creature, so much the more inveterate, in all other creatures, will be the hatred of that Will. Whence it follows that moral disputation is detestable except where it is superfluous; and that the more persistently different Wills urge their maxims on one another, the more hateful they and their maxims will become in one another's eyes.

Discussion about matters of fact is useless, because it is inspired not by interest in facts or knowledge of them, but by political preferences; and discussion about the preferences themselves is worse than useless towards reaching agreement when these preferences are naturally diverse; for all that the most candid and intelligent discussion can do is to clarify those preferences, so that their contrariety becomes more obvious and invincible as the discussion proceeds. There remains one case, however, where discussion may produce union, and that is when union exists fundamentally from the beginning and divergences have arisen by accident, owing to partial knowledge in different quarters or to varying tricks of expression. The discussion ends happily when everybody sees by what an agreement the real desires of all may be satisfied.

It was presumably in just such a case, in bargaining at fairs and markets, that debate first became a habitual art, afterwards rashly extended to theoretical and moral fields where it could only reinforce error and embitter hostility. But the exchange of something that one man has produced beyond his need and that another man requires, is a benefit to both; and contention touches only the amount of this benefit that shall accrue to each. Buyer and seller may spend hours offering a little more and asking a little less, with one or two mock departures and sly returns, until at last a sufficient advantage for the one seems compatible with a sufficient advantage for the other. Then, with a sigh of resignation at a vanished hope of excessive profit, the bargain is struck, and perhaps confirmed by a drink and an assurance of brisk business in the future.

This old ceremonial of trade was tiresome, like hackneyed debates in Parliaments, but not so irrational; at least the two parties had the same standard of value and a common denominator, hard cash, the only thing prized by either, to which their respective gains could be reduced, so as to become comparable. But who shall compare in politics or war, the thing that one side loses with that which the other side gains? And what is the common denominator, even in one's own camp, by which to measure the sacrifices made by agreements with the advantages that agreements may secure? Can the value of liberty be compared with that of order, or that of tradition with that of wealth? I know that the modern English, when first commerce inspired their *ethos*, conceived a calculus of pleasures and pains, by which to reckon all values. Pleasure is indeed the money of the venal soul; but only an artificial and meretricious culture can reduce the good to that quantitative currency, and that not for long, since everything soon ceases to give pleasure if it be prized only for the pleasure it gives. The mainsprings of the soul are entirely spontaneous and generous, and life itself would bring no pleasures if it were not directed blindly on a thousand things not to be attained, and not to be surrendered, without a thousand pains.

Pleasure was indeed identified with the good by many decadent Greeks, including the resigned and gentle Epicurus; but they made no calculus of it. They wished it to be gay, or they wished it to be pure; and content with those fair moments, they were brave enough to face any eventual storm. Pain and death lose half their evil, or all of it, if we do not fear them; and the vanity of existence becomes tolerable, or even amiable, when we have heartily accepted it. But this philosophy of idleness begins by eluding and detesting politics; it does not argue with people about their likes and dislikes; it tries to avoid their passions and to restrain its own; and the clear good it embraces is something ethereal, like gold-dust washed up by a river, a little brighter, but not more useful, than the common sand.

Trade is the home of compromise, but morals are matters of principle. They express integrity in the Will, and compromise involves some infraction of integrity. Either the Will remains firm, and compromise is only provisional and due to *force majeure;* or else the Will itself yields at its source, agrees to be plastic and self-forgetful, for the sake of peace, ease, and good-natured adaptation to circumstances. There may even be a sentimental or mystical glow in this self-surrender. It may call itself love or it may call itself liberty, yet it can be but the swan-song of both, since the first condition necessary to being free or being in love is to exist, and to be something in oneself. Otherwise love could not express a choice or an allegiance; and freedom could not liberate or expand any Will in particular. It could mean only a pullulation of detached whims. Into such a pullulation sentimental philosophy actually empties, and the morality of pure flux is abstention from all morality.

The commercial mind often becomes buyer and seller in one, bargaining within itself. There is a common denominator at hand for all calculations: easy living, which may be secured in two directions: by abandoning every ambition that costs too much, and annexing every source of steady and comfortable income. If you are prosperous, how can you be unhappy? And if you are happy, how can you ever find any fault with yourself? In philosophy, better abandon religion and stick to science. Science is real knowledge; it brings power and money; and it commits you to no final theory, to no oppressive notion of truth, by which your sundry passions might be overawed. There are some truths to be used; there are no truths to be respected. In politics, better be liberal and tolerant; tolerant, that is, about things that really don't matter, but that women and mystics like to indulge in. Of course, to be tolerant of crime would be itself criminal. You must stop all attacks on public health, on private reputations and on private property. Safety in these matters is a prerequisite for living at ease.

Such at least it seemed to rich liberals in the nineteenth century; they were as virtuous as they were luxurious, and any loss of wealth or respectability would have seemed to them the end of the world. But adaptation can go further than they supposed. Attacks on people's reputation become harmless if people have no shame, and laugh at every suspicion, either because they admit it gladly, or because they are indifferent to praise and blame, regarding them both as empty and ridiculous. A critic who thinks he is judging the world, is really only judging and exposing himself. And as to attacks on private property, the progress of democracy or of absolute government (which two may coincide) can remove all the bitterness of that; first, by making confiscation universal, so that if you remain poor at least nobody else will be rich; and secondly, by disabusing you of snobbery and luxurious habits, so that a good healthy standard poverty becomes a matter of course to you, or even a great relief.

One of the first advocates of toleration was Spinoza, and his position is particularly instructive, because he was neither lax morally nor vague intellectually. His liberalism stands clear-cut on a dogmatic background, that brings out its rational principle, utterly contrary to any sentimentality or humanitarianism. It was in the positive interest of the State, he thought, to tolerate all religious beliefs, because these became dangerous only when persecuted, and when tolerated made absolutely no difference in the thrift and loyalty of the citizens. Spinoza's observations were made in Holland where Catholics and Protestants were of the same race and habits, while the Jews, to whom he personally belonged, had no reason to be either idle or disloyal. Perhaps a wider survey might suggest that, while in themselves religious opinions are politically indifferent, the people attached to one religion, either by tradition or temperament, may be less desirable in a particular community than people inclined to different beliefs; Protestants and Jews, for instance, being generally more assiduous and enterprising than Catholics in matters of trade and science. Yet the justice of Spinoza's view is corroborated in the United States, where not only religious toleration but true political equality has prevailed for many years. It has rendered even Catholics perfectly homogeneous politically with the mass of the inhabitants. It has also shown how insignificant differences in religion may become when they are merely religious differences; the only social importance of religion lying in its offering some private sanction, emotional or superstitious, for the common secular morality and ambitions of the age. This morality and these ambitions continue, on a larger scale, the morality and ambition of Holland in the seventeenth century. The tolerant maxims of Spinoza apply perfectly to this society, and are vindicated there; but no far-seeing Spinoza exists to formulate them. American philosophers take them for elementary laws of existence. In Spinoza, on the contrary, and in the seventeenth century, religious passion, even if not sectarian, was dominant. The Jew, become a pantheist, might be superior to religious prejudices, but he could not dispense with a religious philosophy. He craved a sublime peace in his daily labour, an inner freedom in his modest life. The political world was good enough if it suffered the spirit to exist; but it was there, in the spirit, that the State was justified, not in its worldly pride, soon to be humbled; because the power of the universe infinitely exceeded the power of any of its parts.

What, then, may we read between the lines of this argument for toleration, which is the fundamental argument for it? Certainly that discussion should be free, *because it is of no importance.* It can never reach any conclusion except where virtual agreement pre-exists; meantime it is a safety-valve for the opiniated; and in developing and publishing every ignorant view, it confirms the material necessity and advantage of living peaceably together in one great fold, intent on making one's living or if possible one's fortune, under the picturesque shadow of old churches, the refuge of tender memories, or in the midst of revolutionary conventicles, the nurseries of acrid hopes. Government had no other function than to maintain peace, prosperity, and material good order; the rest was to be a silent dialogue between the spirit and the universe. Let the sheep be led to green pastures, and not sheared too much, or out of season; and let the shepherds be sheep too, and content with their own wool. As to ultimate things, were they not all explained in Spinoza's book, and might not everybody read it?

Alas! Spinoza's book too belongs to the sphere of discussion. It admirably defines its own words; but other words insinuate themselves into language, and the old logic becomes obsolete. If only the rulers of mankind could remember that their new words also are words, and that in dominating the mind they blind it to the true sources of power!

VI

A Naturalist Looks at Society

PRESUPPOSITIONS

I. Naturalism

That mankind is a race of animals living in a material world is the first presupposition of this whole enquiry. I should be playing false to myself and to the reader if I did not assume it. All my thoughts, even the most speculative and sceptical, move quite happily on the basis of public sanity, custom, and language. These conventions are not miraculous revelations of the truth, but they are the only available avenues towards it. I should not wish to be a philosopher, if that meant being a prophet with a message. I am content to stand where honest laymen are standing, and to write as I might talk with a friend in a country walk or sitting at a tavern. Otherwise I should be undermining the conventional assurance that my readers exist at all, or that the reported historical facts exist about which I am writing. I assume that here are the sun and the stars set far above us, and the earth beneath, with the sea a little beyond, and all the sea-routes leading to islanded nations scattered about the globe. I assume that these lands have been inhabited by many peoples now extinct or unrecognisable, regarding some of which we have historical records; so that their moral experience was the beginning of ours, is intelligible to us, and often, when pondered, renders our own experience intelligible.

If here I assume these current beliefs without further argument, it is not because it has never occurred to me to question them. I have questioned them perhaps as closely as any man ever did; and I have found that any criticism of them either presupposes them or contradicts and abolishes itself. Trusting these natural beliefs is initially as involuntary and unjustifiable as having been born; yet by trusting them we may re-

George Santayana, "Presuppositions," *Columbia Manuscript Collection.* © 1969 Daniel Cory. Parts of this early version of the introduction to *Dominations and Powers* were published in the section entitled "Preliminaries" in that work.

fine and harmonise them, smoothing away the knots in which they may get entangled. A part of this critical labour I hope to continue here, analysing now, not the logic of animal faith and of common knowledge, but the vicissitudes of human politics.

The nature of these vicissitudes begins to be evident if we simply repeat that mankind is a race of animals living in a material world. Fundamentally all the problems of human society are zoölogical problems: not that a thousand political, personal, and artistic questions do not arise, or that verbal hurricanes and epidemics do not sweep over the nations. They do; and they absorb almost the whole attention of the leaders of mankind, who are then leaders, not because they lead to anything, but because they persuade the people to follow them. Yet these storms are not merely verbal or mental. They betray, on the superficial level of feeling and speech, some fundamental material revolution.

II. Mind Not a Power
but a Prophetic Sign.

If mankind is a race of animals living in a material world, it follows that however far their industry or thought may extend, all will still be rooted in their physical being and material fortunes. Ideas would not exist without the men who entertain them. These men were not produced by their ideas, nor kept alive by them. On the contrary, each generation is brought into the world by ancestors who had other ideas: or if for a time the same ideas and the same state of society can be preserved, it is only when men of a particular type and calibre can physically maintain themselves and physically prosper. The prophet or the beggar must find other people to give him alms: he must eat, and so must his disciples; and if the faith is to endure, they must find the means to fight for it or to propagate it. Whatsoever safety or luxury or intelligence a society may come to enjoy needs still to be secured by physical defences and an equilibrium of customs and interests favourable to that way of life. Those mental and moral qualities would be utterly powerless to preserve themselves if they did not indicate material forces at work, capable of sustaining them. Our admiration will end in tears, unless we bethink ourselves in time of agriculture, and plough and replough the field in which those virtues could flourish.

The physical ground of ideas is directly personal, but indirectly social. Although an idea can exist only in somebody's head, it is institutions that normally preserve and propagate ideas, especially when society is firmly organised and expands from within. Ideas then form an orthodoxy, resolutely ignoring and regarding as dead all ideas native to other societies. When with time the institutions supporting this orthodoxy begin to be undermined by current changes in the material world, the orthodoxy itself gradually loses its authority. Heresies spring up, timid at first intellectually, yet often inspired by the most subversive intuitions and sentiments. Foreign philosophies come to be studied with respect, or actually adopted with enthusiasm, until all possible systems and opinions fly about in an indescribable chaos, like so many pigeons in a dovecot. The loud flutter soon becomes annoying, dies down of itself, or is disregarded as mad and futile by men of character. Perhaps then these men of character, or some small group of them favoured by fortune, will establish a new orthodoxy without meaning to do so, simply by establishing a new order in life and fresh adequate institutions, which by their steady operation will impose a definite circle of ideas.

Thus it is not ideas that form parties, but parties that embrace ideas. Even the stray prophet or voice crying in the wilderness is no pure thought breaking out by miracle at an arbitrary point of time and space. The thought breaks out then and there because human nature in that man finds itself profoundly maladjusted to the society then existing, or by chance grown sensitive to some unnoticed contact with nature. And his cry will be wasted and his prophecy laughed at, unless the same maladjustment or the same sensitiveness is felt also by a group of his contemporaries, capable of trooping together and forming a new body politic. Then perhaps his mad cry, become familiar, will be spontaneously misinterpreted and developed into tolerably applicable precepts and comparatively settled principles. The Church wrote the Gospels; the trades-union will perhaps define the orthodoxy of socialism; and it is always the body, with its organs and its innate capacities, that calls down a particular soul to inhabit it.

A simple reflection may convince the reader that such is the order of nature, and that if any paradox seems to cling to the description of it, this comes only from an inveterate habit of taking words for things. Characters, types, or ideals, in their logical essences, are immaterial; they are eternal ; they are just as near to one point of space and time as to another. Why, then, should any one of them become actual and seem to dominate existence, here rather than there, in me and not in you? Had they any intrinsic power to realise themselves, they would all long-ago have realised themselves to perfection, and we should be left at peace, each soul in the possession of its chosen good. But forms, types, and characters must wait for their occasions. Only the one physically summoned at each point can appear; and then it *must* appear, because the movement of things has fallen into that shape at that moment and the character, type, or form in question has already been realised without being consulted. Yet as it is some form, type, or character that the mind distinguishes and remembers in the flux of events, without seeing the vast flood of natural processes that has washed up that frail phenomenon, we superstitiously invoke the apparition as if it were a manifest god, appearing before us of his own initiative.

Essences have their proper dignity, logical and aesthetic, which it would be far from me to belittle; but they have no power; and when we say they *prevail* or *dominate* over this or that portion of existence, we are using a figure of speech. They prevail and dominate as light prevails and dominates when the sun rises; but as light cannot cause the sun to rise, so characters, types, or laws cannot bring about the occasions on which they are manifested.

III. Language and Ideas

All causes are physical and all values moral: that is an axiom in my philosophy. The psychological sphere is essentially moral, consciousness marking a *success* in organic life: but the whole machinery of this moral triumph is physical. Language, for instance, and its social function, are physical complications, vocal, economic, and historical; and even the spiritual function of language, yielding music and truth, can be exercised only through that physical medium. Words should therefore not be blamed for being only words, symbolic, and wholly unlike their objects. Rather they should be used freely, with sympathy towards the genius of words; so that through the plastic network of their sound and syntax something of the structure of things may be revealed.

I say this in apology for the fact that in some parts of this book I use such phrases as ruling ideas, inspiration, or moral influence. Such expressions might seem inconsistent with my materialism; but they are not, when understood to describe the dominance of a physical agency—an imposing personality, a phraseology, an institution—over simpler human habits.

Higher vital functions sometimes serve to organise lower functions and sometimes to derange them. They could do neither if they were not themselves physical functions having physical organs. But such subtler processes are often hidden from the eye, and can be designated only in a vague globular way by the name and character of their obvious results. So in politics which is not an exact science, the terms used can have only a conventional and dramatic truth. Even in what ought to be physics we are often reduced to the same rude symbolism. The family doctor, looking through his spectacles at a slight eruption on the skin, and pronouncing it *eczema*, will confess if he is candid that this is only a Greek word substituted for the Latin word eruption. He is merely naming the visible fact, the surface appearance. To trace the underlying physiological and chemical processes may be impracticable and not necessary for taking general precautions or giving some relief. So the eruptions and up-boilings of human society doubtless have economic and physiological causes which a complete historical science might trace; but the forces that created animals and that still govern them are not on the animal scale; and the public can observe only gross surface events, expressing them in dramatic language. Hunger, ambition, hatred, and love are the loose emotional categories by which actions are first discriminated; and the refinements by which speech may eventually describe human motives, for instance in Shakespeare, never escape from the same region of spontaneous fiction and verbal fancy.

Seeing, then, that the intimate texture of events, both in ourselves and in the world, escapes observation, we are reduced to naming those superficial features or rhythms which most strike the eye and focus the emotions. The dramatic nomenclature of politics must be accepted, not as revealing a magic world in which some spiritual nebula evolves into material events, but only as the inevitable verbal symbolism by which material events are distinguished and interpreted in the human imagination. A more exact science of life, if we pursued it, would pay for its truth by its abstractness. If it were possible to obtain accurate statistics of human conduct, such information would be irrelevant to the dramatic experience of life, whether private or public; and that mechanical skeleton of history would need to be clothed with the rhetoric of passion and intention before we could recognise it for our familiar world. After all, that which interest[s] the moralist is the phenomenology of spirit; the rest is only the architecture and mechanism of his stage and his stage properties; the play he watches and judges on that stage is a tragic fable, saturated with rival illusions, and spoken in verse.

Illusions form a second reality which may be described with truth. Ideas, however fantastic, grow out of their occasions, and are natural symbols for them. In the proper and widest sense, ideas are *prophetic*. They speak for the Lord, for the dominant power making itself felt in the present, reverberating in the past, and preparing the future. It is no illusion to feel that our words and thoughts are inspired; they really flow from the dynamic process of nature which they describe or forecast; they have some true value as oracles and omens. Their existence is evidence; and they convey knowledge, however partial and qualified, of the course of the world and of their own destiny. This signification of ideas we may admit and retain without any lapse into superstition; and the ordinary idolatrous way of speaking about ideas, purposes, and laws as if they were powers is not only excusable but admirably poetic, if we have the good sense not to press it into a dazed worship of images.

This I say of ideas considered psychologically, as moments and visions in the life of spirit; but the word idea has also an older and purer sense. When any object or event exists, it inevitably possesses some character distinguishing it from other facts and from nothing; and the consequences of fact characterised in one way will be different from what they would have been if the place had been occupied by a fact characterised differently. In other words, the form that matter wears determines the effects that, at that point, matter will have. These forms the Platonic tradition called Ideas. These Ideas, *when exemplified in the facts*, in defining the characters of those facts, prefigure their operation. Thus though forms, Ideas, or essences, taken in themselves, are perfectly impotent, there is a sense in which all natural causes and laws exhibit the domination of Ideas. Concepts, laws, and equations may truly describe the order in which matter, when distributed in a certain way, will presently change its qualities and its distribution.

Taken logically, then, Ideas have the same intrinsic inefficacy as ideas taken psychologically; yet as signs they have an even greater validity. Calculation of events is possible in conceptual terms; and although this formal dominance of Ideas is abstract, and events have many dimensions and complexities not covered in such calculations, often the dynamic thread in events, in their material dimension, may be so traced with accuracy. Such science we call physics. In politics the ideas that prevail have no such validity, because they are not essences exemplified in natural facts, but images or phrases drifting through distracted minds, emotional, ambiguous, and often objectless; so that in politics the wish is commonly father to the thought, nearer than the thought to the heart of nature, and more important for understanding the course of history.

IV. The Psychological Mirage

Modern philosophy and literature tend to be psychological, but psychology itself is an elusive subject, a vague mirage of untraceable images which tends to disappear on closer inspection and to turn partly into animal behaviour, partly into the transcendental being of a spirit witnessing the course of the world. We exist morally as well as physically; we feel and think: so much we may assert with confidence. But our thoughts and feelings are simply an awareness of something going on and maturing in our bodies, under the pressure of circumstances. Experience is, as it were, a spark that flies between the steel of our organisms and the flint of the world. To suppose that our mental life is the primary or only reality, that our feelings, ideas, or wishes arise of themselves or generate one another and determine their own course, is to pass into a land of dreams, and this perversely. For we drop into dreams naturally by relaxing attention and cutting off the control of outer things over our senses; but in making the mere passage of thought, as in a dream, the only reality, we raise illusion to the throne, as if our dreams were not as much, and more passively, effluvia of bodily life than are our waking perceptions.

Such psychologism is only the abuse of an intelligible interest that the modern or romantic man takes in his private experience, focussing his attention upon this, until its occasions and its objects recede into mock reports made for a moment within the dream. And this subjectivism sometimes merges with another normal interest, which the modern or romantic man seemed to have discarded, namely, the interest in spiritual liberation from the world, or salvation. But neither Nirvana nor romantic soliloquy enlightens us about politics; and the intrusion of psychologism into public maxims has been a source of much moral confusion and disaster.

Suffering, hardship, impatience at the structure of society, with hatred and envy of those supposed to be more fortunate, are ancient inevitable sources of rebellion and of slow perpetual revolution in the world; but such unrest, when combined with mystical exaltation and ambiguous prophecies about another world destined soon to appear, takes on the character of a positive delusion and a devastating fanaticism. The enemies of society then think themselves the messengers of God. They draw the sword of Joshua or of Islam or of the Crusades or of some Revolution, and often they are ostensibly victorious. But it is a sorry victory, because on the ruins of the former civilisation another wounded and confused civilisation will arise, under the old natural conditions, and will breed in time a new generation of deluded rebels.

This process, abstractly so hopeless, often has in the concrete very happy temporary results. Each civilisation, judged by perennial human standards, is likely to be, in some respects, better than the old. Irreparable losses are forgotten, dawning pleasures are enjoyed, and in seasons of material prosperity only inexcusable grumblers talk about the good old times, or point to the little black clouds gathering on the horizon.

In order to comprehend these vicissitudes and to enjoy in them what can be enjoyed, it is necessary to remember that mankind is not a flight of wingèd ideas, wishes, and commands, executing themselves in a vacuum, but is a tribe of animals living in a material world. The mirage of psychology is therefore to be discounted, unless we consent that our actions should be as mad as our dreams.

V. Political Implications of Genuine Materialism

It would be vain to discard idealism, if realism were itself a fond image created in the mind and deputed, because we loved it, to be the truth of the political world. The truth of the political world is what it is, apart from all opinion. Such is the primary conviction of an honest mind; and reflection may later recognise that the images by which we conceive the world are mere essences, having no existence there, but serving like words to indicate in our spontaneous sensuous language the different capacities and positions of things in relation to ourselves.

Animal or vital faith, precisely because it asserts the independent being of matter and truth, is diffident about any dogmatic claims of imagination to define those realities. It feels the ghostliness of the psychological sphere, and would not impose human thoughts, cast in terms of essence, upon existent things. These thoughts, like all sensibility, have a true cognitive virtue, since they are a spiritual index to their material occasions; but their virtue is that of a rapid sign; a virtue not to be mistaken either for a dead ultimate self-existence in the image or for a literal exhaustive revelation of anything beyond.

A sign, a language, is something living and transitive. It aspires to report things as they are in some respect, as they would appear from a superhuman station, or at least from as many human points of view as possible. This is a proud ambition, full of perils, yet essentially legitimate. It is involved in being spiritually alive in a material world, where we must cope with surrounding facts. These facts control us according to what they are, not according to what they seem. It is as they are, not as they seem, that sober science and responsible politics must endeavour to conceive them. There is anxiety beneath all speculation; and the fear of being wrong, and of rushing headlong upon fatal dangers, troubles and corrects the intellectual confidence by which we instinctively assume that we are always right.

In politics the philosopher is spared many a pitfall that he might walk into in physics and biology: his field is limited to human affairs. He need not trouble himself with truths deeper than conventional truths. He has to consider real events and real forces, which are all physical, even when they have a mental and moral accompaniment. In this sense he is a man of science, with the responsibilities of an enquirer after the truth, and not, in intention, a composer of historical romances. Yet his contact with the facts need not go deeper than the contacts which other people have had with them, or may have on other occasions. In this sense his field coincides with that of the historical novelist or literary psychologist. He is composing a drama as it might have been lived. But there is this difference: that his interest, if he is not a party man, is not chiefly emotional or centred in the drama itself, as glorious or pitiful; his interest is philosophical and passes from the picturesque surface of those experiences to the causes and conditions that brought them about.

That these causes are all physical is an assumption, or rather an identical proposition, in a naturalistic philosophy. History goes on in the material world, which existed before history began, and by its natural biological developments made history possible. Human beings sprung from the earth and still depend on the earth not only for sustenance but through the agency of a thousand accidents which the changing fertility and quick overpopulation of the earth have occasioned. Yet to climate, poverty, and rivalry the reactions of various men are not identical. Whatever pressure the geographical background may exercise, it would not have produced specifically human societies if men were not physically men, and if their biological, racial, and personal development were not what their inherited nature has made it. The environment fosters and selects; the seed must contain the potentiality and direction of the life to be selected.

I say that human beings have sprung from the earth. I was not present to observe the event; but it is a general presumption of naturalism that men were not let down ready made by a rope, as Lucretius puts it, from heaven. They sprung somehow from the earth; not that in any fallow field, as the earth now is, men would in time grow out of the ground afresh, like thistles; but that in the early plastic state of the planet, shot through by who knows what stellar and ethereal radiations, the potentiality of life, and of all sorts of life, lay dormant. The first tremors and tropes, establishing organisms, probably did not occur on dry land, but as the old Ionians divined, in the sea or the atmosphere. Aristotle observes sarcastically that those early philosophers made the world in turn out of water, air, and fire, but neglected to make it out of earth, as the common man would. The atomists were quick, however, to correct that oversight, their atoms being, I suppose, small stones or crystals. And however childish that image of the atoms may seem to us now, I think that it implies a great truth of physics: namely, that substance or energy must be, and must always have been, unequally distributed, spaced, or concentrated, since otherwise no motion and no distinction of parts could exist in the world.

On the other hand, if we conceive matter not graphically but genetically, as it affects politics, the fact that matter should have assumed the human form, reproducing it *ad libitum* through a human seed, ceases to be a paradox. Matter is essentially only the principle of existence for any and every form. The question is therefore not why, anywhere, matter has taken the form it wears, but why it has not taken some other form; and the answer, I believe, is that it takes whatsoever form it can, given the forms it has taken previously and the method of transformation that, because it had to adopt some method, it happens to have adopted. The radical obstacle to the existence of anything is therefore never the nature of that thing, no matter how delicate or complicated, but the accident that things of a different kind already exist in that region, monopolising that substance, and precluding the formation of the particular thing we have in mind.

Every sort of creature, every sort of government, will spring up out of the earth, if circumstances only allow it. "Earth" here humbly represents the infinite possibilities of Being, reduced by previous local accidents to a particular arbitrary form, with certain limited powers of transformation.

Utopias are all possible—in heaven. As to what may be possible or inevitable on earth, we must certainly consult in the first place the present order of the cosmos at large. Some little lost planet might suddenly bombard us out of existence. Yet in politics we may assume as roughly constant the physical order of nature and of human nature. But all climates and all peoples are not similar; and neither the climates nor the nations, though slightly modifiable, perhaps, by industry, can be changed or equalised by a theory. Their character must be observed and accepted as it is, together with whatever tendencies to transformation that character may exhibit spontaneously. The year has its seasons; so have societies and arts. There are periods of integration, conquest, dominion; there are very brief periods of intellectual and artistic glory; and there follow long eras of confused and monotonous hibernation of the spirit, in which material existence is maintained mechanically, and revolutionised vainly. These revolutions have complex causes, different in each instance, and to be traced, if at all, only by a superhuman minuteness and extent of knowledge; they are certainly not produced by the spirit, usually in abeyance, and in any case not a power. Even at its best, like the daylight, spirit cannot avail to keep itself from fading. But revolutions, in historic times, occur in and by human beings rather than by virtue of external circumstances. Human beings form part of the material world, their psyches being principles of physical organisation, as much as the seed of any plant or the great meteorological cycle by which moisture evaporates and rain falls. In each case the psyche is specific and inherited, without excluding casual variations from the psyche of each of the parents. This personal psyche determines all a man's powers and passions, and his taste or capacity for this or that form of association. Circumstances will encourage, reshape, or suppress these propensities; but without the richly charged individual soul, or the souls of a thousand kindred individuals vibrating in unison, circumstances would continue to compose an empty stage, and a landscape without figures. They become political circumstances when human ambition begins to move amongst them, and to enlist them in its service. Society will then become, under the given physical conditions, whatever the psychic disposition of its members may tend to make of it.

A material interpretation of politics need therefore not be especially climatic or economic or Malthusian, but may take account of those important circumstances in letting loose or suppressing the various instincts and powers of human nature. The initiative of individuals and the contagion of their words and actions must not be excluded: although the persuasions and tumults that sweep through society from such sources are more devastating than fruitful if they do not indicate a happy intuition of that which circumstances, at that moment, render possible and appropriate. Human impulses convulse society, but human necessities construct it.

Nor does a materialistic interpretation of politics exclude a moral judgement upon it, or even a mystical flight beyond such a judgement. Each psyche, in proportion as it is integrated and master of its true will, each society in proportion as it is self-justified, necessarily sets up its ideal to be the measure of all values for its own conscience. Anything else would be mere confusion and looseness of soul. This judgement need not prevent an intellectual comprehension of the contrary or irrelevant interests of others; but such clear insight, in counselling the needful exclusions or even wars in the face of what is alien, only reaffirms the morality proper to oneself. This morality is the ultimate expression of one's nature, by which one lives and is different from nothing; and its moral fervour goes hand in hand with physical health. Sometimes, in exceptional and reflective natures, the distraction and the triviality of life, even of healthy life, become oppressive, and a sympathy with the necessarily excluded goods pursued by contrary moralities renders one's own morality pathetic and almost remorseful. Then a mystical aspiration, renouncing everything for the love of everything, may overflow the mind. Victory or prosperity for one's own people or one's own civilisation will no longer seem an ultimate or unqualified good. It will be counted, if attained, among the flowers of the field, that today bloom and tomorrow wither, only manifesting, in one arbitrary form, the universal impulse in matter towards all sorts of harmonies and perfections. Then all the other harmonies and perfections, not attainable here, perhaps not attained anywhere, will come crowding to the gates of our little temple. And the spirit will be tempted to escape from that particular sanctuary, to abdicate its identity with the society that bred it, and to wander alone and friendless, to be the lover of all climates and the friend of all friends.

The same materialism that justifies ferocity in the jungle may breed impartiality and abnegation beneath the stars.

THE ESSENCE OF SOCIETY

The historical origins of society form a preserve for archeologists into which I will not intrude; but for philosophers things have also a *logical* origin, in that their structure and life may presuppose and complicate simpler structures, whether these actually preexisted separately or not. In this sense a too curious school of transcendentalists maintains that society never had an origin, because nothing can exist except by virtue of its social bonds. Figuratively indeed all existential relations may be called social; for events owe their being to previous events, and things once formed can preserve their existence only by resisting or complying with the present pressure of their neighbours. Something without neighbours, without antecedents or consequents or a position in natural space or time, would not *exist*; it would not be a part of the world, but a mere essence. It would dwell only in the immutable society of all other possibilities.

This baptismal bond of co-existence among all things that are to exist in the same world is sometimes exaggerated by saying that things are nothing but their relations to one another, and that morally too a man is nothing but the functions he exercises in society. I think, however, that if a man were not first something intrinsically he could never be found in forced relations to anything else. What he is in himself, his essence, has indeed inescapable *ideal* relations to other essences, as a straight line is essentially distinguished, by its constancy in direction,

George Santayana, "The Essence of Society," Humanities Research Center, University of Texas. © 1969 Daniel Cory. The old handwriting suggests that this reflection was written late in Santayana's life.

from all curves that essentially change their direction at each point. These ideal eternal relations suffice to give character to the straight line, and make it discoverable, if it ever exists or seems to exist; but definition does not produce any cases of it. In order to acquire existence that essence has to be found, or to find itself, in a mesh of relations that are not ideal and inevitable, not possibilities eternally collateral to its own essence, but extraneous, accidental, variable relations, the surprise and pressure and inconstancy of which prove that it has been born into this world, and compelled for a time to cut a figure there, precariously, confusingly, treacherously, and perhaps painfully. It is this second inconstant realm of being that we call *existence*: but so far is our accidental and changing position in it from being our essence, that it is the violence and groundlessness of that position that prove to us the terrible paradox that *we* exist.

BIOLOGICAL IDEAL OF SOCIETY

By a chronological accident, monarchy among us has become associated with tradition, and republican institutions with reform. It happened in the seventeenth century that monarchy, which had been an agent in political unification and expansion, became the instrument of vested interests, artificial privileges, and foreign dominations; and against these insurrection was naturally directed. But ideally, the most stable order in society would be biological, instinctive, and not committed to any ruler. Life would seem to each individual wonderfully fresh and free, while he and his contemporaries repeated the same round of transformations and actions that had delighted their ancestors. Government is not needed to create order but only to check disorder. Like medicine and law, government exercises a double function. Organically, and viewed from the animal side, it is a parasite, and at best remedial; perhaps it prevents a greater evil. Yet in so doing government becomes

George Santayana, "Biological Ideal of Society," Humanities Research Center, University of Texas. © 1969 Daniel Cory. A reflection intended for *Dominations and Powers*.

an art, gives exercise to special passions and virtues, grows into the very focus of social life, thinks itself its own excuse for being, and perhaps turns into a devastating incubus.

In a perfect animal society, such as we imagine the bees or ants to compose, that human parasite, government, would not exist at all. There would naturally be differences in size, health, and strength between individuals, and even differences of function such as go with sex and age; but the queen bee, like the cock in a barnyard, exercises no government; it is merely a generative centre, as a spring would be a centre for drinking or a roost a centre for sleep. In human society these organic differences could be extended and intensified by education and the use of instruments: there might arise classes and even castes, if expertness in special directions were proved to be hereditary; but if each man spontaneously chose and exercised his profession, all would remain perfectly free and politically equal, without the need of any government to coerce them. This social order, being insured by pre-established vital harmony among all functions and wills, might remain identical for ages; as long, indeed, as the health of that society or the conditions of its life were not undermined.

Such a happy people would be intensely conservative. Whatever difference of occupation or taste there might be among them would leave every class and every individual perfectly satisfied with the arts and pleasures of that station; nor would there be jealousy between those having the same vocation, since each would prefer his own degree and quality of performance: so every parent prefers his own children and every poet his own verses, without setting up any conceited and indefensible demand that other parents or other poets should prefer his offspring to theirs. It is when one's own virtue is clouded that fate begins to seem unjust; because then some impediment prevents one from becoming oneself and doing or thinking what one's heart was naturally set upon. And it is the interference of circumstances or of other men, when this seems to be the cause of one's failures, that provokes anger with the order of nature and of society, and sets the unhappy mortal being at war within himself, against everything that surrounds him. He will then make an alliance with those he hates less in order to destroy those he hates more: and the victorious band will form a government, revolutionary, or reactionary, and in either case vindictive.

Is then a changeless cooperative happy society the ultimate ideal of republicans and democrats? Not avowedly, nor in these times, because the dominant images in the modern political mind are revolution and progress, with the spectre of tyranny, aristocratic or clerical, to be feared and finally laid. Yet behind the urgent cry for reform there is often, if not always, a classic confidence in finality. Reforming parties call themselves *radical*: that is, they aspire to extirpate evil by the roots; and, then, apparently, the eternally natural and just form of society would ensue of itself. War is preached to end war: institutions, parties, and nations are suppressed in order to safeguard liberty. There seems to be in the background the conviction that all human troubles are artificially imposed, that wicked men and wicked governments have wantonly destroyed the order of nature. Only a wildly romantic philosophy dares to maintain that war is a good in itself, that progress has no goal, and that life requires perpetual self-contradiction.

Nor is the implication of finality merely logical. The constitution of the United States was meant to last for ever and is expected to do so. It has actually lasted amid much ruin of monarchies and republics everywhere, in spite of a complete transformation in the extent, population, and condition of the country. It has been amended, but amended legally, according to its own provisions; and in one remarkable instance an amendment, on trial, has been revoked. This elasticity is a sign of life. The character of the nation may become utterly unlike anything that its founders expected; yet their principles were simple and abstract enough to represent, at least verbally and legally, a fit framework for the material coordination of old and new interests. In the concrete the United States are a much-governed country: new legislation is piled up, like the tower of Babel, to further all manner of enterprises; but the impulse to advance these projects is still spontaneous and confident. The much-governed community dreams of more regulations, and still feels vitally free.

It is when society is chaotic, when the individual is distracted and insecure in himself and circumstances are hopelessly unfavourable that direction by another becomes a possible help, perhaps the only possible salvation. Yet government from without is inevitably imperfect and unstable. Impulses in two organisms not initially adjusted to each other and capricious in themselves cannot meet without friction, and each will impute its own defeats to the perverseness of the other. At the same time, in a crisis natural leadership asserts itself, and is instinctively accepted by the crowd. And the natural superiority of the leader grows by exercise, becomes expert, surrounds itself with sub-sidiary organs of information and control, and becomes a government. This is an artificial, imperfect, substitute for biological order; it in-duces vices in the ruler as well as arts, and brings unnecessary burdens on the people as well as needful security. Yet the monarchial system— and all government, in act, is monarchical—being guided by perception rather than habit, is more sensitive to change in things than is a pre-established institution. A monarch, when he really rules, is a greater innovator than a society content with its inherited constitution, which it probably thinks divine and alone right.

INHUMAN SOCIETY

When the order of the body politic and its accretions are left to chance, like vegetation in the jungle, the units of society remain hu-man, but social life becomes inhuman. If we shudder at the cruelty and waste of such chaos, and at the oppression and distortion that each liv-ing organism suffers from the blind pressure of every other, we need not for that reason imagine that human society should form a Levi-athan, such as is pictured in the book of Hobbes under that title; a monster composed of a tightly packed mass of human beings, and armed in either hand with a monstrous sword and a monstrous crozier. To defend such a Leviathan would be idolatry of the worst type, since the idol that crushes everybody is inanimate, and the crushed creatures are animate centres of life and of spirit. And if the folly of such idolatry needed further proof we might find it in the futility of that holocaust: for such an artificial monster, dead in itself but composed of living units, is a corpse, already in the act of decomposition and devoured by the worms that are its substance.

The problem for political art is not to transfer life fom natural to artificial organisms, but rather to transform the medium in which living

George Santayana, "Inhuman Society," *Columbia Manuscript Collection.* © 1969 Daniel Cory. A draft, written after 1945, in preparation for *Dominations and Powers.*

organisms have already arisen, so that they may flourish there more freely, and the jungle may become a garden. A garden has neither the substance nor the form of a living plant, but is so cleared and watered, so traversed by paths, so walled in and so sown and weeded that, while each plant flowers and yields fruit at its best, all together form a spectacle delightful to the master-eye that is able to survey it as a whole. This intellectual dominion is not that of a stranger or a tyrant; it is the sympathetic response of each open flower to the air, the light, and the varied shade and fragrance of all its neighbours.

Still, the growth of our political jungle are not plants but animals, running about and burroughing the soil to their own advantage; a zoological garden where the beasts are their own keepers. And nothing infuriates a busy animal, intent on its chosen food or breeding-hole, than to be disturbed by other animals chasing other plunder or snatching away his own. This happens almost always even in the desert, by the intrusion of beasts of prey, large or minute; so that life becomes a perpetual war against other life. The broad field and steady opportunities offered by inanimate nature, where labour finds normally its expected rewards, almost disappear from the minds of men living in a closely political society; and instead they struggle against a babel of rival interests and usurped rights, in the midst of which no settled arts can flourish, but the intellect is narrowed into fox-like meanness and intrigue, with no assurance of success, and an incessant flow of contradictory alarms, disappointments and treasons. Such is the life of professional politicians; and such they make the life of the public that they lead. The wilderness leaves man poor and unprotected against material plagues; but society, when overwrought and disorganised, plunges him into a vortex of rival enterprises, most of them unnecessary, that offers him only a choice of artificial slaveries and of false hopes. The non-human world at least is friendly to the disinterested spirit; but the human world seduces the mind into hectic passions, merciless to one another, and each vain in itself.

Yet it is only because man is a social animal that he can find society where none intrudes, in great spaces, amid superhuman sympathies. Were he a beast, he would never be able to raise his nose from the ground, unless it were to tear and devour some victim or some enemy. The cure for inhuman society cannot be found in material isolation or in solitary ignorance; it must be sought in a rational economy, material and moral, to be established in the human world. Kindly arts may at

once protect mankind from distress and give them congenial employ-
ment. To make room for these arts, however, it is first necessary to clear
the jungle. One of the many species that this jungle has bred must
transform it into a park and an orchard after its own heart. Other
species and abnormal or incompatible developments in the dominant
race itself would have to be excluded from these cultivated precincts,
not with curses or detestation but discreetly, allowing the exiles to dwell
freely outside, or perhaps retaining such as could be tamed and rendered friendly, as we now include a few useful beasts of burden or at-
tractive cats, horses and dogs in our domestic economy. Rationalised
society would still touch at the margin much alien life; insects and wild
animals, insane or criminal persons, and perhaps, as always in an-
tiquity, "blameless Ethiopians," or other childlike or intractable races,
relegated to their confines and left there undisturbed and unexploited.
In any case, however completely an all-absorbing human society might
dominate the surface of the earth, the deeper and all-controlling forces
of nature would remain unharnessed, and would continue to support
human life and reason with an ominous step-motherly coldness and frequent frowns. The attempt to humanise and rationalise the universe
can end only in illusion, by ideally substituting an invented world for
the real one; unless indeed this attempt turns against the pride that
prompted it, which was legitimate pride in the human sphere, sets up
the ways of nature at large into a model for man, and fanatically
tramples down our political garden again into a jungle.

The reader may perhaps wonder what I mean by this last suggestion.
The devastation that we have lately seen in the world was due to an attempt at establishing ruthlessly a particular national and social order;
it was not an inhuman revulsion against artifice but an inhuman
insistence upon artifice and upon political unison. It was inspired by
dreams of racial and cultural omnipotence, that is to say, by a childish
impulse armed with the weapons of pedantry and mechanical invention. It failed before the massive resistance of a less strained, more
humane, more deeply rooted civilisation. It was by no means to the
jungle that Fascism and Nazism wished to reduce the world, but on the
contrary [to] but an engineer's and schoolmaster's ideal of rigid and
universal order. All the wanton branches of the human tree were to be
cut off in order that one vertical stem should flourish in solitary perfection.

The possible return to the jungle which I have in mind would be prompted instead by the love of anarchy. There is perhaps less danger of this historically, because a deep love of anarch[y] would disarm the anarchist himself and limit the disorder he could cause to his own bosom. But spiritually—and I would always keep the spiritual effect of politics in view—the love of anarchy is a real danger, for its omnivorance amounts to indecision and indifference in the will, and such indifference may seem to bring a mystical peace. And so it might if the spirit were really absolute and independent of any physical organ. An equal love of everything might then save it from all contradiction, and make it invulnerable. But in fact spirit arises only when a modicum of order has been established in a living organism, and a measure of harmony between the impulses of that organism and its natural opportunities. If in a spiritual life so rooted, an equal love of everything should arise, it would paralyse that spirit, or dissolve it [in] utter distraction. It would be a case of vital fever or madness. For the spirit to renounce moral and political preferences would be suicide. By introducing an ideal jungle into its own life, it would contradict and renounce the original animal will that permitted spirit to exist at all, when a vital order first arose in the sea or in the jungle.

PARADISE LOST

A prudent tyranny seeks to domesticate its subjects in a preserve which it calls a paradise, patriotic or ecclesiastical. Here they are invited to enjoy certain fruits of civilisation: security (save from official exactions), authorised pleasures, some sorts of abundance, and a somnolent faith and labour. For a man who is not a rebel by nature, existence in such a medium is not intolerable; private passions and private wit give enough scope to his spirit, and he is not sorry to leave the procession of the great world to the richly caparisoned elephants that march in it. But always, in the midst of any Eden, there is a tree whose fruit is forbidden: you must not hear the rustle of lost possibilities, you must

George Santayana, "Paradise Lost," *Columbia Manuscript Collection.* © 1969 Daniel Cory. A "little essay" intended for *Dominations and Powers.*

not relish the flavour of foreign things. They are declared beforehand
to be all indigestible; they would indeed disarrange your home diet, and
very likely, if you took to feeding on them too exclusively, you would
die poisoned. Yet who knows? Your heart may feel a secret affinity to
the untried: you may have been, at home, starved all your life on the
husks of a foreign orthodoxy. Even if you were content before, the mere
discovery of your limitations may turn them for you into an evil; and
you may prefer danger to confinement.

The apologue in Genesis puts the case for submission in the strongest
possible light. In the Garden of Eden tameness ought to have been without a sting. Adam and Eve were being victimised or bidden to love and
obey their oppressors. They were free from hunger, forced labour, old
age, or disease; there was no possibility of quarrels except between man
and wife, and tiffs in the absence of all rival spouses would not have
been of long duration. Their browsing life was not embittered by un-
satisfied passions or rebel memories, or tales wafted from happier lands.
Nevertheless the fable is constrained to be tragic. Even this blandest of
tyrannies could not secure lasting allegiance. There is a radical flux in
nature, and morality can never arrest it. The mind, like the very surface
of the earth, takes in time a new slant; even without express prohibitions or talk of forbidden fruits, the old ration becomes wearisome.
The serpent in Eden therefore has a secret accomplice in the deepest
texture of existence, beneath any specific animal nature or any dictates
of reason. To sane human nature and clear reason Adam and Eve
would appear strangely frivolous; indeed, if we admit that all their
impulses were under rational control, their conduct becomes a sudden
madness, as if the devil had bewitched them. But that alleged rational
guidance of life is a fiction; it represents an ideal never reached, and
even if reached, never stable. Romantic moralists, who are in sympathy with nature rather than with art, therefore assure us that the
Serpent was no devil, but creative spirit itself under a comic mask; and
that the alleged Fall was in reality the beginning of moral experience.

The fact, however, is hardly that this mutability is a good in itself;
perhaps under favourable circumstances a normal life might be sustained indefinitely, as it seems to be in some animals and even in some
nations. Such a normal life is not static inwardly: every man and woman runs through youth and age with a fresh spirit, through continual
unprecedented accidents; but the ulterior points of reference for these
adventures are fixed by law and religion, and the wise can tell us before-

hand what our own wisdom will discover. This, if the wise are wise enough, happens even to the romantic adventurer: his evolution is not predictable in detail, but its method, its violence, and its vanity can be seen at a glance.

Whether, in any movement, the evolution is a progress will depend on the presence or absence of suppressed instincts and warped powers. If the soul had *needed* no more scope than Eden afforded, the soul would have sinned outrageously, would have debauched and mutilated itself, by breaking away for the sake of mere change; but in that case we may well believe that it would not have broken away. Such unnatural variations would not have seemed tempting, but obviously absurd and horrible. Your perfect poet will not wish to speak foreign languages: he can speak of all things better and more penetratingly if his words have been interwoven from the beginning with his native impressions, and Satan would never get a hearing by assuring him that if he tasted the polyglot dictionary he might become even as the philologists, knowing all the worst ways of saying everything.

Unfortunately the serpent that lurks in every earthly paradise is no interloper. There is an unreconciled residuum, a centrifugal possibility, in every portion of the most perfect organism: and a cry of rebellion in one quarter is echoed everywhere by a rising murmur of discontent: though probably the causes of friction are different in different quarters, and disruption, if it gathers head, will destroy more rebels than it will satisfy. Yet somewhere, out of chaos, a new order may spring up, and re-establish for a while a different, no less imperfect, equilibrium.

THE REVIVAL OF AUTHORITY

It is an ancient impulse in man to invoke a divine sanction for his customs and institutions, and even for his greater crimes: folly itself seems to be sanctified if it is deeply enough seated in the world. So

George Santayana, "The Revival of Authority," *Columbia Manuscript Collection.* © 1969 Daniel Cory. Santayana's subtitle is "I—In Government" indicating that the essay, written between the two wars, was to be part of a longer piece.

Herodotus represents the Trojan and Persian wars as earthly manifestations of an eternal quarrel between the goddess Europa and the goddess Asia. Similarly President Wilson referred the late war, after he
became entangled in it, to a divine epic necessity destined to suppress
all war and to make the world safe for democracy. Others, whose home
myths were different, nerved themselves to the same struggle by fancy-
ing that they were once again defending Latin genius and religion
against the assaults of barbarism: or—what is the same thing turned
round—that they were stepping forth proudly and resolutely to perform a crowning act in a providential drama, in which dominion perpetually passes from old or dissolute nations to nations that are young
or ruthlessly organised. This bombast is no accident: it represents the
essential difference between people who follow custom or passion instinctively, and those who attribute to them a superior authority, and
follow them deliberately. It would be nothing that any party or nation
should be animated by the will to dominate: every child and every
criminal is so animated too; the point is that the party or nation should
invoke the authority of universal nature or of some glorious destiny to
sanctify its private impulse. It then makes a virtue of its passion, or perhaps of its madness, and identifies morality with a steady determination
to suppress all impulses save those in harmony with itself.

Harmony is indeed, as Socrates taught, the principle of morality, as
well as of beauty; it is what in modern language we call organisation.
But for exclusion, assimilation, and definite heredity, there would be no
life; and the high points of civilisation and intelligence are reached
when the greatest resources are gathered up and dominated by some
one nucleus of order, by some definite traditional body. On the other
hand the celestial machinery invented to account for this fact is
needless and fabulous. Events, unless my philosophy is sadly mistaken,
have diffuse causes in the jumble of previous events; and the sequel
stultifies all prophecies and romantic logics, even when in some verbal
sense it may seem to fulfil them. Thus, geographically, there is still a
Europe and an Asia, and we are told to expect terrible conflicts between
them, as if they were a brace of fighting-cocks; but what are the corresponding moral entities, and where do they begin or end? Modern
Europe and America are what a Greek would have called Asiatic, in
scale, organisation, luxury, and religion: while Moslem Asia is at least
as much an heir to Hellenism, in ways of living, and feeling, as the West
is in letters; and as to externals, the Chinese and the Turks may soon

be indistinguishable from Yankees. The continents of Herodotus remain, but both his goddesses have perished.

The same fatuity appears in the myths of our own day: events have curiously belied the idealisms by which they were supposed to be explained or sanctioned. The "manifest destiny" pursued by imperial Germany with such extraordinary resource and conviction, has ended in smoke; there is not only a momentary pause due to circumstances, but a moral change of front. This change of front was indeed announced by Spengler—an authorised herald of German myths—when he still expected a military victory. Germany would guide the world, but henceforth only in the paths of material greatness, no other leadership of greatness being possible in the coming age. Germany would thus do for the vast herds of mankind rather less than Napoleon might have done for them, and little more than America is actually doing: for if there is to be a domination of the world by mechanism, it is not now to Germany that the domination is likely to fall. Inventions are soon generalised; while the man-power and the natural resources lie rather in China and India, in Russia and the United States.

Nor is it clear that the major premise of the Spenglerian prophecy is sound, and that the earth is about to be subjected to a homogeneous mechanical regimen, without national or local characters. Perhaps various peoples, like the Japanese, may adopt the requisite mechanical equipment only the better to defend their moral diversity. The special form and spirit thus preserved in certain centres would then be likely to spread over the comparatively amorphous parts of the surrounding world, as the Greek form and spirit spread, diluted, over the East with Alexander and over the West with Rome. In the same way the maxims of the French Revolution and the English parliamentary system have spread over the modern world; but where not native to the soil they have proved absurd excrescenses, without use or vitality. It would have been simpler and healthier if each nation or city had bred its own traditions and had remained faithful to them. This conviction is now deeply felt and loudly expressed in many parts of the world, in Asia, in America, in Italy, in Spain, in Poland, in Ireland. Perhaps the epidemic of catch-words by which international democracies are swayed may not avail to obliterate the natural constitution of society in different classes and in different places.

There must always be a Germany, as there must always be a Spain;

but it would seem as if the Germany of yesterday, like the Spain of the sixteenth century, could never be restored: the clock has run down, and the key is lost. And if we turn to the other camp, where is the victory that was to ensure universal peace and democracy? We find everywhere disgust and confusion and ominous rumblings: plutocracy uneasy, parliaments discredited, governments impotent; and if a note of youth or hope is sounded anywhere, it comes from the national autocracies set up in several states, notably in Italy and Spain, where the incubus of a foreign liberalism, hypocritical even where it is native, has been thrown off, and the true interests of mankind have begun to appear in their ancient simplicity: order, friendship, beauty, union.

But the chief, the unexpected, the tremendous by-product of those vain convulsions has been the Union of Socialist Soviet Republics. This too is an autocracy, but not national: it avoids using the name of Russia, and aspires to be universal. Here is an armed atheistical sect, with a doctrine proclaiming its right and its intention to govern the whole world. Here crime—for (not to mention rivers of blood) it is crime to trample on living interests, material and moral, at one's sweet will—here, too, crime appeals to mythical sanctions: the courage of the faithful, in their own sufferings and peplexities, is fortified by a thundering philosophy, which assures them that fate is on their side and that their speedy triumph is certain. It would be easy to mock this prophecy and to proclaim in one's turn that these promises will fail, or have failed already, if by success we understand a realisation of the bright ideal conceived in the beginning. But delusions of this kind are elastic: their original sense is soon lost in some new meaning which necessity or a changed imagination may presently read into them. There is therefore no knowing, even after the fact, whether they have failed or succeeded. Did the Roman Empire succeed, or Christianity, or Islam, or Prottestantism, or liberalism? Such movements have a momentum which may long be traceable materially after they are spiritually extinct; they may have served to give a new form or equilibrium to human customs and sentiments. In dissolving and merging with other influences they may initiate a new civilisation.

The Bolshevist system, like the Fascist, is intolerant; it intends to impose a regimen, a task, and a mode of sentiment on everybody within its fold. In other words, its ambition is to occupy the heart, and to guide life from within in all its manifestations, instead of merely controlling it at its periphery, as if the State were a menagerie of miscellaneous creatures, that needed only a local or an international police to keep them from biting one another.

Intolerance, in the nineteenth century, had a bad name and seemed identical with tyranny. But intolerance is an integral part of form, a biological principle of health. If you are anything, you cannot be, or consent to become, anything contrary to your essence. As the body rejects poisons, so a community, if it has moral definition, must reject treason or dissidence or disaffection. It has no place for the essential alien: not because the alien need be wicked or mistaken or inferior, but because he is foreign here, incompatible with this experiment, and out of this picture. All societies are intolerant in so far as they are morally definite: a liberal regimen can leave everything important free only because it leaves everything important out.

Under a liberal regimen the middle and upper classes could live very safely and comfortably and could freely improve their minds. Unless a man took up politics as a sport or a hobby, he could forget that there was a government at all, except at intervals when there was much shouting because the persons of the government were being changed; and after they were changed he observed no difference. Property was safe; taxes were fixed and moderate, or else indirect and invisible.[1] Custom and law—which were ferociously intolerant—provided for his personal security. Being providentially endowed with a religion, a home, and an income, or easily able to acquire them of his own initiative, he only asked not to be pestered by meddlesome priests, policemen, taxgathers, or recruiting sergeants. There existed convenient churches, universities, railways and steamships, luckily all privately endowed and privately managed, for his education and travels; academies and international empresarios [*sic*] amply provided for his tastes, and fashionable society for his pleasures. The fields were still green and open for walking, or even for hunting; and it was pleasant afterwards to sit by the fire, and read of the discoveries of science or the curious speculations of philosophers; and then, after a hearty dinner, tucked deliciously in bed, it was easy to fall asleep between smiles and tears over some great sentimental novel. Naturally, in this liberal

1. In Santayana's first draft this paragraph began with the words, "The nineteenth century was an age in which. . . ." "Under a liberal regimen. . . ." was a later substitution, and only a part of the paragraph was changed to reflect it. Hence the change from the conditional to a direct description here.—Editors.

paradise, the mere idea of intolerance seemed hideous and intolerable. What possible right could anyone have to interfere with this happiness or to encroach on this liberty?

Unfortunately the world is in flux, and the prosperous, whatever may be their prosperity, are "like little wanton boys that swim on bladders, but far beyond their depth." Those periodical rows, when the government was being changed, were continually loosening the moral fabric of society; each election, with its factious hatreds and false promises on every side, was a lesson in disaffection. Meantime the growth of industry and of population was undermining the social fabric materially. The many who had no home, or a hateful one, no education, no income, and no religion somehow did not find felicity in naked freedom. A man to whom nothing belongs wishes at least to belong to something. He will be glad of a vote as an acknowledgement of his rights and a testimonial of equality, or as a weapon to be used vindictively, to destroy everything which he does not possess; and the State itself will seem to him the chief of his natural enemies until it becomes socialistic and begins to provide for his personal needs. Meantime his free church or club or trades-union will be the sole objects of his loyalty. These societies, at first nominally voluntary, become inevitable for him, and compulsory: he must live by one or another of them, or he can have no life. They are the nuclei of a new regimen and of a new intolerance, despotic to those within and merciless to those outside. The more completely these new organisms absorb the allegiance of their members, the more anarchical the old national State becomes, with its disastrous elections and its weak governments, and the more superfluous: its only function seems to be to create frontiers, maintain armies, and produce wars. Yet since geographical and economic necessity compels the inhabitants of any region to acknowledge some common authority, there will be no choice in the end but to organise the free societies in which people actually live, industrially and morally, into a single compulsory society. The State will then be a union of social Soviets.

Such is the character of the new autocracies, no less in Italy and Spain than in Russia. Indeed, Italy and Spain realise this ideal better, because the misfortune of Russia is that its revolution has been made by outcasts and doctrinaires, in the interests of a class-war and of the dictatorship of the proletariat, so that its doctrine includes a chimerical philosophy of history that expects events to move dialectically and an absurd theory of value that measures value by hours of labour, and not by the excellence of the result, while its practice disregards or suppresses half the spontaneous associations—such as the Church and the nation itself—which required to be included in a fair political synthesis. It is precisely these living Soviets, carrying the moral interests and traditions of mankind with them, that the new governments of Italy and Spain are embodying in their constitutions; because the men who guide them, though resolute, are not fanatics but large-hearted and rich in human experience. That a particular religion, nationality, or military organism should exist anywhere is a historical accident, as are all the specific traditions of mankind at any particular stage; but these accidents are the very substance of politics, which a just and truly representative government exists to harmonise, not to destroy. It would be a pity to suppress in human nature or in tradition, precisely the most human and most civilised elements; in order to begin again at the bottom, with a pack of animals. Is it not enough to antagonise wanton invaders or heresies, precisely for threatening and not being able to share one's traditional life? Why turn furiously against one's own bosom, and try to extirpate there our home passions and profound inheritance? The intolerance of revolutionaries is not only more sweeping than that of conservatives but less excusable. Not that there is anything sacred, or even reasonable, in things as they are. Almost always, things as they are are absurd and odious, and there would be little harm in destroying them root and branch, if such violence merely hastened their disappearance, which although many a fond soul may regret it, is always inevitable in the end. The great evil of destruction is prospective: not what revolutionaries destroy condemns them, but what they produce. For what they produce is simply ruin: true beginnings do not come from revolution but from unintended and unnoticed seeds, falling in the fallow field, or perhaps in the furrow, ploughed with some other intention. But for such happy accidents, revolution would produce nothing, and merely render difficult the continuance or genesis of definite organisms, whether better or worse than those which it had destroyed; since there is nothing more obdurately stable than a desert, or less fertile than moving sands.

Intolerance flows from moral integrity: far from being a vice, it is a consequence of health and vigour, the thermometer of virtue. Yet except in the rare instances where harmony is spontaneous, this virtue must have a sinister side; it must be the unflinching enemy of much that flourishes outside, and of much that might flourish within. Sacrifice is inevitable, because in a living synthesis each person or each passion has a head of its own and is not adjusted *a priori* to any eventual harmony. To forbid, to demand, to lead, to modulate—in a word, to govern —is therefore inevitable, if anything definite is to be achieved or maintained: such is the price of order, of greatness, of virtue, of life itself. This cruel character of existence, with the insecurity and imperfection of its best achievement, may tempt the philosopher to turn away from life altogether, or to aspire to live only in the spirit, repenting, as it were, of all those shameful limitations and injustices which are imposed upon him by his station in time and place, by his human nature, and his tribal morality. Nature, however, cannot repent: every child and every nation is born unregenerate, in spite of all sour prophets or shining redeemers. Until destruction overtakes this world, it must live on on its own terms, succeeding here and there, through intolerance and victory, in establishing for a time some modicum of harmony; because if no special regimen were imposed anywhere, but all were toleration and freedom, chaos and nonentity would have already returned.

It is unreasonable, therefore, to blame intolerant governments or moralities for those constraints which are proper to organic existence: but we may note certain limits beyond which moral integration is impossible, so that the effort to attain it becomes a vain violence. Virtue, as man may possess it, whether in the soul or in the State, is a synthesis of impulses which are initially independent; and this tremulous organisation is faced in nature at large by overwhelmingly greater forces, which are alien and indifferent. Virtue may accordingly overreach itself in two directions: at home, by exacting perfection, abroad by claiming universality. In either case, its constitutional intolerance becomes a trespass, aggressive not conservative, arbitrary instead of natural, malignant rather than holy. These trespasses of virtue are the cause of the bad name which intolerance has had in the modern world; for no one notices his own intolerance, which, in himself or his party, everyone calls high principle or zeal for progress; and in the looseness of his own ideas and traditions, he would find oppressive almost any definite regimen that could be proposed to him, having no natural roots in his own soul.

Saint Francis could preach persuasively to the birds and fishes, because he understood their relation to God, and God's relation to them: if he had bidden them learn to sing the Latin psalter or come and be fried in the kitchen, they would have pecked his eyes out or bitten his shins. If we wish to hold any reasonable communion with alien natures we must rise to the point of view of God, our common creator, who is not a moralist. We may then, in our affectionate detachment, see the humor and sweetness of our comradeship, and the necessity of our conflicts; and even in these we shall understand both sides, with a religious chivalry, and be brave without being angry. Such was the spirit of the classic poets in describing battles among the gods, or even among men. They saw the glorious vanity of it all, and how nature is but a confused and painful Olympia; but the manliness of their souls kept them from slipping even for a moment into disloyalty to their own side; better perish bravely than suffer change, which would be but a slower way of perishing, and less honourable: and their readiness to die, far from weakening their determination to live beautifully, kept the beauty of their lives inviolate. Here was morality in its place and unyielding integrity without arrogance or unreason. If some sentimental sparrow had chirped in Saint Francis's ear, that he might just as well stop chanting the psalter in choir, because the woods were God's first temples, and music was purer without words, the Saint would most assuredly have wrung that silly bird's neck; and if some blustering whale had replied to his sermon by bellowing that men, too, were mortal like whales, and that there was no pure spirit in them and no heaven for them, the apostle of charity would instantly have perceived that a devil had taken possession of this whale, and with a violent exorcism would have driven the fiend out of that innocent monster, and sent it, freed from the errors of thought, to spout the white sea-spray with a vengeance.

A sense of brotherhood with all forms of existence, however strange, whether it comes through spiritual insight, or through an initial sympathy, such as in the joy which children take in animals, implies security in one's own being; the child does not yield an inch of his own ground out of consideration to his pet's wishes, nor is a clear spirit tempted at all to forego its intellectual dominion and whoop with the savages or burrow with the worm. On the contrary, what chills this natural sympathy and suggests the preposterous desire to impose human morality on nature or human logic on God, is the sense of insecurity in oneself. Terror does not create the gods; but it creates the mania to humanise them. And the same terror creates the passion for regimenting other men, and compelling them to think and to act as we do. A truly lordly spirit, or a truly humble one, perfectly content and sure of itself, would love to be surrounded by giants and dwarfs, by persons of all nations and moralities: without contaminating one's own soul, they enlarge its field and add to the gaiety of nature. But unfortunately it is seldom given to an incarnate spirit to be safe: its food and air, if not its inner resolution, are always being filched away from it, or poisoned. Nature is overcrowded with seeds: you must trample on others to make room for yourself. This is the reason why on earth there is a recurrent ambition to establish universal empires, religions, or systems of thought. Terror, and uneasiness at being oneself, are at the base of it; as now-a-days we all dress alike, because each of us is ashamed of his looks. Uniformity is our refuge from nullity. No brave and spontaneous organism would put forth such a claim: but a dreadful consciousness of weakness—and inferiority—drives us to abolish all differences, and to hide our ugliness, and bolster up our illusions, by imposing them on other people; or (what comes to the same thing) by adopting theirs. This is why religions and political parties carry on propaganda, why women want votes, why uneasy minds dream of a universal language or government or philosophy. The field of human affairs being now grown narrow, so that every race and every mind, to its confusion and destruction, is intertwined with all others, no organisation promises to be staunch unless it is universal. But such need of universality, where it is real (as perhaps, in commerce) is a geographical accident. There would be no speculative insight in a philosopher who wished to extend human logic to the universe or human morality to God. God, as the true sages tell us, is great: and nature, even if not great in the same sense, nor raised above particularity, escapes any given particularity by continually changing it for another, and the finite mind, too, may escape through irony from the limitations which it cannot escape through omniscience.

LIBERALISM AND DEMOCRACY

The accidents of political development in recent times have associated liberalism with democracy, but the two things are separable; and in the future as in the past may probably be divided. The Roman Empire was liberal, after democracy had become impossible; because the very apathy of the people is favourable to toleration and the encouragement from above of a harmless diversity in life and mind, partly from cynicism and partly from kindliness. On the other hand, many ancient cities and some modern religious communities have been democratic without being liberal. The very intensity of their democracy—the single mind and temper irresistibly swaying the whole people—excluded the individualist and made him the butt of mockery, ostracism, and abuse, merciless as only a unanimous people can be merciless. Indeed though I am not fond of paradoxes, I will venture this assertion, which may seem a paradox to the reader: that to be liberal is contrary to the genius of democracy. Liberalism is individualistic, respectful towards things alien, new, or unknown; it welcomes diversity; it abhors compulsion; it distrusts custom. Does democracy, or can democracy, share any of these feelings? It would be a violent tyranny to make majorities absolute if, in a democracy the majority and the minority were not much alike. To yield on a question of procedure, of persons, of minor policy is easy for the minority; that minority is not thereby robbed of any fundamental liberty or outraged in any rooted habit. But to yield up one's soul, because the devil has a majority of one, is not in human nature. Democracies must either have a single soul—the minority being in agreement with the majority in every important matter—or it must not touch the soul at all, but be itself only a matter of procedure, a convenient form of government so long as government is of no great consequence. In both cases the officials might be chosen by lot almost as well as by ballot—because where there is unanimity any one on whom the lot fell would fairly represent the people; whereas if the government is perfunctory, and without directive influence over the

George Santayana, "Liberalism and Democracy," *Columbia Manuscript Collection.* © 1969 Daniel Cory. A notebook entry.

lives of men, it is idle to quarrel over the possession of that shabby sinecure. It falls then, without much inconvenience, to one group or other of hungry professional politicians, who on both sides have no grander or more sinister aim than to keep their modest salaries in their own hands, or in those of their friends.

THE ULTIMATE AIM OF POLITICS

Politics undertakes to secure the best possible order of society. We might say that the best possible order would be that of reason; but I have given reasons for thinking that reason has nothing to do with the concrete interests that are the factors in political life; nor can reason supply a criterion by which to pass judgement on those factors taken singly, or determine how and by whose specific sacrifices they shall be combined. The separate factors are judged by someone's instinctive sympathy or aversion, by actual preference or moral sense; and every fresh election and every added negotiation proves that conflicting interests are combined or compromised not according to reason but according to the weight of numbers or of other material forces; the result being simply the domination of some of the rival interests over the others.

This fundamental prevalence of unreason is no ground for invectives, since it follows from the axiom that mankind are a race of animals living in a physical world; and the same consequence follows from the generative order being fundamental in society. Reason is by no means absent from the process; but it figures there not as a first cause but only as an incident in the generative march of events, and arises out of their incidental harmonies. Nature out of inexplicable elements breeds an astonishing wealth of atomic and astronomical systems, of vegetative and animal organisms; and the impulses proper to man, who is the agent in politics, are so contradictory in each individual and in each

George Santayana, "The Ultimate Aim of Politics," Humanities Research Center, University of Texas. © 1969 Daniel Cory. The manuscript is written in a very old hand. Intended probably for *Dominations and Powers*.

society, and so inconstant in both, that reason has no means of determining impartially which elements had better prevail in each case.
The dignity of each earnest love, and of each noble undertaking cannot
be reduced to a common measure.

I can see but one criterion that must be acknowledged to be rational,
namely, that it is irrational to attempt or prophesy the impossible. This
does not prevent the romantic soul from prophesying and attempting
it, but at the cost of discarding reason as unworthy of the heroic will.
Any scoundrel, cries that soul, can devote himself to getting what can
really be got: the brave, the inspired, the indomitable spirit will gladly
perish pursuing the impossible. This is a case of generative exuberance
in the moral sphere: genuine vitality losing its moorings and sailing
irrepressibly into the void. There is a way, discussed elsewhere, of em-
ploying the generous energy in this madness in a rational cult of the
ideal: but in politics only positive and socially visible results are expected: the cult of the ideal must be left free to the spirit in its free
arts and free friendships.

We may therefore throw this sop to reason at the gates of the political
realm: *No one who seeks the impossible should enter here; or he will
never get out.* Reason is a faithful Cerberus; it releases its masters.

We may interpret this divine riddle by repeating that an *ideally* best
possible order of society can exist only in the estimation of some individual; there are therefore as many *ideal* societies as there are socialistic poets; but no political spirit can be at home in the world or brave
and happy in itself until it has virtually allied itself with the powers
that control destiny. Now to bring about such an alliance is the office
and test of rational religion. Politics therefore will never achieve its
ultimate object until it has led mankind to such a religion. This true
religion would represent the relations that bind all men alike to nature
or to God; yet it would not be a political religion, because it would be
in each spirit in its most hidden and private depths that those relations
would be discovered, honoured, and heroically welcomed. By such a
religion life would be enhanced, as it is enhanced by music or poetry,
by knowledge, and by festive ceremonies; things that are ends in themselves and form parts of the criterion by which the statesman's art
itself must be judged. But it is one thing that true religion should form
a part of the end or aim of moral economy; it is quite another thing
that religion should profess to secure material advantages for mankind
by miraculous means. When it assumes this function religion is either

a government serving the spiritual needs of a religious people,[1] or else a conventional device, hypocritical and deceptive, for enveigling men to behave in a way useful to the secular interests represented by the government. It is only religion of this instrumental kind that I call political religion.

Official Christianity is an offshoot from Judaism and from the beginning down to the present, in both its Catholic and Protestant forms, remains a political religion. It is a varying development, but not a heretical one, because it conceives religion to disclose and to cultivate the true relations of man to the powers on which his existence and welfare depend. It is physics, and physical economy, extended to alleged circumambient realities, perhaps known only by prophecy and revelation, but constantly at work and eventually to become overwhelmingly apparent, and open in the end to material and scientific exploration. God and the other world antedate, control, and will outlast this world of matter and of secular history: they are therefore realities of which a prudent and farseeing man must take account. Whether cultus or morality or the sudden feelings of the heart are most efficacious in dealing with those hidden but all-important powers, is a minor question; perhaps all three methods may work in different measures at different times.

The prophets that emphasised morality against the cultus, or the psalmists who emphasised the heart against both the cultus and formal morality, were therefore perfectly orthodox reformers within the Jewish tradition. Yet emphasis on morality has an heretical tendency, as emphasis on the heart has also because if these things are prized for their own sake, and turned into an ultimate good, in defiance of material prosperity, the whole fabric of earthly and post-earthly economy is shattered. The crucified thief, for having in his last moments one humble and just thought, enters that very day into Paradise; the lilies of the field are better clothed than Solomon; and the birds better fed than an agriculturally advanced community. Of course the thief has had a rough life and a cruel death, the lilies soon wither, and the sparrows drop dead; yet to a poetic and mystical insight those facts, though sad, seem inevitable and irrelevant: the point is to have had one humble and just thought, to have been beautiful for a moment, to have once flown and sung. And the temptation presents itself to

---

1. Santayana substituted "a government . . . people" for the original "sheer superstition."—Editors.

substitute these spiritual graces for all practical arts and for all earthly wisdom; and if we fall into that temptation, we have discarded all political religion, and set up a poetic or mystical religion in its place.

The Catholic Church has always continued to maintain the physical and positive existence of heaven and hell, the resurrection of the body, the personal psychological character of God, angels, and devils, and the material efficacy of sacraments and prayers. Yet a double danger besets this orthodoxy. The more you insist on the physical reality of the supernatural or ultra-mundane, the less spiritual your religion tends to become; and the radical change of emphasis in Christianity is forfeited, which made salvation depend on a change of heart and a profound alienation from the world. At the same time, such a load of invisible physical realities and such an ultra-mundane economy of salvation strained the credulity of mankind. The incubus of the world, far from being lifted, has been redoubled and made an eternal nightmare. Good sense throws such an incubus off, and this fictitious political economy discredits the religion that preaches it.

For this reason the Protestant princes that re-established a frankly political religion in their dominions had such good fortune. The Jewish nerve of Christian orthodoxy could be restored to active control. The heart could be turned back to its natural allegiance, yet with all the unction and self-righteousness of a converted soul. Only real benefits in this world were to be asked for or worked for; but this was to be done with a sense of having purified religion and morality from the heathen complexities of a petty supernatural economy. Plenty of moral commotion and speculative liberty remained to be awakened in the inner man, when the inner man was so inclined, and social unanimity in this sphere was not expected or desired. Where social unanimity was desired and largely secured was only in the sphere of public custom and institutions, and in the general direction of effort towards prosperity. The problem for these political societies was only the *distribution* of wealth, both among nations and among social classes. On these points there was perpetual war, which still continues; but there was no serious concern about relative value of wealth and of freedom from wealth. Wealth with the requisite virtues for securing it and the wealth-preserving ways of enjoying it, grounded the only sort of liberty that a decent citizen would desire. A savage, idle, or mystical liberty would be disreputable. You must be civilised and bound by duty; and your duty is defined by the material interests of the community. You must keep your inmost aspirations in harmony with these interests. Education, public opinion, and a prosperous active life will help you to do so; and if you do, you will find that the performance of duty is its own reward. This conviction, perpetually fostered and warmed within you, will be your rational political religion. Very different was the turn taken by Christianity in the beginning. John the Baptist had indicated it beforehand: "Repent, for the kingdom of heaven is at hand." "The kingdom of heaven" is a vague phrase, but whatever it meant, it certainly was not the material interests of the community. It was to be a miraculous cataclysm, crushing that "generation of vipers." Officially and under pressure the Jewish prophecy of a reign of God was still admitted; but in spirit it was despised and discarded, all interest being transferred to the ascetic discipline of the individual, which of itself would render those prophecies indifferent. When in the Gospels the Jews put test questions to Christ, about paying tribute to Caesar or about what husband a woman should have in the kingdom if she had had seven husbands in this world, the replies elude the problem by abolishing the conditions that create it: in the kingdom there will be *no* husbands or wives, and you may let Caesar have your penny when you have given your heart to God. So in regard to religious professions and spiritual brotherhood, the legal priority of Jews and of saints is acknowledged, but sympathy and love go as much or more to the outsider and to the natural man. The condition of both is pitiable, but in all alike there is a potentiality of salvation, a spark of spirit that may be kindled into flame; and there, in the realm of spirit, all earthly distinctions lapse together. Religion, in its essence, knows nothing of politics.

Now, this inward holiday of the mind, which may accompany any kind of labour, creates no revolt from politics politically. Politically the spiritual man, if a bit passive, is perfectly docile, peaceful, and inoffensive. His transcendental insight does not even forbid him to be a party man, if as a man he leans towards some party. He will consent to be, in this world, what God has made him; but as a spirit he will perceive how accidental that station is, with all its intrinsic commitments and duties; so that in playing his appointed part in the world he will not be deceived by the world or by his own stake in it.

This detachment in cooperation, recommended continually by Indian sages, was not unknown to pagan philosophers. The Stoics cultivated it in one form and the Epicureans in another. But for Christians, with their Jewish traditions, it could be only a rare and fugitive thought, or a personal sentiment that might colour one's life but could hardly be uttered publicly without running into heresy. Orthodox Christianity, though it preached and practised an ascetic morality, remained doubly political: political in its prophetic view of nature and history, of heaven and hell, and political in its own work and organisation as a Church, with a mission in society, straining every nerve to convert the heathen, to educate the young, to control the family, and to revise all science and philosophy. Christianity was bound to dissolve, or at least to subordinate, the natural ties of races and peoples, and to substitute for them a new and militant social bond, the bond of faith. Christendom became the moral fatherland, the veritable nationality, of all Christians; and it imposed upon them all the duties, sacrifices, and wars that any worldly empire would impose. The inevitable enemies, to be conquered and assimilated (because as individuals they were not enemies but brothers, souls redeemed like ourselves by the blood of Christ) were the pagans, or the Moslems: the Jews also, although Christendom was not unwilling to retain a few recalcitrant Jews in its midst, as hostages, as it were, or exiled witnesses to their own perversity. And within Christendom the whole organisation of society was required to respect the organisation and mission of the Church; so that Christianity, besides being a political system in itself, claimed the right to exercise supervision and censorship over all other political systems.

There was, however, an inner difficulty or dualism in Christianity not found in thoroughly political religions. Christianity had begun by announcing the end of the world, and its ethics and sentiment were a preparation to meet that end inwardly, by indifference towards all worldly arts and ambitions and a compassionate, forgiving, mystical summons to abandon the world, and lay up one's treasure in heaven. Heaven might be described as "another world," and a set of laws, punitive and admonitory, might be prescribed for admission there; yet no Christian thought of heaven, when once reached, as still the scene of adventures, perils, and changes of heart. Those who reached it were safe, saved eternally, rescued from the world of politics altogether. So that the whole prodigious engine of creation, redemption, and militancy in the world, as well as of sin and sanctification in the soul, had its period and its limited purpose. One day the spirit would cry, "It is consummated," and after that there would "be time no longer." Thus all life would be a preparation to cease from living; for what could life be without time and change? And all creation would become but the contents or *Inbegriff* of a diviine vision suspended in eternity. Christianity, in this direction, was not a development of Judaism at all, but a religion akin to the Indian. It entered the world and became a part of the world with the avowed purpose of destroying the world by severing the soul from it; and it reduced this life to an indispensible but odious trial through which the soul must pass in order to prove and clarify its love for something entirely different from the world. Christianity was thus a stranger within the gates; even, we might say, a spy and a traitor, that accepted a domicile in nature only in order to condemn and betray nature, and restore something contrary to nature which nevertheless seemed to sleep in the heart of nature, namely, a safe infinity of pure light and sheer bliss.

This mystical or purely spiritual principle is theoretically incompatible with the Jewish political foundations of Christianity; and in the first centuries, when speculation was rife, various heresies, notably the Gnostics, attempted to reduce Christianity to its novel spiritual element and to shake off all affiliation to Judaism. For philosophic minds, however, there was already pure non-political religion in the form of Stoic and Neo-Platonic traditions among the pagans; but these traditions left the natural world in possession of the field, with only a sad commentary upon it made by the helpless reason of individuals. The times required stronger drink; and the Gnostics, and the other anti-Jewish heresies, could not be content with a mere criticism of political religion and its useful superstitions, but embraced extravagant speculations of their own devising, with an idealistic and moralistic mythology, and they sometimes combined exaggerated ascetic precepts with dangerous mystical revels. A critical spiritual philosophy should never attempt to compete with popular religions, or to found a new one. What can be done was well illustrated some centuries later by the sudden success of Islam: a great rational simplification of popular religion in doctrine and institutions, with a claim to revelation for a suitable morality and worship, which did not preclude mystic abstraction or exaltation in a few saints. But those speculative Christian heresies had no political wisdom, and no self-restraint: their insights therefore evaporated, or subsisted submerged and prudently qualified in Christian orthodoxy.

Christian orthodoxy is too deeply rooted in Judaism to condemn, in principle, either matter or time or local influences or bodily existence:

the ascetic call to repentance must be a call to reform nature, not to transcend it. The supernatural comes in to restore the truly natural, which an accident—the misused free will of man—had introduced into the world. The great cosmic order is divine; so is the true and ultimately triumphant political order and moral hierarchy in the world. Paganism was not a worship of this true order of nature but of worship of devils; there were angels and saints, more powerful than those devils, that controlled the same forces of nature and could ultimately correct their operation. Christ had begun his ministry by casting out devils; and in one sense that was the whole ministry of the Church. For this reason, as soon as the Roman Empire relaxed its opposition to the Church, well grounded as that opposition had been in principle, the Church could form an alliance with the Empire, even take office under it, become a branch of the government, and lose that secret dissolving and paralysing virtue which had seemed to animate it. And in fact, in the new barbarian North the monks proved later to be the pioneers of civilisation; and when a most picturesque moral order, under the joint influence of chivalry and Christianity, had actually filled the world with castles and monasteries, it was easy and not unedifying that artfulness and merriment should flourish in Christendom, together with poetry, music, wit, and fashion. The age, without ceasing to be an age of war, became the age of love—a love not quite such as Christianity had recommended, yet one that Christianity could tolerate and even sanctify. Indeed, Christianity could sanctify a great many things; and slowly it might have widened and softened its toleration of nature, until little difference would have subsisted between Christendom full-blown and the old paganism rotting in its ripeness.

There were gifted men of the Renaissance, like Shakespeare and Bacon, Machiavelli and Erasmus, who without meddling with the spiritual side of religion, saw no difficulty in carrying on human life, and enjoying all its phases, on the basis of naturalism. Christianity, in such hands, could have remained, as classical mythology remained, a harmless traditional rhetoric in which to express and to judge the various conditions of men and their various feelings. The spiritual life in Christendom would have known how to transcend this naturalism ideally without deranging it politically. But Christianity was itself, fundamentally, a political system resting on faith in the supernatural; and naturalism could not be restored without either destroying Christianity altogether, or revising and controlling its supernatural claims so as to keep them always friendly to the political principles and aspirations of the age. In the Germanic nations the thing was done easily by reforming the Church and turning it into a branch of the national government; in the East such a reform was not needed, because the Church was already politically captive; and it was only in the Latin countries that the ethics and politics of naturalism came into open conflict with the ethics and politics of Christianity. These differences affected the form and the suddenness of the inevitable resolution, but not its necessity or its ultimate issue. Religion, in a stable and harmonious civilisation, must either cease to be political at all or else must catch the political inspiration of the hour and drape it in some half traditional poetic vesture.

I am afraid that the images in which nations traditionally Christian can clothe their inspiration will not soon be fresh or poetical. A deadly positivism and a gross vanity possesses them; and people who have any taste or any spiritual sensitiveness will simply sit silent and shudder. This may help traditional Christianity to survive or even to revive as a private or mystical solace: the believer, when he enters a church or turns his thoughts to religion, will simply feel that he passes into another world, leads a separate parallel life, as if he were already half dead, and half risen again. Yet this would itself be an unstable and local state of things. Politics, like physics, is a compulsory pursuit. You cannot live or act without virtually making assumptions and taking sides in those matters. But spiritual religion is not compulsory. It visits a few souls in the beginning. It suggests hidden harmonies or invisible powers; and reverence for these imagined presences gradually establishes certain pauses and certain cautions or ceremonies in performing daily actions. These habits, without the original visitations of the spirit, are imitated by the vulgar. They seem to presuppose complexities in nature and in morals which remain mysterious; and a vast net of superstitious practices and mythical notions may come to entangle the practice of life. When the incubus becomes unbearable, or too obviously absurd, scoffers will ridicule the whole thing, and bold men will defy pious opinion in their actions. Such rebellion is restringent; it tightens and dries up the soul that is compelled to reject and criticise and condemn everything beautiful. A long winter may intervene before the mind can awake again in its vernal innocence, exercise its originality without fear, and fashion its poetic world while keeping its foothold sure and free upon terra firma.

Perhaps political religion has been a mistake biologically. Like an amphibious animal it is reptilian, ugly, misbegotten. It had better divide into its two potentialities, and limit itself in each to a special function: then both halves of its soul may create perfect bodies and live happy lives. If politics and morals and hygiene understood their natural principle, they might take classical naked forms, humble in their perfection. And if religion understood its poetic and passionate essence, it might expand through the heavens and in the heart, without deceiving the natural man about his natural status or his political good.

VII

Free Spirit in the Moving World

FREEDOM

Words are often names, not for persons or individual objects, but for ideas, for essences; and as words, and the logical relations of words, fill the reasoning mind, an affinity seems to exist between mind and logical form. But form is inseparable from existing matter; and since it is this perceptible form that distinguishes one part of nature from another, and "makes" each part what it is, all "reality" and all power may come to be ascribed to form, to intelligibility, to reason, or (as a synonym of these) to mind. Here the argument glides equivocally from logic to psychology, from form to the perception of form, from essence to spirit; and by this path we may arrive dialectically at the eloquent conclusion that spirit creates and constitutes everything.

There was once much superstition about words and names: they seemed to have a magic identity with their objects. Something of this feeling remains in philosophy about essences. The forms that things take seem inexplicable unless the form existed first, and compelled the matter to mimic it. But how should forms or essences *exist*, when they are logical terms only, qualitative only, timeless, homeless, invariable, and each eternally identical with itself? And how should such forms be *powers*, when before they are exemplified in some fact they have no temporal relation or point of contact with events?

There are two ways in which forms may be conceived to be powers: either of themselves, by their intrinsic authority, as the numbers three, seven, and ten have been suppose[d] to impose themselves on things by their own magic; or else forms may be conceived to exert power through some mind that regards them, is fascinated by them, and causes the body to imitate or execute what the mind conceives. Or else without any noticeable or relevant effect on the body, the mind

George Santayana, "Freedom," *Columbia Manuscript Collection.* © 1969 Daniel Cory. Possibly an alternative to the chapter entitled "Freedom" in *The Realm of Spirit.*

may be conceived to constrain the outer world, by force of will or direct command, to assume the form that the mind contemplates.

This second method may seem the less mysterious, and is illustrated continually in our voluntary actions, when we think of what we shall say or do, and then say or do it. On analysis, however, this case turns out to be only a double instance of the other, and to reduplicate the same magical process. For when first an idea occurs to us, we must ask whether it did so by its own power, or by some subterranean process in ourselves bringing that idea to light. In the latter case it would not be the idea, but the ground of that idea in the vegetating psyche, that produced both the idea in the mind and its realisation in the world. Such vegetating dynamic processes in the psyche, like those that generate a flower from a seed, can hardly have any graphic resemblance to the forms that result from them. We have therefore, in such a hypothesis, abandoned the notion of power in ideas, and are attributing power only to material processes. All we could say would be that certain forms attained during that process, or at the end of it, were more visible or more interesting to us than the process in its entirety; and that therefore, sentimentally and verbally, we were satisfied with those interesting aspects of the event, and ignored their origin and dynamic context. Literature, like sensation, cannot help doing this, and thereby creates a second poetic or dramatic world, very thin, but very manageable to the mind. It is only in science and philosophy that we are called upon to study the mechanism of the substratum.

Or might we say that the spirit, of its own initiative, may evoke ideas which it afterwards decides to adopt and to realise in action? We should then be giving the name of spirit to something that pre-existed and that possessed a soil, fertilised by past experience, out of which certain new ideas rather than others would be apt to spring. I think such presuppositions and such metaphors proper enough in literary psychology, where "mind" and "soul" are names given to so much of the psyche as it manifested in memory or soliloquy. The psyche so manifested certainly pre-exists, and with the organs of sense, dream, and passion supplies abundance of fresh imagery continually to the spirit. We can often trace, as reflection proceeds, the labyrinthine conjunction of this suggestion with that, the ripening of a plan, the budding of an idea. Even more customary is the quick improvisation of words and purposes in the heat of action. All this is perfectly unpremeditated, and may surprise and distress the spirit in retrospect as much as it excited the spirit in the performance. The spirit proper is the witness throughout, but not the agent. The agent everywhere is the person, the self, the animal whose form of life may be called his psyche, his character or his Will: latent principles of organisation and reaction, which consciousness brings to light spasmodically, now in scattered whims, now in clear planning. The fountain of impulses, words, ideas, and actions which is in a man, and which is much more deeply himself than his consciousness, may show any degree of spontaneity and freedom, according to the plasticity of the organism, the wealth of its latent heritage, and the circumstances that stimulate it to new growths. We are in the work-shop of nature, in the realm of matter. To attribute these movements and leaps to spirit would be a lapse into blinding metaphor. The most important decisions occurred before we were born, in the concretion and spontaneous variations that made each of us an individual.

If there were no realm of matter, and pure spirit, endowed with absolute freedom, stood before the whole realm of essence, from which to choose the object it would think of or the idea it would realise, the choice would not be attributable to anything antecedent. Neither pure spirit nor pure essence have [*sic*] any bias. Essence offers an infinite field of choice, spirit an infinite capacity of selection. When an image or a feeling of any sort actually arose, the event would be absolutely groundless and inexplicable, like the existence of this universe rather than a different one. If we insisted (on account of our acquired human habit of attributing one thing to another) on giving a reason for this contingent miracle, we could not possibly find that reason in spirit, which before experience begins, or apart from the miscellany of experience, is merely the empty category of thought or sensibility, without any indication of possible objects or their variety. But variety does appear, in a certain sense, in the realm of essence, which is a manifold of items, as well as a sea of infinite possibility, the sea being qualitatively infinite only because each of the drops is eternally individual. It would therefore have some meaning to say that, on the apparition of a particular idea to a virgin spirit, a special privilege or power to assert itself had appeared in that idea; whereas it would be utterly meaningless to say that spirit had chosen that idea, when it could have had no previous notion of that idea and no latent bias in its favour. Bias and latency are marks of some material evolving substance, contingent but restless; and if images or laws imposed themselves on spirit without the intervention of matter, they would seem to have imposed themselves by their own magic, and created themselves by a sort of arrogant whim.

What difference, if any, is there between saying that certain Platonic laws or ideas compel existence to obey them, and saying that Existence, in its absolute contingency, happens to show that particular aspect? I think there would be no logical difference; yet the two ways of speaking belong to opposite moral climates. If forms are conceived to impose themselves on matter, those particular forms would seem to have won a previous victory over all other forms in their own realm of essence. This would imply as it were a battle in heaven before the creation, and the triumph of Michael over Satan. We might consequently expect that the regimen thus once for all established in eternity would assure us of a constant physical and moral government in this world. If on the contrary we conceive this world to wear by chance the form that it wears, nothing would forbid it to lapse gradually or suddenly into some other form, and a freer field would seem to be open to our impatience or our romanticism. These contrary suggestions are arbitrary. Michael and Satan might still have another bout, and reverse the celestial order: while the inertia of natural fact and natural process, however contingent they may be logically, is as likely as any mythical decision to keep the stars rolling in their courses. The contrast we feel between the two ways of speaking shows how deeply mythological instincts still govern the human mind.

Suppose now that by some magic an idea has presented itself to the mind: a second magical operation is involved in carrying out that idea, either in action or in some material object. An *idée-force* is an ambiguous thing. The force can hardly come from the idea taken strictly, as an essence; for then its power would be exerted equally and perpetually in all places and at all times; and if it was exemplified in some particular event, though nominally that event might be attributed to its influence, the occurrence of it then and there would really be determined only by the circumstances. The sun might alone shed its lordly light; the motion of the ripples would be requisite to catch and to reflect it. Such is the case in any Platonic system, in which the ideas are essences or divine thoughts. But in modern psychology the intention is different. An *idée-force* is a concrete moment of life, a state of the psyche which brings an idea to consciousness and, by some nether process not specified, also carries it out. That the efficacious process should not be specified is essential, if we are to retain the superstitious feeling that the idea itself is a power; for how should an immaterial fact, an intuition, insert itself among material events? And how should the specious image transfer itself to the material object, or to the material act? It all happens dramatically, and is observed *ex post facto*, from the ouside; and we are reconciled to the miracle, not only by habit, but by two circumstances proper to our psychic life. One is that the idea hardly ever appears alone: if it appeared alone nobody would ever think it a power. It comes preceded by a flux of impressions and sensation, representing in consciousness the whole movement of the organism and its environment; and the idea is half executed before we notice it. We notice it, indeed, only because it is already half executed. There is therefore a real force at work, multiform and unseizable by the senses: and the idea, carried by that force, becomes our sign, our name, for the movement afoot, and for its issue. That the issue should respond to the idea, so that we can regard the idea as controlling it, follows from the fact that the result appears to us in the same sensuous and dramatic terms as the cause: not that the idea ever passes, in its own shape and person, into the dynamic process at work, but that the later phases of this process wear much the same aspect to our senses as the earlier phases did to our prophetic imagination. The realisation is therefore not a miraculous realisation of the idea in the fact, but the natural continuation and fulfilment of the idea in another idea.

Another circumstance that naturalises for us the miracle of will accomplished is the *moral* harmony and continuity between the project and the achievement. The project was already a solution: it was already a miraculous invention of thought, coalescing out of vaguely felt subterranean currents and impulses to act; it was a premonition and an incentive. If presently the premonition (with some variations) is realised, and the incentive draws us to achieve the promised result, the soul is profoundly satisfied, finds it most natural that the world should cooperate with her own designs, and accepts full responsibility for a result which she welcomed, and into which her action flowed, although in some unknown fashion. We easily appropriate and defend a state of things that we like, even if we had no hand in establishing it; but when in our physical capacity we have had a hand in it, we appropriate and defend it with all the more reason. We meant it should be so: we foresaw, desired, and willed it. What more, in way of initiative, could conscience demand? Or if later the result turns out to be disastrous, and contrary to some deeper need of ours which for the moment we had ignored, we are covered with confusion at having conspired to bring that result about, and blame ourselves for it: most justly, because the self, the psyche, was guilty of distraction, was disorganised, and suffered its organs to do, and its fancy to wish, something that its heart on the whole detested.

Such is the basis, in the idolatrous mind of man, of a strange superstition, to the effect that the forms things wear are inexplicable unless chosen, that is, unless they had already been taken (and not chosen) by an image in some mind. But why did that mind form that image? Not because it willed to form it; since in order to select and accept it as the right form, we must first have thought of it. And when once that particular image had appeared to us automatically, why were we pleased or allured by it? Evidently we are moving in a region of verbal conventions, proper to social life. In our daily conduct, habitual or deliberate, we either positively first think out what we shall do or at least anticipate vaguely what we shall soon be doing, as when we sit down to write a letter, or decide to go to bed. We may then say truly enough that we should never have written those words in the letter unless we had first thought of them, and should not have gone to bed unless we had felt or seen that it was bedtime. But the first time a creature lies down and goes to sleep, he cannot have first thought how pleasant and usual it would be to do so. The head nodded, the eyes closed, the limbs curled up in pre-natal comfort; and the idea of going to sleep and the notion of a bed could not have arisen until many a time one had dozed off and been awakened, and the function of a bed had been performed by a heap of hay or of rags, a strewn cloak, or a sunny corner. And as for the first time a man speaks or thinks of words to be written down, there is manifestly a determination of those sounds and of their meaning by his vocal organs and by the occasion. He will be repeating what he has heard, or inventing what he is capable of putting together. The utterance, even when meaningless and parrot-like, will be spontaneous. He would not imitate were he not a capable mimic for that sort of sound. He would not understand his own words, if he had not a predisposition (that a parrot has not) to turn to the thing signified, and follow it up in its own medium. His thought is thought, and not mere babbling, precisely because in its spontaneity it is guided and fed by circumstances which are not thoughts; and his action is rational when, in its freedom, it represents his constitutional powers adjusted to occasions that make it possible to exercise those powers. It is always, therefore, the forms already realised in matter that determine the new images that may appear to the fancy, and also determine the values which these images, taken as plans, may have for the Will.

That an image should ever serve as a plan at all, so that a man feels that his mind is governing his action and transforming the world, far from proving that images have magic power to realise themselves, proves the opposite. For whence should the image come, or how should it be prophetic, if the very process that is to carry out the prophecy had not, at its inception, suggested the image? And why should this image be interesting or the body know how to carry it out, unless the very capacity and impulse of the body to carry it out had generated and appropiated that image, recognising it at once as a fit ideal and goal for action? The psyche, therefore, being a form of organic life already in substantial harmony with ambient forces, feels her contacts with them in the form of images and passions fit to express and prefigure her destiny in the world. Her ideas are, or may be, excellent counsellors: not because they control the world magically, but because they proclaim her prevalent interests and the development that she may be able to give them.

That facts should be contingent, and should have a determinate form for no possible reason, is in any case logically inevitable. We should gain nothing in rationality by having the physical world at our beck and call, or being able to transform our own nature into something different. This Will to change, this power to create, would itself be a contingent fact, and an arbitrary preference. We are not condemned to be wholly irrational. Matter has relieved us of that reproach, and taken the initial responsibility on its shoulders. Our premises in life are established for us; also the directions in which harmonies are possible among these extant forces. Our own force thus has an intelligible task before it, and as far as may be turns into the triumphant spirit of this singular world.

Thus the dominance of mind or of art, which may seem to be a miraculous efficacy of spirit, is really a natural efficacy in the psyche: the psyche not being a spirit, but an organisation of life in the body which has spirit for one of its immaterial radiations. Two factors conspire in the psyche to render this dominance of mind possible: *scope*, that is, range and accuracy of the response of the organism to circumstances, and *timeliness*, that is, a congenital harmony between the impulses of the psyche and the prevalent movements of the surrounding world. Scope without timeliness may, if integrated, yield genius, but not success; while timeliness without scope is mere vulgarity. Napoleon, for instance, exercised in his day an astonishing control over things and persons, because he had a clear intuition, made accurate by long study, of the forces at work, and the likely turn of events, such an intuition as a good chess-player has in making his moves; and at the same time his temper and passions were those of the new age, enthusiastic and rhetorical in form, materialistic in substance. He could guide the Revolution better than the revolutionaries, because he understood the true force of the Revolution much better than they and knew that what it was after was material comfort and wealth, without overarching superstitions; and he could check the Revolution better than the conservatives, because he invoked no outworn superstitions in doing so, but fed the modern mind on the glitter of its own idols. If he failed, this was because the modern mind and the Revolution were, at bottom, out of line with the reality of things. They were Utopian, they were rhetorical; he was often Utopian and rhetorical himself; and his realistic intelligence could not avail to dominate the remoter forces at work or the subtler fires of the human heart. He misjudged England, Russia, Spain, and Germany. Perhaps he misjudged—we are still watching the experiment—the willingness of mankind to equalise their civilisations and to renounce all moral individuality.

SPIRIT NATURAL YET TRANSCENDENT

If spirit were inwardly free from animal bias, if it were simply truth aware of itself, it would never pass judgement upon its objects, and would nurse no anxiety about its own fate. We seem to approach such intellectual purity and selflessness at certain moments, and the ap-

George Santayana, "Spirit Natural Yet Transcendent," *Columbia Manuscript Collection.* © 1969 Daniel Cory. Probably an early draft for *The Realm of Spirit.* The title was supplied by the editors.

proach is a triumph, because intellect, like the other forms of spirit, is secretly sacrificial and aspires to lose itself in the truth. Yet even the most impartial science and purest contemplation bear radical marks of their animal genesis; they have a point of origin in time, a centre of survey, a limited scope, and a transitive movement. Even when the terms traversed in thought are proper to the object (as necessarily happens when the object is an essence) these terms are picked out by a subjective selection, and traversed at a subjective rate and in a subjective order. The soul has so much at stake in the world that our intellectual functions are little but emissaries and scouts sent out to survey our claims and to spy on our enemies. Our very pride of insight and our desperate fidelity to cold fact betray our vital predicament. We are afraid of our own imagination: free thinking would be mad thinking. In thought as in action we find ourselves alternately baffled and audacious, submissive and exacting. There is danger for us in going wrong and tragedy in going right.

Consider, for instance, the perpetual demand of the intellect for reasons. This passes for a rational demand, and whole systems of metaphysics have been built up, and confidently imposed on nature, in consequence of the alleged necessity that there should be a reason for everything. It is felt that reality everywhere should have arisen in answer to some prior or inward demand which, if fulfilled, would explain existence and show it to be very good. Could there be a more pathetic confession of animality in the mind? Nothing is allowed to exist unless it be demanded: but demanded by whom? By something non-existent? No: by the poor blinking animal soul, needing air, needing food, bent on preserving through all hazards and labours a particular precarious hereditary life. If spirit were separable from animal existence, if it were even independent of animal interests in its own motions, it would make no demands. It would see with absolute clearness the inevitableness of omnimodal being in the realm of essence; also the inevitable contingency of particular facts, if particular facts are to exist at all. It is as impossible that there should be a further reason in the one direction as in the other. The question: *Why?* marks expectations, presumptions, ignorances, and surprises: feelings proper to animal minds. A psyche is an experiment in domination, an effort to incorporate everything discoverable into the service of a single life. All facts must be justified by home habits. Nothing must startle or disconcert our nest, or spoil our confident plans: or perhaps, if our home habits have grown too staid and boring for our romantic temperament, just enough, and not too much, excitement must be provided for us by unpredictable accidents. As for the realm of essence, that must be ignored altogether, or reduced to the grammatical categories current in our language: it may then seem that all essential relations between forms have been established for our convenience. There would be a reason even for logical necessity: and reason would be reduced to the pleasant enjoyment of human prejudice.

Indeed, if spirit be conceived as I conceive it, if it be the perfect actualisation of life, the notion of a pure and passionless spirit becomes self-contradictory. Such a spirit would not be a form of life at all. It would mirror the temporal and logical relations of facts in every direction impartially, as the truth exhibits them, or as speculative theology might conceive them to lie open to the eye of God. Every fact would be faced squarely, as unrolled at its actual date, and, if it were a living fact, in its felt quality. But at the same time all these facts, each intrinsically present, would also be past as viewed from their future, and future as viewed from their past. Transformation, though it might pervade the universe, would forfeit that tension and dramatic novelty which it carries with it in the existing world: the notions of achievement and collapse would coincide and cancel one another, because the very process that was birth in one respect in another respect would be death. Chaos would be as perspicuous as order, and universal war in existence would be compatible with eternal peace for the spirit.

Far as this is from being the condition of the human spirit, even in the purest raptures of the saints, something must suggest it to us, else why should we ever have framed the notion of such impossibility or attributed it to divine mind? On the one hand, indeed, God is the truth personified, and in that capacity must be passionless: but I suspect that there is a deeper and more intimate source for this demand that spirit should be sublimated into pure truth, and should finally rest in peace. Like so many ultimate mystical ambitions, this may seem self-contradictory. You cannot be at peace, if you have ceased to exist; you cannot be a spirit, if you are nothing but the truth of things in general. Nevertheless, at the very origin and first occasion for consciousness there is transcendence: because, as we have seen, consciousness is not seated at any point in the field of consciousness; it has scope, temporally, morally, and pictorially; so that if some feature in this given field be identified cognitively with any physical moment or locus, that physical moment or locus is transcended in thought, and placed in a setting which overflows it on every side. There can be no self-transcendence in facts, or in states of substance; there can be only interaction, or succession, or derivation between them; and it is precisely these relations, subsisting in the realm of truth, that spirit comes to actualise intellectually, thus transcending each of its objects in the very act of conceiving it.

SPIRITUAL LIBERTY

Vital liberty, considered genetically, hangs on unimpeded functioning in some psyche astir in the world. Sometimes, however, at least in man, the psyche functions within itself, for instance in dreams; so that, viewed subjectively, this fantastic activity might seem to be less impeded and therefore vitally freer than sensation and action in rude contact with other bodies. This point of view can lead reflection and theory into great extravagance. For in fact the psyche when perfectly enclosed and autonomous passes into dreamless sleep; and it is then that bodily growth is healthiest and order best restored to the waking mind. Dreams for the most part are inconsistent, fugitive, and troubled; they seem the floating wreckage of frustration; they escape clear memory even when memorable, because then waking fancy is apt to transform and improve them for dramatic purposes. That dramatic fancy deeply troubled is at work always in dreams has only recently been discovered. Formerly, when dreams were studied earnestly, it was under the spell of superstition, that took them for prophecies or warnings or divine instructions. Now an important though still ambiguous science has begun to recognise in dreams sporadic ebullitions of fancy, air-castles built automatically by the momentum of incipient passion or suggestion. Life has a proclivity to blind experiments; and when experiment is not canalised by some present occasion for action, it runs

George Santayana, "Spiritual Liberty," *Columbia Manuscript Collection.* © 1969 Daniel Cory. Written in a very old hand.

wild, and out of the debris of old impressions generates fantastic occasions and absurd troubles.

Imagination with the eyes closed paints as any painter does without
a model; the pictures tend to be both feeble and monstrous. The mind
necessarily works with pigments of its own manufacture. A grazing
animal cannot breed pastures and rivers within itself; it will simply feel,
in terms of sensation and impulse, an effect of those bodily presences
or contacts. So in the human mind there is no occasion or possibility
of reproducing the material world in its profound dynamic structure
and secret essence on which that mind depends for its very organs, its
food and its fortunes. Mind belongs, for all its earthly roots, to quite
another realm of being. While body acquires useful habits and a working equilibrium with the world, the vocation of mind is freely to
articulate its native sensibility, in time with those physical adjustments, into the purest idiom and music of thought, framing in this way
some symbolic picture of the world and of its destiny. So in time the
waking dream of our animal psyche may become the life of reason.
Feeling will have been elaborated, in contact with things and by self-
development, into a language or system of sensuous and ideal signs,
that may figure to the spirit, as far as imagination avails, the places and
the exact motions of all besetting powers. Blind sensation and impulse
will then have become articulate ideas; and in the end these ideas will
compose a panorama and epic history of the world, dominating it
spiritually, as far as spirit in man can be concerned in the world. All
material buffets will then have been turned into strokes of the brush
and the chisel, and the world into an eternal theme for intuition, freed
from the writhings of the monster that gave it birth.

Dreams are therefore as remote as possible from exemplifying the
free life of spirit; they represent rather its initial helplessness and servitude, condemned to be roused by every accident, distracted from
every congenial or fertile thought, and tormented by utterly unnecessary nightmares and terrors. As day-dreams show spirit in the act of
dissolution and vagrancy, so night-dreams, when vivid and overpower-
ing, show some strain in the psyche getting morbidly dominant; so that
if ever it persists in waking life this strain deranges perception and
thought and produces madness.

Presumably all matter is affected in some degree by whatever goes on
elsewhere in the dynamic universe; while the range and accuracy of
sensibility anywhere will depend on the elaboration of organic struc-

ture at that point. In a psyche like the human, already kindled into spirit, intuition might combine the absorbing immediacy of sensation with all the cognitive validity of science. It is not by enacting existence that understanding of existence is attained. The rush of action and passion only tosses the spirit from one casual and broken commitment to another; life is then but dreaming at high pressure. The proper virtue and divine freedom of spirit begin to appear when, shocked and thoroughly awakened by some irrational trial or sharp disillusion, reflection surveys that episode, and virtually the whole drama of existence, feeling at once the magic of each of its parts and the vanity of all. This is logically possible. The detail of all truth is once for all what it is, and there could be no occasion to re-enact it all and no advantage in doing so; nor is its literal infinity a theme suitable for any living mind. But being incarnate in an animal psyche, spirit must have a station in space and time, from which perspectives capable of synthesis and dramatic emphasis are open in all directions; and it has moments of surprise, of discovery, of delight, and other moments of reflection, equilibrium, and self-denial. At each moment, with varying objects and varying scope, such a living spirit gathers up what is relevant to its specific endowment, frames an image, defines a virtue, adores a visiting god; and in that intuition and that worship attains its perfection and liberty.

Liberty for the spirit is therefore by no means a power to initiate or alter other existences or to prolong its own. It is sent like Christ into this world by an older Generative Power. Were it left to itself, as modern idealism professes to leave it, spirit would simply vanish, like music without a living voice or a sounding instrument. Friendly influences of nature playing upon a germinating body kindle there the first sparks of sensation and light. Many a wound also awakens pain in the spirit and torments it with confusion and darkness; and the diseases and vices that debase the body pollute and torture the spirit too. It is then that the spirit cries in religion for mercy and grace, and in politics for vacant freedom. But it can be only good nurture and good government that will ever liberate it from distraction; a free rein for miscellaneous life in the world can only vary its troubles. Not that the world, in its generative impulses, is the spirit's enemy; but that universal Will is bred out of chaos; and one experiment in form is for ever thwarting and defeating another. Only in sheltered nooks and calms between battles does the rare germ mature, of which spirit is destined to be the ultimate flower; nor will that inmost potentiality ever be realised without many trials, crosses, and contaminations. For spirit, in its essential vocation, transcends humanity and transcends existence: it is the Word that distinguishes and names all things; the Light that falling on them equally and together would reveal them in their Truth; the Love that divines in each its half-manifested virtue.

Spirit is a form of Will, else there would be no sense in speaking of its vocation or calling it the supreme expression of vital freedom. But it is a form of Will supervening on all the others, as reason is a passion harmonising particular passions. But spirit dwells in all the vital movements that it transcends, and for this reason is a much more intimate and kindred monitor than either reason or conscience. It has no axe to grind; it forgives its enemies, and is universal in pity, as well as in intelligence. Its specific vocation cannot be invidious, since it simply shares, collects, and intensifies that intellectual power which animates all self-transcendent thought or affection. In this universality, it even shares the insecurity of any specific aim. It is as frail in its existence as it is dominant in its scope: an unsubstantial flame, purely luminous in its own nature, intense and far-flaring when fed by ignitable fuel, but bending with every gust, and daily dying, buried under some avalanche of rubbish. Yet wherever, amid such treacherous accidents, this flame bursts out for a moment, it leaps ideally from time into eternity. For in all life, even in all existence, there is a divine affinity, which in spirit becomes actual vision, living hypostasis of some ideal form. This self-transcendence, in the inanimate world, appears only passively, in movement, rhythm, cyclical tropes or laws; in the organic realm it becomes reproduction of each species; and in the human mind, intuition, memory, and inspiration; and moral self-transcendence accompanies intellectual synthesis, imitating in miniature the ideals of divine omniscience, justice, and love.

It is by reaching, at moments, this absorption of life in eternal themes that spirit is liberated from the hindrances that envelop it at its birth and distract it in its career.

VITAL FREEDOM

Vital freedom is simply life undivided and unimpeded. Far from hanging on the groundless choice of an empty spirit, such freedom presupposes a natural organism with determinate impulses and capacities.

Nor is this psyche like the "mind" of literary psychology, a *tabula rasa* or clean piece of paper, miraculously adhesive, such that flying phenomena might sometimes stick to it, or at least leave marks upon it of their contact, to constitute respectively perception and reflection. Such a passive sensorium, even if we assume that it felt these impressions, would have no faculty of comparing or regrouping them, so as to think; nor would it have any means of linking them with action or weighting them with animal interests, as they are weighted in human discourse. Before significant discourse or vital liberty can make their appearance, living creatures must have arisen with a congenital tendency to grow and develop its action in particular directions. In so far as any creature is able to do so, it is vitally free. In so far as circumstances, instead of allowing and feeding such native movements (which we call life), impede or prevent them, the creature struggles under compulsions, prohibitions and conflicts that defeat its natural free will, or confuse and deflect it, or finally crush it out altogether.

In man, however, this natural free will is seldom perfectly unified. When the psyche is highly complex and sensitive to many different influences it pursues now one good, now another. Where impulses dominate by turns, the creature seems merely versatile; but when several impulses or passions persist together, the man vacillates, feels that he contradicts himself, each element in him hating and spoiling the others. Then, when a particular character and profession is adopted by him officially, other affections may secretly survive, and his whole life may be embittered by forced virtues that he feels to be his enemies and disgraced by vices that he dares not call his friends. Then suddenly, perhaps, the tables may be turned. In the name of vital liberty he may publish to the world that his only vice, and the ruling vice of society

George Santayana, "Vital Freedom," Humanities Research Center, University of Texas. © 1969 Daniel Cory. A fragment of what might have been a longer essay written late in Santayana's life; the title was provided by the editors.

has been hypocrisy; that his suppressed passions and thoughts were all legitimate and amiable; that freedom is the root not only of genuine virtue but of universal sympathy and justice; and that all nature and all history are animated equally by the spirit of life. The glory of this proclamation, however, is likely to be short-lived. Vital liberty is indeed the essence of all genuine virtues; but these virtues must be opportune; they must be compatible in each man and in each society; and the freer rein they all have indiscriminately in the jungle, the more cruel the survivors among them will seem to the miscellaneous multitude of innocents that will be sacrificed.

Simple animals enjoy vital freedom by nature; a complex animal can recover it only by achieving moral integrity. He needs to become a disciple of Socrates and learn to live by the knowledge of his radical self and of his total circumstances. Unfortunately so complex an animal as man has prolonged dissimilar phases in his moral being and probably various societies or careers requiring of him divergent developments. Has he any true self? Has he any fixed, authorative, trustworthy environment? He has to earn his living; or if not yet, he is dragooned into a crude and intolerant regiment of youngsters, where everything is prescribed, or else by a regiment of pedagogues, where everything is forbidden. If he is a favourite of fortune, he either becomes the slave of convention, or the sport of every accidental temptation to be free, not in the exercise of his veritable natural powers, but in miscellaneous experiments and tiresome adventures. As he grows older, his possibilities will be slowly buried under the crust of his habits. He has no vital liberty, but can't help going on in his old round. Yet under all these masks and incrustations there still lives a human being that had other potentialities; and the fact that they slumber in him as if unborn, is betrayed by the impatience he feels at being so perpetually bored, so perpetually driven to do this thing and that, which are notoriously not worth while. He is not even the victim of a master-passion, in which, however tragically, one ray of vital liberty might have found its way out. He has never had a chance to become himself, but has suffered from a pervasive cramp by which a part of his psyche, like a cancer, has paralysed the whole.

TWO MEANINGS OF LIBERTY

Could there be liberty before anything existed? Or could anything exist without being something in particular? Could anything possessing a particular character *exist*, if it did not find itself surrounded by a particular world? This reflexion appears to exclude a kind of bottomless initiative which people are sometimes tempted to attribute to themselves. It is not merely that they are not held down by any obstacle, and can jump in any direction from the spot where they stand. That would be simply the vacuous freedom that, at least logically, surrounds anything existent. It might conceivably change in any one of an infinite multitude of ways. I am thinking of something more intimate: of the root of freedom in oneself. Is this inner freedom all vital, all the on-rush of movements already afoot, a contingent automatism; or is there here also a sphere of vacuous liberty surrounding the kernel of organic life? In lazy thinking, for instance, a given train of images or words may be arbitrarily crossed by an image or word absolutely irrelevant: yet if you notice the intrusion, your mental life has been deflected in a way that, in some cases, might prove important. The intruding word or image might be attributed to the grace of God or to a temptation by a devil: or might it (and this is the point in question) be attributed to one's own absolute freedom? In other words, can what seems absolutely groundless, have its ground in one's unconscious choice of it out of the infinite realm of vacant possibilities?

I may seem to be relapsing into the vain controversies of other days concerning freewill and necessity: but though my arguments may be of that ilk, my subject and aim are wholly different. Of causes or necessity I do not speak, nor am I interested in attaching blame to anybody or in escaping it. Blame is not a philosophical category. Everything existent seems to me equally contingent, including the uniformities that we may think we trace in nature or in human habit. Everything of that sort might have been different, or may become different. I am concerned only with the nature of that kind of liberty which society and

George Santayana, "Two Meanings of Liberty," Humanities Research Center, University of Texas. © 1969 Daniel Cory. Written in a very old hand.

government may notoriously grant or deny to the individual. When, in what sense, in what relations, is it possible to be free?

The conclusion to which I am led is that this possible liberty is exclusively vital: that is, it lies in the exercise of the instincts or gifts with which the individual finds himself endowed. Vacuous liberty to exercise other faculties, which he has no gift for, is no benefit to him; rather an evil, because by the power of suggestion, fashion, or vanity he may be tempted to profess interests which are not his own, and to neglect his true capacity and moral advantage. And his social duty in this respect is to do to others as he would have them do to him: to impose no alien or artificial virtues upon them and to afford them the greatest scope possible for developing their ingrained disposition and powers.

It makes no difference whether a man's bent is innate or acquired, provided it be acquired organically, so that his inner life adopts it and he lives spontaneously and happily in following that acquired bent. Education may therefore serve to awaken latent or congenial capacities, and to train them: so far it is truly e-ducation, or the bringing out [of] the vital nature of a man. But instruction and training are worse than wasted if they bore or distract the child with profitless tasks, and perhaps disgust him with all concentration and discipline.

It is under such unhappy influences or in sheer abandonment, that a man may imagine that his true self is infinite and indeterminate; that it is always something new and unimagined that he really longs for; so that if only he had complete vacuous freedom before him he would be a sublime genius, or even God in person. His politics will then be anarchical. He will deprecate all definiteness in custom, law, science, or art, and think that by fishing uneducated in the vacuous infinite he may expect to draw a miraculous catch. And meantime, if he does not become a criminal, he will be little better than a madman.

Now madness, or an originality for which there is no thoroughfare in the world, may by chance be exciting and wonderful in itself, like an opium dream: but politically and morally, or even hygienically, it is a misfortune. In some other world it might be virtue to cultivate that form of life, but in this world, and for a human being, it is a vice. The turn by which a human psyche developed that vice was an instance of liberty misplaced. True and vital liberty for that psyche would have developed ways of living rooted in itself, and possible at the place and time in which it found itself. Even the cultivation of ways of living impracticable in the circumstances of the moment, but rooted in the psyche, though tragic, would not be insane: it might even be heroic. On the other hand, the current ways of life, if contrary to the innate bent of the individual, make social existence for him a veritable servitude.

It follows that the vacuous infinite is not a source of freedom in any case. That which a being morally and vitally vacuous may draw from chaos, transforms intuition without either liberating or satisfying the soul. It begins a new chapter, which may be happy or unhappy in itself, as a dream may be, but does not belong to the same story as the man's life in the world. It is always, in that background, an accident and a defect in composition. The root of freedom is always the will already alive, the person already possessing definite interests and tastes. If accidents intervene from the irrelevant infinite they do not enlarge liberty, but renew fatality. The root of freedom is nature.

THE WORLD

There is a just selfishness in each happy moment. Not that other moments, whether called mine or other people's, are less important. Each is all-important to itself, and dyes the universe for one instant, from one centre, with a different and genuine colour. But the other dyes are not visible here; why should they infect the spirit now? If you make *this* depend for its peace on *that*, you destroy the peace of nature. Nothing is made worse elsewhere by what is good at each point; *carpe diem*, not by being lazy or reckless, as if there were no future and no other sensitive souls, but by being collected, and content with your interior life. The great engines of action, the stellar universe, the revolving earth, the politics and industries and sports of mankind will carry you with them of necessity; they are the medium of your life. In that vortex, according to your powers, you will play your allotted part, and spirit far from dissuading you will profit by your action, as it does by the economy of nature at large, if only its own house be

George Santayana, "The World," *Columbia Manuscript Collection.* © 1969 Daniel Cory. Probably a preliminary draft for *The Realm of Spirit.*

in order. The Indians give good counsel on this point: live the life of the world, *but with detachment.* Charity is not infected by the diseases it cures or the sins it forgives; and meantime it cures the soul of her own sins and diseases. The human world would be an ant-hill like any other, if spirits did not suffer in it; let them be liberated from their attachments, and floods and earthquakes will not disturb them inwardly, nor the certainty of death, but only render the spectacle more impressive, and the joy of inner liberty more complete.

The detachment of sense differs from that of intellect. A childlike, flowerlike spirit may care nothing, because it knows nothing, of the rest of the world, and be happy in the moment. This may be a spiritual joy, but precarious; and probably at the next moment utter distress will follow, because of some small accident. Intellect is in one sense more cruel, because it knows the troubles that it regards with detachment, and connects them speculatively with their causes, and results, many of which may be excellent in themselves; but this ironical wisdom is more broadly based than innocence was, safer and steadier, and even more beneficent; because it may give warning and direction in action, even when indifferent to the issue. The passions, even the most instinctive, like love, are enormously histrionic and rhetorical. They would be wholly so, and as easy to shift or abolish as fashions in dress, if the impulse to feign and to dramatise were not itself natural. But, when once imagination, language, and vanity exist, actions cannot be accomplished without an orchestral accompaniment of unnecessary sentiments and redundant words. The intellect, surveying and possessing all this superfluous experience, turns it into history, into vision, which of itself sublimates the events concerned, and detaches the spirit from them as dangers and lures while preserving them as reports. For this reason spirit is so well satisfied with fictions, and so rich in them. Ultimately, when the predicaments of time, place, and person are escaped, the outer reference of mind to matter may lapse; poetry will seem better than prose, and myth better than history. Only the inner dependence of spirit on matter will remain, its roots in nature, from which it draws its vitality, its contingency, and its limits. Spirit, being a form of life, cannot exist except in a world, and when sane it will always feel that a world of the not-given surrounds it. In other words, it will feel that it is incarnate and not perfectly free or independent. Intuition will have to be bent into knowledge or into error, neither of which it is in itself. In itself it is imagination and emotion. In this direction free spirit will pull; and for this reason spiritual men are often poets or believers in some extraordinary religion. Facts, nature, history, even clothed as they must be for the mind with the wedding garment of intuition, are not enough for such spirits. Facts must be transformed and enlarged even more than direct perception or conception transforms them. They must be imbedded in a purely imaginary world, or superseded by it, so that the impulse and fertility of spirit may have their way; and that since this spirit, being incarnate, must live in a world, at least it may think that world perfectly fit to live in. There is still a world for poetry; and even for music, though a different world in each case; I mean, that the imagined movement comes impelled out of something at work beneath, and is deployed and left suspended, in a medium of sound or of adventure where a myriad other movements might continue it. Poetry and music are processes not merely in the realm of matter but also in intuition; they are given as progressions; not all the parts are equally vivid, but all are involved, and given at least potentially in the perspective present at any time. These sequences, suspensions, and culminations occupy intuition with essences present only indirectly, suggested and promised, but not quite given now: that they hide, that they threaten, that they fade away, that they return redoubled is the essence of this excitement. Spirit is compelled to play a game in fiction, as it does in real life. It is still in the hands of Power, launched into commitments, overwhelmed by catastrophes, no less thrilling, if less dangerous, than those in the real world.

Music, poetry, and religious prophecy while they withdraw the spirit in a measure from common life, therefore do not liberate it, the new imaginary life being often more ominous, more compelling, than the old one. A nightmare is a worse tyrant than worldly drudgery, the only advantage being that we get rid of it sooner.

We see by this how interior to spirit is spiritual good. We gain little by substituting fancy for truth, or heaven for earth. We should gain little by being always young, rich, or admired or by revolutionising the universe and living in Utopia. There would come the same pains for different reasons, or the same tedium in a different routine. All real liberation is inward; in that the fact or the image before us ceases to disturb, even physical pain becoming a mere sensation that confronts but does not derange us, because we have now identified our Will not with the Will of the psyche that is suffering and perhaps dying in that struggle, but with the Will of the spirit that perceives the fact, and perceives all the circumstances that make it natural and transitory, and balance it with a myriad other moments, equally important and equally futile. This pain is not annulled by that insight: rather it is eternalised in its wretchedness and relativity. God can never wipe it out. Yet that cry for us is soon lost in the yielding air of the infinite; and terrible as it continues to be in itself, it cannot ruffle an intuition that extends beyond it and is rooted so much more deeply in the equilibrium of things. For frail as intuition is in its existence—a firefly in the summer night—the whole truth is focussed there for a moment and virtually knows and proclaims itself in its serenity.

FREEDOM OF THOUGHT

One of the most passionately claimed of freedoms is the freedom of thought; yet it is one of the most vacant since thought is not any specified thinker and the field open before it is an infinite unspecified field. Moreover, in a psychological sense, when this freedom is claimed it must be already possessed, for in being claimed it is being exercised. The hint, at least, of some unprecedented thought must have entered the mind, with a promise of being fresher (and why not truer?) than all the old wives' tales on which we were brought up. Here expectation and surfeit, two distinctly vital feelings, begin to people the empty prospect.

In Christian tradition there has been a particularly distressing tension about one form of freedom of thought called "freedom of conscience." This touched a crucial dilemma within the accepted religious faith. To have rejected religious faith altogether, as did those in whom the spirit of the Renaissance was clear and dominant, would not have troubled the conscience; nor need it have seriously troubled the ruling powers, civil or even ecclesiastical. The middle ages were rich in ribaldry and li-

George Santayana, "Freedom of Thought," Humanities Research Center, University of Texas. © 1969 Daniel Cory. A "little essay" meant probably for *Dominations and Powers.*

cence; and even the Spanish Inquisition never touched professed Jews
or Moslems, unless they had pretended to be converted. Abuse of power
had appeared in perhaps forcing them to be christened; but the primeval human right to disbelieve was never questioned. Even among
Catholics, total disbelief, though lamented, was not persecuted; Rabe-
lais could be published; but heresy, which attacked the Church in the
name of Christianity, seemed intolerable treason within the camp and
roused political and social alarm, rather than religious sorrow. Only
faith in doubt can raise a disquieting question within the conscience.
Was it right for religion to change its prescriptions or revise its creed?
And if so, was it for the learned only, or was it for the heart, to make
the revision?

In any case, thought while it exists is free and intangible inwardly;
but it has no power either to initiate or to prolong its free thinking. It
could not have existed before it began to think, and its present thought
cannot perceive or command what thoughts there may be elsewhere or
in the future. The existence and continued exercise of any thought depend on the vital powers of some psyche, so organised and fed in the
material world as to precipitate spontaneous ideas. This psychological
flowering is invisible and inaudible save "in the sessions of sweet silent
thought"; and to these tyranny has no immediate access. But most
people would not care to think if they were forbidden to talk; it would
be wasted trouble. It is freedom of speech, therefore, that is ordinarily
meant by freedom of thought. Unspoken thought eludes the purview of
politics. In politics freedom of speech is limited rather by custom than
by law; there are words and ideas that everyone uses in men's society
that are not allowed before ladies; and so a government, according to
the susceptibilities of the dominant class, limits the public expression
of thought to language that gives no general offence and inflicts no
personal injury.

All matter from the beginning was "free" to think, but for the most
part it was not able. Were thinking a disembodied faculty, as spiritual-
ists believe, not all the rush and fury of matter in the universe could
stop or even ruffle cogitation: the trouble would be only that no cogitation could then ruffle the world. Tyrants would have smiled at free
thought and free thought would have had no occasion to denounce
tyrants. Indeed, were thought intrinsically possessed of absolute freedom, I can see no reason why any idea or judgement should ever have
taken cognisance of any other, or been troubled by it. For then diversity

in thoughts would never have become contradiction, since they would have had no common stamping-ground and no common object; nor would diversity of affections or appreciations have excited any protest; for they would have exerted no influence and threatened no contagion.

There is indeed little inclination in political or even in ecclesiastical authorities to persecute pure thought, nor have ideally inspired poets or artists ever found tyrannies dangerous. The eye of orthodoxy could wink, if only practical scandals were avoided. It was the most democratic of multitudinous juries that condemned Socrates; but we do not read that the wise men of the East, however bold their speculations or original their lives, were ever victims of the despots by whose gates they sat; on the contrary, they seem to have been allowed to utter their proverbs and recite their fables—often rather pointed—like any harmless itinerant beggar or sanctified madman. Like the jesters at medieval courts, they moved in a realm of vacant freedom, and there could be no occasion to disturb them there. But when thought is not itself inwardly free and pure, when it is the voice of impatience, envy or intolerant libel, thought is not so much thought as the first growlings of anger and threats of assassination: by which a tyrant is naturally disquieted. The free-talker will then be banished or put to death, not because his thoughts were original but because they betrayed and diffused the most rudimentary of impulses to violence. In such cases thought proper, far from exploring too far its infinite freedom, joins in the quarrels of matter and becomes itself a slave.

The same reasoning applies to the discursive movements and ideal visions of spirit, when spirit forgets its station in this world. I cannot think that pure cogitation could ever have been so invidious and perverse as to rise in arms against itself for having eleswhere formed a different conception. The venom in disagreement is secretly material; the rivalry is dumb fear of being undermined, hunger for the safety in ignorance, or for the applause of the inconstant chorus of fools. Freedom of speech is demanded in order to conduct propaganda and compel this dangerous crowd, willy-nilly, to be of our own opinion. Especially when this opinion is not scientific or even defensible: for then nothing could confirm us in it so securely as the public concurrence of the whole world.

That which troubles tyrants is not free thought but the propaganda or the silent contagion that, while nominally diffusing an innocent fancy, really betrays and prefigures a dangerous material revolt. He is watching anxiously over the cohesion and vitality of that conjunction of political forces, perhaps only momentary, which raised him to power; and he forbids the thunder in the hope of dissipating the storm. All is a desperate physical struggle, not a quarrel among the muses.

ON DESPISING THE WORLD

Contempt for the world was once much preached by Christian missionaries; but they could never say that the world, in spots, was not beautiful to the eye or interesting to the curious mind or that for the fresh heart it was not rich in pleasures and excitements. Moreover these same preachers were compelled to assert that this contemptible world was the work of God: that is to say (if we may interpret this dogma critically), that the world was pregnant with all kinds of perfections unrealised only because in their blindness they crowd one another out and become enemies.

Nor is it any initial aversion that brings moral contempt on the world. On the contrary, disgust with it arises from an initial love that experience turns into a kind of universal pity, if we think of the world as animate, and into a universal distrust, if we think of it as merely a set of opportunities and means for action. Great things may be afoot, and you may take part in them gloriously, if you are on the winning side; but your glory will be a sort of drunkenness, disturbed at its best, and dragged out into a miserable sequel; and the only clear gain that will remain to your spirit (if there is a spirit in you capable of rising above that tragedy) will be the catharsis, or purification of the will, by which the world is at once loved, understood, pitied, and renounced.

The modern revulsion of feeling on this subject had a rational foundation by accident only. Those preachers of *metanoia* were often personally worldlings. Often, to denounce sin and vanity was a rhetorical tradition of their office, not an impulse of their hearts. The

George Santayana, "On Despising the World," *Columbia Manuscript Collection.* © 1969 Daniel Cory. Intended for *Dominations and Powers* or for *The Realm of Spirit.*

honest man of the world, hearing those denunciations, felt little moral or intellectual force in them superior to his own tastes and passions. He therefore returned the contempt that was expressed for his rational interests, as he thought them, and despised the hollow rant of those tiresome prophets.

And false those rantings really were not only when insincere but also when they appealed to imaginary alternatives to the world or material rewards for forsaking it. The promise of paradise, taken symbolically, might represent a true insight or experience of ancient sages, whose language was inevitably poetical: but if those promises are taken literally, and if we renounce our doubtful ambitions in this world for the sake of sure rewards and perpetual joys in another world to follow, our worldliness is not overcome but stimulated. We are not converted, only doubly fooled. Scorn for this imposture practised on the innocent sharpens the resentment that a man of the world naturally feels when fanatics denounce his habits and even his affections.

Now scorn of deception was one of the genuine reasons for withdrawing from the world. The world is in flux, and the spirit, as well as the acquisitive instinct, looks to the permanent. Sense takes every image for a substance; and love of possessions hates to see them melt away. Hence the whole elegiac tone of reflection, and the intellectual search for substances and laws on which we may count for ever. But the substance of this world is itself fluid; and the laws in it, when not imaginary, reveal only the method of this flux, not any ultimate issue.

Surprise, novelty, irrelevant excitement are the joy of children; and if we disregard catastrophes in store, to dance with the dancing waves and rush down with the rushing torrent may be the ideal of life. It will be monotonous; but if we are sufficiently absorbed in the transition from moment to moment, the repetition will no more tire us than the planets ever tire of going their round. This is the very ideal of existence in the realm of matter. It is man's ideal as an animal also: and if, having less elbow room than the planets, he must expect many a knock and a short life, it is virtue in him not to mind; as it is also to arm himself with every sort of weapon, so as to hit back smartly, broaden his orbit, and die just in time and victorious. How much more fun, he may say to himself, in this than in going round silently and safely like the planets a quite unnecessary number of times!

Now this somewhat swaggering and reckless tone marks a youthful way of facing the world; yet it contains in principle all that is philosophical in the contempt of the world: for it denies neither the goods nor the evils of life, nor is it afraid to face fortune; yet it rescues the spirit from servility to fortune; and judges the issue, not by wordly standards, such as length of life or range of dominion, but by the ideal beauty and nobility of the life lived, and by the degree of freedom and spiritual clearness attained in living it. Contempt has lost all its rancour: it smiles, yet in smiling it dominates the checkered prospect, covets nothing, yet possesses all things in idea. Philosophy does not insult the world, but shows it its own face in a mirror, and willingly dismisses all facts, as the facts by changing are always dismissing and forgetting themselves. A liberated spirit on the contrary forgets nothing, endows that fugitive world with a kind of immortality; and living there ironically with its treasures laid up in the realm of truth escapes all the delusions of life and the ignoble part of its sorrows.

ILLUSION OF
LIBERTY IN THE ROMANTIC MIND

To render us vitally and morally free, definiteness and constancy are requisite in our characters and in the direction of our endeavours. We could not be morally free or virtuous if we did not have definite faculties, definite preferences, and definite enemies. This is admitted, perhaps without intending it, by those who look at morals from the political or humanitarian point of view: nothing would shock them more than the suggestion that the best possible life might be that of a vulture, solitary, cruel, and fearless. Even the opinion of Paul Valéry, that life reaches its perfection in the porpoise, might not seem to them morally serious. Why not? Because they assume humanity, in every sense of this word, to be the foundation of goodness. And so it is, for the average man: but this degree of determination is insufficient for grounding any high excellence. A tolerably human and humane man

George Santayana, "Illusion of Liberty in the Romantic Mind," *Columbia Manuscript Collection.* © 1969 Daniel Cory. A reflection, entered in one of Santayana's notebooks, occasioned probably by reading Bergson.

may be commonplace, full of small vices and devoid of any heroic virtue. The integration presupposed in genius or in sanctity must be far
tigh[t]er than that: it will require passionate concentration upon something less than all human interests in scope, and more than human in
elevation.

This is readily felt by those moralists in whom the spiritual and
poetic and emotional life predominates: but such preoccupation with
the inner man often leads them to ignore or deny the organic basis
requisite for those higher flights; and it is they, very likely, who will
insist on liberty of indifference, in order that the soul may break away
altogether from earthly influences, and may work miracles.

In a great religion or mature philosophy, which generations of attentive souls have worked out to ultimate issues, this demand for indetermination in details is apt to vanish, because in those systems the
truth or fate or the will of God has united all the accidents of time
into a single picture, itself arbitrary and groundless enough, but marvellous, on which the mind loves to dwell; and it seems a more devout
task to trace harmonies and responsive echoes within this total reality
than to inquire whether at each point a different event might not have
been possible, and perhaps better. In Christian theology, however, the
demand for internal accidents, or private free-will, has always persisted, because God is here conceived in a double relation, first (He-
braically) as the ruling Power in all things, and secondly (Platonically)
as the Good ultimately desired by the human heart. Therefore, as sin
and suffering and eternal rebellion in hell are not good, and cannot be
turned into goods for the sincere human heart, they cannot be attributed to God even in his capacity of dominant Power. There must
therefore be another ultimate power or accident or weakness: there
must be a radical incalculableness in things, to relieve God of responsibility for the actual results of his Creation.

This traditional motive for clinging to indetermination, as an expedient in theology is reinforced in modern times by psychological
self-scrutiny. Viewed longitudinally, the mind is no more characterised by new beginnings than is the life-history of an insect. There is
the same awakening out of almost nothing, the same wonderful transformations, the same flutter, the same seed-sowing, and the same collapse. But viewed introspectively, vertically, from within, as an
emotional stress and revelation, at any one time, of one's own inexplicable, ill-defined, unstable existence, the mind is a passion on the

wing. There are no causes discoverable for its being; no finality in its visions, no limit to its possibilities. All discoveries and all knowledge, from this point of view, float across the mind, like so much drift-wood down a stream: and the deeper your inward sense, the vaguer its deliverance. The root of emotional or conscious existence seems to be sheer potentiality; and from this root all the branches and flowers of thought seem to grow as they will, to have their season, and, if they wither, to leave behind them nothing but the old indetermination of being, whence perhaps something different may be developed later.

Moreover, this passion on the wing, which the soul finds itself to be, may be romantically deployed in a legend; the epic of a mysterious adventurous past, a crucial present, and a glorious future. There were felt uncertainties throughout, chances and risks and plans conceived in moments of inspiration and then executed, amid the buffets of accident; the purpose grew as we went, and built in the end perhaps better than we expected. Indetermination here is not only a confession of welcome ignorance—because it would have spoiled the story to have known the *dénouement* at the beginning; it is also a sincere description of the emotions of surprise, of self-unravelling, of intentional experiment with which self-consciousness is filled in the act of living. If, as in modern philosophy, self-consciousness be accepted as the sole seat of reality and ultimate model of truth, indetermination must surely be declared to permeate the world.

The works of Bergson are all the more instructive because in their sequence these works beautifully illustrate their own doctrine of progress. One master-impulse, one inspiration, runs through them all; yet the end was by no means foreseen at the beginning; the movement of thought is seen to waver, to lean here to one conception and here to another, as the subject matter varies, and to culminate (in so far as such a method can culminate at all) in a rather surprising underpinning of the original position, supporting it in one sense, yet exhibiting it in such a different light, that the upshot seems entirely different.

We begin with a passionate yet cautiously expressed assertion of the nature of inner experience, as opposed to the mechanism of material causes or even that of sensations and ideas. The inner man, in his heart, feels and observes that he is free, that he forms his thoughts and his wishes by a continuous spiritual effort, that these wishes and thoughts are always new and evolved amidst many open alternatives by a secret elemental impulse which is his very self. The vulgar material world, conceived and constructed by the intellect, is a mere fiction, perhaps useful in practice, but incapable of generating by its odious mechanical ticking that continuous mounting life and those crucial sudden resolves which are the most obvious data of experience.

Bergson in this merely repeats (why should it require such continual repetition) the protest of Berkeley against the "minute philosophers," of Goethe against the French materialists.

VIII

Philosophers

NOTE ON DEMOCRITUS

At that dawn of intelligence, direct observation of nature far from discouraging bold guesses, encouraged them, and gave them, as in religion, the flush of inspired assurance. That trust in intuition is not yet wholly lost by sanguine philosophers: but science has outgrown it. If metaphysics, then, is to be banished from materialism, materialists should leave to scientific men the gradual transformation of such theories as the experiments with matter lead them to conceive, without any claim to having reached any ultimate or direct view of matter in its intrinsic constitution and movement. Meantimes, the presupposition of all natural science remains materialistic: for matter is simply the name for the dynamic reality that confronts us in observation and action, external to our bodies and coterminous with them. That this physical world, of which our bodies are an integral part, and in which our spirit is an involuntary guest, exists before and beyond the spirit in ourselves, is the first unhesitating transcendent assumption of perception and intelligence: it is the fundamental dogma of animal faith. And it is a true assumption and an enlightening dogma, because it reveals true spirit, which is nothing but the internal sensitive witness, or as it were, the audible music made by the material movements and crises of animal life.

George Santayana, "Note on Democritus," *Columbia Manuscript Collection.* © 1969 Daniel Cory. A notebook entry.

NOTE ON LEIBNIZ

Leibniz in his *Monadology* has attempted to compose a possible society of pure spirits. There is an infinite multitude of solipsists dreaming, each without any organ or any previous experience to impose his dream; yet by miracle all their dreams confirm one another's fictions, so that whenever A dreams that he kicks B, B dreams that A kicks him. The idea of each is bred in the other by spontaneous imagination—a beautiful instance of the generative fertility of psyches; but psyches are tropes in a physical world, in matter that is in constant dynamic interplay with surrounding matter; and when animals of the same species breed, feed, and fight together, it is inevitable that the pressure and peculiar influence of each should be felt by its neighbours. There is then society in nature, and when its member[s] are cognisant of their condition at all, that society is recognised by their action and feeling and then pictured by images in their minds. But if there were no society in the realm of matter the dream of it in an orchestra of spirits would be not only a miracle, but an illusion, and an illusion without any ground, value, or even symbolic truth. Pure spirits, as Saint Thomas Aquinas teaches, must be each of a different species, and it is in God only that they read their knowledge; that is to say, their knowledge is all generated in them without other causes than the primeval fertility and contingency of existence. That many spirits should breed corresponding dreams, and being in contact only with primal fertility, should falsely conceive themselves to inhabit and undergo life in a society of prisoners running about and knocking against one another in a non-existent cage, is the most childish of fancies: childish in its groundlessness on the given hypothesis, and childish in feigning not to credit the obvious natural facts on which it is modelled.

George Santayana, "Note on Leibniz," *Columbia Manuscript Collection.* © 1969 Daniel Cory. A notebook entry.

NOTE ON BERGSON

"The inertia of matter he calls matter, the energy of matter he calls life."

In some places Bergson seems to admit a matter which not only resists and divides the unitary (yet formative!) current of life but also possesses a complete form of its own: e.g., the stellar universe, and the whole process of nature as modern mathematics tends to conceive it. He tells us that mathematical physics can ultimately define an absolute, i.e., may define something really existent in the exact form in which it exists. But elsewhere, and repeatedly, he points out that a mathematical universe has no scale, no duration; that it would run through its infinite successive phases "in no time." The drag, the delay, the enacted tempo of this process distinguish the real process, then, from the mathematical formula describing it: and as the substance of this drag or duration is the *élan vital* itself, we see that the absolute reached in physics is, after all, the same as that found in personal introspection. Moreover, in another phase of his speculation, Bergson has identified matter with the pictorial world infinitely comminuted: shuffle the images of sense fast enough, and they are reduced to the primary vibrations of matter. But images are simply terms, distinguished by spirit in the experience of spirit; and even when pressed to an infra-human acceleration and instantaneousness they could be, intrinsically, nothing but phenomena for spirit: so that, here too, matter turns out to have no other substance than spirit itself. Why, then, is it called matter? Because the force of antithetical terms, such as matter and spirit, comes from some *special* sphere or function suggested by them. In a pure monism it would make no real difference whether we called the one reality God or nature, mind or matter, water or fire or will, since in any case this substance must be the seat and source of every kind of distinct existence. The "life," therefore, which in Bergson['s] philosophy is the substance of matter, might as well have been called "matter," and been deputed to be, incidentally, the substance of life. The point in contrasting the terms is moral. The great

George Santayana, "Note on Bergson," *Columbia Manuscript Collection.* © 1969 Daniel Cory. A reflection written on notebook sheets.

stream of "life" is said to run through "matter," because in the total flux of existence we may distinguish *morally* certain formations which we call higher living or organic, from a background of other forms and processes which are indifferent to us, except as occasion, food, or obstacle to those "higher" existences. It is this *moral* perspective that reveals the *élan vital*, and that opposes it to the relatively inert, recalcitrant, or self-repeating background that is, relatively, material. So that here again the principles of Bergson's physics are only a hypostasis of his romantic impatience, and the dichotomy in his universe is a projection of his moral and personal bias. "Life" is "dynamic," and "matter" "static" only if we mean morally dynamic, and morally static: because nothing could be *materially* more swift, explosive and self-transforming than matter; or more self-repeating, conservative and hereditary than life. But where a form interesting to the romantic imagination first arises or suggests itself, the force at work is said to be life: and when that form lapses or becomes habitual, the force at work is said to be matter.

VAIHINGER

In the year 1888 at the University of Berlin, I remember hearing Georg Simmel delicately describe ten different philosophies, each of which professed to distil the central and only valid meaning of the Kantian revolution. Of these systems perhaps the most incisive was that of Vaihinger, which has now been re-edited and sensationally set before the public as the "Philosophy of the As If," or as we might say in modern English, or rather American, the Philosophy of Bluff.

Vaihinger admits that in the wisdom of the Sage of Koenigsberg bluff was not the only ingredient; but he collects a hundred pages—by far the most interesting in his book—of quotations from Kant's writings; and if these passages could be allowed to stand alone they would

George Santayana, "Vaihinger," *Columbia Manuscript Collection.* © 1969 Daniel Cory. This essay may have been intended for Santayana's autobiography, *Persons and Places* (New York: Scribner's, 1944).

seem to establish a curious paradox: that in that famous philosopher's meagre little body there had lived a desperately romantic soul, and that those labyrinthine paragraphs hid the most pessimistic of doctrines. Probably the truth is that Kant, the man, began by possessing the humane virtues and sanity of the Eighteenth Century, and that in his person he never lost them; but like many of his contemporaries he tended to admit principles which, if carried out ruthlessly, would undermine all sanity and virtue. For instance, Kant proved to his satisfaction that the human mind creates its idea of the world; an assertion which might pass for a truism, at least with anyone who has considered the history of science or the biological basis of thought. But in proving this harmless assertion, he seemed to himself to be proving another also: namely, that the human mind creates the world itself, which is nothing but the human idea of it: and this second position, when generalised, implies that no idea can have any object but itself, that knowledge is impossible, and that no truth exists, to be the standard of ideas. We are thus brought to the edge of a veritable abyss, yet we are not frankly pushed over; for it is a rule of this game to maintain a perpetual equivocation and never to ask whether we are speaking only of our idea of a thing or of that thing itself.

Let us, however, in order to play the game, leave this equivocation for a moment unchallenged. Kant's next move will be to set up, on moral grounds, certain tenets which he called postulates of practical reason. Leibniz and the psychological idealists had accustomed the learned to the sentiment that each mind is shut up in its own shell and each man confined to his personal experience; yet practical reason leads us to postulate objects on which our action may be directed and whose presence and character may be signalled to us by our senses and thoughts; every sense and every language making this report in its own terms. By animal faith or by religious faith (which are two forms of practical reason) we may accordingly reach a sufficient knowledge of the powers, divine or natural, by which our experience is controlled: and this without denying our psychological isolation, which is only another name for our personal existence and spiritual integrity.

According to such a view, the first, perhaps the only, postulate of practical reason would be the existence and order of the material world; and we might go on living confidently in it, like the other animals, our critical philosophy having rendered us soberer, but not less natural men. I say soberer, because we should now recognise that our assur-

ance in regard to matters of fact is presumptive only, however safe and
true the presumption may be; and also that, in its substance, our
knowledge is a phase of imagination, a creature of the thinking soul;
so that while our bodies are busy in the world of matter, the report of it
which reaches our minds is an echo only, and a poetic image.

Such, however, is not Vaihinger's view, nor on the whole was it
Kant's; for Kant's practical reason did not postulate the existence of
the material world. This world for him was only an idea of pure
reason, or of science: and we may be surprised to learn that what
practical reason postulates is rather the existence of free-will, of God,
and of immortality. Here we might well exclaim with Cicero: *Ubinam
gentium sumus?* Where on earth are we? For we do not seem to be on
earth at all. Yet we are: we are at Koenigsberg in East Prussia; we are
listening to the public deliverances of a professor, an official of a
Lutheran State; and we are witnessing the difficult fusion in his mind
of religious tradition and the system of Leibniz on the one hand with
the scepticism of Hume and the sentimentality of Shaftesbury and
Rousseau on the other. The word "practical" must not mislead us, as
if it referred to action in the world, and to its implications: "practical"
here means ethical, and the implications concerned are those involved
in puritan moral sentiment. God, free-will, and immortality are indeed
the postulates, not of the arts of daily life, but of an attenuated Protestant theology and of a puritan moralism seeking to justify itself
metaphysically. Kant was not thinking of practice at all, but of conscience; and he was expounding the possible postulates of conscience
when conscience has become superstition.

Very well; let this be the second move in the game, and let us consider the resulting position; which is not a little puzzling. For here again
there is a crucial question which we are forbidden to ask. We must not
inquire whether these, or any, postulates of practical reason are
articles of faith, suppositions which are believed to be true in fact, like
the postulate that the sun will rise as usual tomorrow morning, although pure reason may not be able to establish them; or whether on
the contrary they are *mere* postulates, like the postulate that if I take
a ticket for the lottery, I shall draw the big prize, not believed to be true,
yet needed as a false lure or mock goal in the game of life. If God, free-
will, and immortality existed in fact, we should still need to posit them
as objects of faith; for since they would exist on their own account they
could not possibly be parcels of our personal experience or imagination,

as are our ideas of them. Such faith would be clear, it would be modest, it might even be true; but if Kant had stopped there, without insensibly slipping into the opposite view, how would he have differed from a poor scholastic, and where would have been his new, colossal, and earth-shaking philosophy? Yet the alternative position, to which logic might seem to drive him, and which Vaihinger tries to assume, is plainly untenable. For if the postulates of practical reason were unequivocally false, it would surely not be virtue to live as if they were true, but folly and crime. Can practical reason compel us to be foolish, and can the essence of duty be never to cease from crime?

I might postulate that an aged uncle was about to make me his heir, and I might hope, without believing, that some day when I opened the morning paper, behold, my postulate would turn out to have been true; so that the debts contracted by me in the days of my postulate might then be actually paid, and I might pose henceforth as an honest man, or at least as a lucky scoundrel. Or without waiting for a fabulous uncle, my practical reason might postulate that I was already in possession of boundless wealth, though pure reason might show me to be a pauper; and I might proceed to sign cheques lavishly in consequence, until arrested for obtaining food, lodging, raiment, and love under false pretenses. Which of these kinds of postulates does the As If philosophy recommend?

Perhaps the benign Kant inclined to the former, and *hoped* that an unknowable uncle might turn out to have existed: but Vaihinger has no such evanescent weaknesses. The heroism and pessimism of his position, which he attributes to Kant in spite of the latter's benignity, requires that the postulates imposed upon us should be avowedly false. Indeed radical transcendentalism, pure subjectivity, and profound paradox require this interpretation; without it, why should Vaihinger, or why should Kant, be a revolutionary genius? The same, in all its romantic violence, was the attitude of Fichte, and also of Nietzsche. It forms the core of the philosophy of *Bluff as the Principle of the Universe*.

Goethe noted with approval that the new German philosophy came to turn dogmas into postulates; and as a matter of method, something of the sort has happened in the sciences, of which Goethe perhaps was thinking. His own philosophy, however, was not of this kind. Where he did not lean on Spinoza, who was an honest dogmatist, he set observation above hypothesis, and disliked to think of any mechanism behind the fair face of nature: her secret was rather to be learned by intuition of her luminous aspects. For this sentiment Spengler, a botanist in history, esteems Goethe to be a great philosopher: and I should agree, in so far as intuition of sensuous or poetic essences seems to me a happier exercise of the mind than the investigation of causes; yet the latter, as Virgil says, is the concern of practical reason, and makes the happy farmer. In any case, the expedient of postulates is something intermediate; bluff, like doubt and like lying, is a marginal phenomenon. If no one ever really held a good hand, the wiliest and most taciturn gambler could never bluff. It is assured knowledge of fact, filling in the background, that lends plausibility to hypotheses and to postulates; and, if they are true, supplies their ulterior verification. Even when, on intellectual grounds, our expectation is of the slenderest, we entertain the possibility that our suppositions may be true in fact: otherwise the assumption would be meaningless. And not only are postulates marginal in origin, but in their moral force they are unstable; for it is psychologically impossible to accept a postulate and to live by it without presently believing it to be true; in other words, without turning it back into a dogma. Megalomania, indulged, becomes insanity, and sensation, acted upon, becomes perception and belief.

There was a subtle irony, doubtless unconscious, in Kant's choice of his postulates. Had he postulated that which practical reason actually needs to assume, namely, the existence and order of the material world, it would have been only what every sane man assumed already, what in practice everybody believes, and what every turn in life confirms. But he chose rather to postulate the existence of free-will, of God, and of immortality, for fear that they might be forgotten and that people might live happy without them. Absolute conscience itself, which seemed to him to dictate those postulates, might then be eclipsed. Faith in things true or probable or at least possible would have been but base earthly wisdom in his eyes, and disgraceful heteronomy: the autonomy of absolute conscience positively demanded that we should live by the light of postulates which we were willing should be false. Otherwise the purity of the moral will would have been contaminated with considerations about matters of fact.

Was this a merely personal extravagance? Far from it: it was romanticism revealing its principle; it was subjectivism attempting to be logical. A critic looking for proofs or refutations might prize it as a *reductio ad absurdum* of all modern philosophy: but a critic himself somewhat romantic, and interested in the life and passion animating no matter what folly, will prefer to think of it as a symptom. The romantic hero need not be a philosopher: he need not trouble himself to assert or deny the existence of God or matter, hell or heaven. He is necessarily an egotist, and can be concerned with these things only as with the giants and dwarfs, the weeping maids and rollicking taverns of his adventures: they will be foils for his courage and food for his dreams. Nothing is altogether real to him except his capacity to feign: his pose is the centre of his universe. And eventually this pose will be more exciting, and more sincere, if it is somewhat paradoxical. Heaven, he will say to himself, if it existed, would be a bore; hell might be better worth trying; God and matter may be real, but the one is a tyrant and the other a nuisance. He will defy God by his heroism and exorcise matter by his subjectivity. After he has denaturalised these objects in this way and made their supposed reality relative to himself, it will not take much critical acumen on his part to perceive that he need not believe in them at all. Yet in that case, with what counters shall he play, and on what shall he exercise his virtue? Evidently on the *idea* of these, or of other such things; on the *illusion* of their existence. Thus, by the sheer force of his romanticism, he will be brought to the philosophy of false postulates, and to the vital duty of bluffing.

The revival of this doctrine (which might seem rather out of date) is perhaps a symptom of our times: while the philosophers are returning to scientific cosmologies, the uncertainty of these systems, and the uncertainty of everything, brings the notion of living by assumptions, yet without faith, near the public mind. Our contemporaries are deeply engaged in bluffing; not lavishly, for some ulterior clear purpose, but helplessly, by virtue of the commitments under which they groan. You or I may feel that these commitments were unnecessary, but we may lack the courage and the time to criticise them. Therefore we go on bluffing in religion, in art, in politics, in sport, even in science and in our airs of happiness. No doubt bluff has always prevailed in some measure in human society, because society is necessarily artificial; suppression and hypocrisy are inevitable, if we set about to establish order in public or integrity in private. Men must live up to their assumed characters, as they must live up to their clothes. But the peculiarity of our age is that the safety valve is closed: we see no issue out of our vanities. Bluffers in other ages, when they felt ruined and sick of the game, knew how to repent; they could turn with a clear mind to re-

ligion, to patriotism, or to superb understanding. Today if we turned to
such things, most of us would be conscious of bluffing more than ever.
We therefore often accept this necessity with bowed heads, somewhat
in Vaihinger's spirit. We nerve ourselves sadly to play the game out,
whatever it may be, in which we find ourselves engaged. We have
habits, affections, responsibilities, which it would be too great a wrench
to disown, ignorant as we are of any better allegiance. We therefore
suffer our discredited postulates to carry us, if they can, a little father
on the road to nothingness.

INDEX